ADVANCE PRAISE FOR
Forever After: NYC Teachers on 9/11

"I have always believed that the most powerful moments of learning come through the eyes of children. These moving firsthand accounts vividly capture this simple but precious lesson. I recommend this book to all parents and teachers."

—**Deborah Meier**, New York University, author of
In Schools We Trust, Many Children Left Behind and *Keeping School*

"Just as school was starting, two huge, fuel-filled aircraft smashed the World Trade Towers, raining fire, chaos, and death on those within and below. In these mesmerizing, previously untold stories, teachers from nearby schools tell what happened as they led their children to safety and counseled them in the days that followed. These are stories of ordinary men and women acting with extraordinary caring and courage, but the tales are told with the searing simplicity of Hersey's *Hiroshima*. If ever a horror confirms our understanding that learning is mediated by love, surely this is it . . . this book is not to be missed."

—**Thomas Sobol**, Christian A. Johnson Professor of Outstanding
Educational Practice, Teachers College, Columbia University

"The terrorist attacks of September 11, 2001, changed the way that we define 'homeland security.' After reading the stories chronicled in *Forever After*, I am confident that you will change the way that you define 'heroism'!"

—**Gregory A. Thomas**, Director of Security for the New York City
schools on September 11, 2001 and author of *Freedom from Fear:
A Guide to Safety, Preparedness and the Threat of Terrorism*

"In the days following the September 11 attacks, teachers throughout New York City faced the extraordinary challenge of helping their students cope with their feelings and work toward some kind of understanding. Many rose to the occasion despite the turmoil and heartache they themselves were experiencing. *Forever After* gives voice to these unsung heroes. The compelling stories collected here are a credit to the profession, and the insights they contain make this book must-reading for all teachers in these times when tragic world events are occurring all too often."

—**Tom Roderick**, Executive Director, Educators for Social Responsibility Metropolitan Area

"This book has the power to transcend a specific catastrophe. It gave me a renewed zeal for the work I do and an insight into what I can say and how I can react when one of my 2nd graders asks, 'Could that happen here?'"

—**Joanne Bell**, 2nd-grade teacher, St. Charles, MO

"Finally! A story about New York's true 'unsung heroes,' the teachers of New York City."

—**Ann Lipson**, high school teacher, Manhattan, NY

"An astonishing collection of reflections with unique perspectives that reveal so much about the courage of these teachers in New York City. I felt their vulnerability as each person displayed their quiet acts of heroism, setting aside their fears and anxieties and risking themselves for their students during and after that horrific day."

—**Mary B. Mumbrue**, 4th- and 5th-grade teacher, Winnetka, IL

"Not enough has been written about the role of the teacher during and after 9/11. I compliment Teachers College Press for publishing the essays and helping to make not only other educators, but the public aware of the incredible impact the teachers of New York had and, of course, still have, on their students."

—**Rochelle Shereff**, high school teacher, Manhattan, NY

"A powerful looking-glass into the very heart of our community—our schools."

—**Christopher Lewick**, 2005 Presidential Award-winning high school mathematics teacher, Byram Hills, NY

"A powerful and vivid collection of personal accounts that capture the heroic efforts of NYC teachers in the aftermath of tragedy. Up until now, these stories were not known."

—**Nadia Pervez**, high school teacher, Long Island, NY

FOREVER AFTER

New York City Teachers on 9/11

Edited by
TEACHERS COLLEGE PRESS
with Maureen Grolnick

Teachers College, Columbia University
New York and London

Published by Teachers College Press, 1234 Amsterdam Avenue, New York, NY 10027

Library of Congress Cataloging-in-Publication Data

Forever after : New York City teachers on 9/11 / edited by Teachers
    College Press with Maureen Grolnick.
    p. cm.
    Includes bibliographical references.
    ISBN-13: 978-0-8077-4715-5 (pbk. : alk. paper)
    ISBN-10: 0-8077-4715-7 (pbk. : alk. paper)
    1. September 11 Terrorist Attacks, 2001—Personal narratives.
    2. Teachers—New York (State)—New York. I. Teachers College Press.
    II. Grolnick, Maureen.
    HV6432.7.F667 2006
    974.7'1044—dc22   2006015926

ISBN-13: 978-0-8077-4715-5 (paper)   ISBN-10: 0-8077-4715-7 (paper)

Printed on acid-free paper
Manufactured in the United States of America

13 12 11 10 09 08 07 06   8 7 6 5 4 3 2 1

To the NYC teachers of 9/11
who kept our children safe

. . . and to teachers everywhere
whose stories of day-to-day commitment
are seldom told

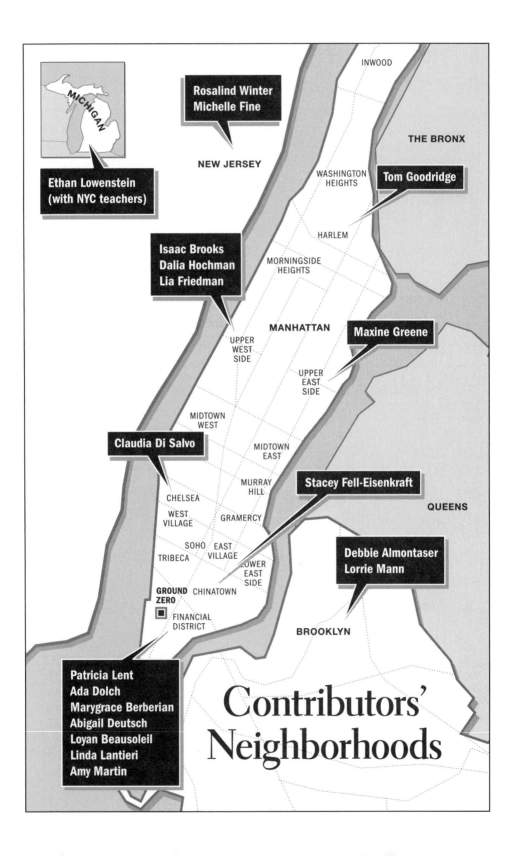

MICHIGAN

INWOOD

THE BRONX

Rosalind Winter
Michelle Fine

NEW JERSEY

WASHINGTON
HEIGHTS

Tom Goodridge

Ethan Lowenstein
(with NYC teachers)

HARLEM

Isaac Brooks
Dalia Hochman
Lia Friedman

MORNINGSIDE
HEIGHTS

MANHATTAN

Maxine Greene

UPPER
WEST
SIDE

UPPER
EAST
SIDE

MIDTOWN
WEST

Claudia Di Salvo

MIDTOWN
EAST

MURRAY
HILL

Stacey Fell-Eisenkraft

QUEENS

CHELSEA

WEST
VILLAGE

GRAMERCY

SOHO   EAST
TRIBECA VILLAGE

Debbie Almontaser
Lorrie Mann

LOWER
EAST
SIDE

GROUND
ZERO   CHINATOWN

FINANCIAL
DISTRICT

BROOKLYN

Patricia Lent
Ada Dolch
Marygrace Berberian
Abigail Deutsch
Loyan Beausoleil
Linda Lantieri
Amy Martin

Contributors'
Neighborhoods

Contents

Beyond Incomprehensibility

MAXINE GREENE

A T FIRST THERE WAS a muffled crash, not unusual among the city's sounds. Here and there a teacher felt a chill of alarm, and children looked toward her anxiously. Still, she saw to it that the classroom work went on: pupils were welcomed, bookbags unbuckled, newcomers hugged a little, to be made to feel at home. Seats were assigned at the tables; pencils and pads were passed around. The familiar routines enclosed the classroom, a protection against the unknown. But something was wrong. A kind of heavy silence seeped under the doors—a silence punctured by shouts, screams, the peculiar thud of running feet. Children huddled together. A few began to cry . . .

Then there was a second thunderous sound, loud enough to be heard blocks away. Was the city being bombed? Some thought of London during the war, of families hiding in subways. Would the rising cloud of smoke and dust smother the school? Would a fire drill protect them? Two or three parents, panicked, ran in and seized their children. The teachers, particularly those in schools close to the Twin Towers, found a new certainty, a new determination within themselves.

They were teachers; their vocations defined by responsibility for the young. There was only one thing to do: save the children. Depending on where they were, depending on who claimed to be in charge, they found different ways of responding. Some instructed the children to stand in line, two-by-two; then they moved outside into the white dust. Here and there teachers began chanting familiar songs, rhymes. Certain ones, not knowing where to go, followed the crowds over the Brooklyn Bridge. Holding frightened children, when they could, by the hand, taking off their high-heeled shoes in order to run, finding unexpected help from strangers offering water, even saying they would carry the little ones. Others ran along the waterfront on the West Side: They could see high school youngsters boarding boats in order to cross the river.

There was pure horror when the first tower fell, and then the second. . . . A few young ones saw people falling, thought they were watching debris hitting the ground; one made out a pair of eyes. Remembering, teachers summon up experiences of flight and endless trudging walks. And they recall groping for explanations, for directions. How does one cope with events unaccounted for by ordinary understanding, by whatever meanings have been funded over time? Broken glass; empty ambulances; sheafs of flames from the windows; strangers embracing each other on the streets. And there were immigrant parents who could not speak English, who had to be notified; and, for a while, teachers felt the same way: expelled from the familiar world, from their homes.

Then there were the pictures on the fences, on the walls. Men and women, desperate, looking for the lost ones. Many school people remember wondering how they would help children deal with such loss. And later they had to help numbers of pupils deal with the last-minute cell phone messages, the words of love spoken just before death. There was a widespread consciousness of a lost invulnerability. Teachers, perhaps particularly, have struggled to help their students, especially the very young ones, to feel protected, to feel safe. Looking back today, they are aware of the new pedagogical demands made on teachers at all levels. Children and young people are exposed to all the tragedies and ambiguities of the time by the media, and teachers cannot be true to themselves or their students if they gloss over the dark spots in contemporary history: the falsifications that thrust us into war, the false promise of "mission accomplished," the sight of wounded soldiers being loaded into trucks, the bloody children being carried away in their fathers' arms. What can be done to counteract numbness? How are teachers to deal with a spreading apathy, a deadness of denial?

Recent events have sharpened the questions latent during 9/11 and the fearsome days that followed. Some children had to be transferred to different schools—they and their teachers felt themselves groping, dislocated. The accounts of the dispersal of children and their families after the Katrina tragedies brought back memories of 9/11 in intensified form. There are pictures of homeless little ones being comforted by teachers they have never met. There are accounts of teachers, their own homes destroyed, camping out in school buildings to make sure they would be there for the children in the morning. And there have been continual reminders of the importance of opening schools after catastrophes: schools as havens, as agents of continuity, as reminders that there would indeed be a future.

There has seldom been such a need for multiple literacies, for acquaintance with a range of subject matters ranging from physical sciences to social sciences to the humanities. Teachers are moved to think of neglected "facts" (the levees in New Orleans, the opportunities to escape, the difference between high and low ground); the problems of AIDS and other diseases avoided in numerous classrooms; the pros and cons of high-stakes testing; the workings of commercials. Again, "Dick and Jane" literacy is no longer sufficient at a moment when even young ones have to be helped to distinguish between information and knowledge.

John Dewey once wrote that facts alone are mean and repellent. Imagination is required, he went on, to open the way to intellectual possibility. Adrienne Rich has written that poetry begins in terror and ends in possibility. So may it be with the teachers writing in this book. Their stories remain incomplete, even as they confront the incomprehensible. The challenge now, as most of these teachers know, is to keep the towers from falling over and over, to summon up images of the possible, images of building anew.

Preface

CAROLE SALTZ AND MAUREEN GROLNICK

1. The Presence of Teachers, Forever After

This book began as many things do—with an awareness of something missing. So much was missing in September 2001 after the 11th: so many people gone, the landscape emptied, assumptions disrupted. Shaken, confounded, we stood at many points along a continuum that had abruptly stopped. Things rushed in to fill the gaping holes, to comfort us—or not. Local, state, and federal government reassured us relentlessly that we would put "paid" to our losses, but for me at least this was cold comfort and only increased my unease. Instead, comfort was located in the everyday, in my neighborhood and local community.

For some of our children, the missing was forever: an unimaginable tragedy. For most children, it was a lesser loss; certainly easier for grownups to ignore, perhaps not a loss at all, but the apprehension that they could not trust that the things that were would always be. My own daughter, Katie, was 9 at the time—a student in a New York City public school. I know the sadness that suffused her days and nights; our small family circle was too small to support us supporting her. Perhaps to help the waves of shock recede, New York City schools resumed two days after September 11th. The routine helped. Doing something helped. But doing what we did before was not okay.

It was in Katie's classroom that recovery began. Isaac, her 4th-grade teacher, sustained her (and us) daily as he quietly drew out from his kids the questions—frightened, curious, angry, funny—

that were living just below the surface. He could have chosen to continue teaching as if nothing had happened. Instead, he threw out his regular curriculum and put big maps of the city and of the Middle East on the walls of his classroom. He welcomed parents in for as long as we needed to be there. He sat with the kids for hours and listened hard. He wrote the questions and the ideas down tirelessly on big white pieces of paper in bright magic marker and helped to organize ideas, until the children understood what had not been understood before. I guess all of this would fall under Social Studies, but poems were read, science experiments took place, many kinds of learning happened. He trusted and was trusted, and that made all the difference.

I imagined this scenario in classrooms around the city, maybe even around the country, but I read and heard nothing about what happened in New York City classrooms on or after September 11th. Why were the important voices of teachers missing from the story of September 11th?

Why, as the fifth anniversary draws near, is something still missing?

Five years ago, tentatively, we began to think of a book of teachers' writings. I first asked Isaac if he would participate. Once he agreed, we began to gather a most amazing group of teachers, school leaders, and students to work with us. They made time within their already too full days to attend a small series of workshops—cosponsored by Teachers College Press, Teachers and Writers Collaborative, and Project Renewal—to write their stories of September 11th.

Isaac's story is contained within these pages, as are the stories of educators throughout New York City. Some simply retell their experiences, and in doing so allow readers to know their struggles to keep children physically and emotionally safe on that day, with no blueprint for action. Others bring us into the present as they think through what they have taken away from the experience to make them stronger and more thoughtful at their craft. And still others talk about leadership and the lessons learned.

Maxine Greene and Michelle Fine, eminent scholars, offer their views on the importance of the issues raised in the collection. They were there from the beginning, in Maxine's living room not long after September 11, 2001, when we invited that first small group of teachers in to talk about 9/11. Our hope for this book is to open a conversation among educators, parents, and the community—a conversation that can move us all past the idea of a "simple" evacuation plan when we consider the legacy of 9/11 for our schools. We hope as well that the book will remind us of the strength, purpose, and goodness of those who commit themselves to the teaching profession. Educators in particular must be capable of "thinking beyond the incomprehensible" (from Maxine's Foreword) and as this book shows, teachers who can teach children through difficult times may turn adversity into understanding.

—Carole Saltz, Director
Teachers College Press
March, 2006

*   *   *

2. Teaching the Present, Forever After

Someday the events of September 11, 2001 will be on a test.

In the days and weeks following the attack, the teachers whose work is collected in this book didn't know what might be on such a test. Events jumped the curriculum. These teachers were teaching the present

Was the Civil War fought over slavery? What *really* caused World War I? Did the New Deal end the Depression? Should we have used the atom bomb in World War II? Were the Russians really going to attack us during the Cuban Missile Crisis? For most of us, these questions were first (and sometimes last) asked and answered in school.

Willing or not, those of us who teach are the appointed custodians of a past that is rational and just—a past that, in the end, makes some kind of sense. We evolve ways of integrating terrible events into a bigger picture. If we are "progressive," we look for ways of turning student questions back on themselves, even ways of teaching more by answering less. But even when the question of a cause or justification remains unresolved, an event still means something because something happens next. Writ large, American history progresses.

The teachers whose work is collected in this book didn't have it so easy.

On September 11th, my long career as a teacher and high school principal was 6 years behind me. On that date, I was tucked safely away as an education book editor in New York City. I could watch the towers burn from my office window, and it shames me to remember that, in my horror, I comforted myself with thoughts of relative safety—safe not just from the inferno of the World Trade Center more than 120 blocks south, but safe from the overwhelming responsibility of being in the schools: *How in the world would I have found the presence and the wisdom to do the right thing, to make good, or even adequate, decisions in the moment and, for now and ever after, to say what it all meant?*

The teachers whose work is collected in this book were not so safe.

The incomprehensible events that my colleagues and I taught about all happened in the past. No one ever asked us why thousands died at the World Trade Center *the day before yesterday*? Or, "Will there be another attack?" Or, "Why do they hate us?" Or "Should we strike back?" These are not questions best answered with another question. Unhappily, they are also not questions with answers. Far beyond finding "opportunities" to learn, the teachers in this book had a crisis of fear, confusion, and anger thrust upon them, even as they were struggling with their own feelings and understandings. When their students asked "why?" they were asking their teachers to interpret events as they happened and to make sense of them in a way that resurrected the rational and just universe of their very recent past—the universe of September 10th.

History doesn't usually enter the K–12 school curriculum until we know for sure it's important and until its meaning is agreed upon. Years after its beginnings, the civil rights movement was important. It had heroes and martyrs. It was a good thing. It was finally in the book.

The teachers whose work is collected in this book were teaching the present. They could not resurrect the universe of September 10th, nor did they try to. Instead, decision by decision, they struggled with their students to find their places in the universe we've always lived in—the very uncertain and morally ambiguous present.

We can only acknowledge what we see and hear, both past and present. We have honored the victims of September 11th and wept with their families. We have stood in awe of firefighters and police who ran towards the World Trade Center, while we ran away. We have listened to the stories of our children, captured by the teachers who enabled them to talk and draw and write, but we have not heard from those teachers themselves. In the weeks and months following my personal encounter with relief and safety, I could only imagine what they were doing, the decisions they were making, the questions they were answering. I could not see or hear them. When I met with the teachers whose writing is collected here, their work became real to me. I talked to people who were doing what good teachers do: teaching the students they had in the world we are given.

It's time they were in a book.

—Maureen Grolnick, Editor
April, 2006

[We wish to express our gratitude to some of the people who helped immeasurably in the creation of this book: Catherine Chandler, Judy Berman, Nancy Shapiro, Meredith Sue Willis, Linda Lantieri, Ada Dolch, Isaac Brooks, and Maxine Greene]

One

Moving Back and Moving On

PATRICIA LENT

I ran as fast as I could. The two 8-year-olds holding my hands ran as fast as I could. I'm not sure how they kept up with me as I hurtled forward in that river of running. We ran, as fast as I could, north, up the avenue, *go go go,* our backs to the one tower. Only one tower. Was it possible?

As fast as I could was not nearly fast enough. *"It's falling!"* the men yelled, arms waving. And I ran, imagining behind me the tower falling like a monstrous steel redwood. One hundred and ten floors coming after me, after us. Better to be running when it hit. I remember thinking *"will it hurt, will it hurt, will it hurt?"*

I held the children's hands tightly, too tightly. I was propelled by terror, not bravery. Terror in my brain, terror in my blood, terror in my hands.

Hours later and for days afterward I would watch the towers implode on TV. Not a redwood after all. I would see the cloud of dust and debris chase up the street—the cloud that we outran, running as fast as I could.

I would remember, a day or two later than that, that a child (10 years old? 11?) had said, *"Look! Even the dogs are scared."*

AT THE MOMENT that the first plane hit the World Trade Center, I was standing in my classroom at P.S. 234, watching 24 third graders unpack, chat with friends, and prepare for morning meeting. It was the 4th day of school. We'd enjoyed an unusually smooth beginning to the year. We were in the 2nd

year of a 2-year loop. I had taught 20 of these 24 children the year
before. We knew one another well. We knew how to get along and
how to get things done; we knew how to tackle problems and how
to celebrate accomplishments; we'd shared our passions and we'd
developed common interests. We'd already been through a lot together. We would draw on every bit of our shared knowledge and
experience to get through the year ahead.

Despite my school's location only a few blocks north of the
World Trade Center, I saw very little in those first moments. I heard
a screeching roar and the slam of an impact. I saw a gray glittery
cloud of smoke race past our windows and up Greenwich Street. I
heard shouting and screaming, and I watched my students rush to
the windows.

I later learned that in many classrooms in my school, teachers
immediately gathered their students in their meeting areas. Our
meeting area is a place of trust and safety. It is the place we go
to share ideas and feelings, to discuss important issues, to grapple
with problems, and to come together as a community. It is the place
we needed to go, right then. But my meeting area is flush against
a wall of windows. Although I had no idea what had happened, I
knew I needed to get the children away from all that glass.

I instructed them to sit at the three tables nearest the door. And,
sensing they needed something to do, something to hold, I grabbed
two baskets of picture books and passed them out. Months later,
a child would say to me with an incredulous tone, "Trish, do you
remember what you did that day? You gave us books to read." "I
remember," I'd respond. Looking me right in the eye, she'd say,
"The book I got was about airplanes."

While the children talked and turned pages (I don't think anyone actually read), I went to close the windows. Craning my neck
south, I saw the huge burning gash in the near tower. I thought
bomb, maybe accident. Except for one glance south 2 hours later,
that was the last time I would see the Twin Towers. I turned away
from the windows and toward my class.

Within minutes rumors about planes, fire, and mayhem began
to circulate through the school. I was torn between an urgent desire to know what was happening and an equally urgent desire to
insulate my students from frightening news. I pushed the rumors
aside, I willed myself not to know. I closed our classroom door and

A third grader's drawing of the moment before the crash.

focused my attention on what was right before me: two dozen children caught in the middle of unimaginable events, and looking to
me for direction. I would learn over time that what was happening
outside—those events that were reported on the news—were not
the same as what was happening to us. Right here, in our room,
we were waiting and wondering and whispering. Parents were on
their way. Our class was about to disperse.

   I knew it was important to remain calm, to speak softly, to listen
carefully. I also believed it was vital to be as honest as possible. I
remember crouching beside the tables, looking into the children's

faces. "Are you scared?" I asked. "I'm scared too." I felt certain that although the children did not need access to all the facts and all the misinformation, they did need to know how we adults were feeling, and they needed to hear us say it out loud. Over the course of the year, I would learn to share feelings of sadness, loss, doubt, hope, relief, exasperation, and even joy.

Meanwhile, the adults in the building were trying to gauge the seriousness of the situation and choose an appropriate course of action. But we had so little to go on. Incredible as it may seem, the first announcement made over the loudspeaker merely informed teachers that outdoor recess would be cancelled for the day. In the hallway outside my room, two parents debated whether or not to take their children home. "A school is one of the safest places to be, in a situation like this," I heard one father say. And then he looked at me and asked, "Right?" When a mother showed up at my door to collect her child, I assured her that the children were calm and quiet, and I tried to persuade her that it might be better if we all stayed put. Other parents rushed past me and my assurances and hustled their children out of the building. All year we adults would struggle with uncertainty. How would we make decisions, who would make them, and should they be based on information or past experience?

Then came the second plane. I felt a jolt between my shoulder blades. I felt a surge of dread and doubt. A parent raced into my room shrieking her daughter's name. The word *terrorist* was suddenly everywhere. A new announcement instructed teachers to bring their classes to the gym or cafeteria, and advised parents in the building to take their children home.

It's hard to tell this story without sharing every detail. But I'm going to move quickly through the rest of that day. Not because those hours weren't important. They were. But I want to get to the days, weeks, and months that followed September 11th. They were also important.

So we headed for the gym. I recall locking eyes with another teacher in the hallway. My face crumpled. I felt relieved that my back was turned toward my students.

Parents and babysitters and family friends streamed in and out, picking up children and dropping off snippets of news. We made lists, lots of different lists, trying to keep track of who was still in

In this child's drawing, an orderly line of grim-faced children follow
behind as I move through the hallway with long, urgent strides.

school. Someone passed out pretzels. Someone else distributed paper and crayons. We waited a long time. We played a halfhearted
game of Simon Says. Children drew pictures of the World Trade
Center, and of birds and butterflies. Lights flashed. Fire alarms
sounded. (I later learned that was when the first tower fell.) Those
of us left in the building were told to move down to the storage
basement. Finally a decision was made to evacuate to P.S. 41, an
elementary school in the Village nearly 2 miles north. We set out
walking in a long line, but moments after we got outside, the second tower began to fall. Some teachers and students were caught in
a black cloud of dust, others were forced back inside the school. My
group ran north, hand-in-hand, as fast as we could.

Eventually we slowed to a walk, melding with the crowd moving north. "Trish, why did you tell us it was safe in the gym when it
wasn't?" a girl asked me. "I thought it was safe, but it wasn't. We'll
be safe where we're going."

Small clusters of students and teachers began arriving at P.S. 41. We were given a place to wait and food to eat. Eventually all the children were picked up. Eventually all the teachers went home. Walking the two blocks to my apartment, I felt dazed and drained, unsure what to do now that I had only myself to look after.

Once home, I watched the news hour after hour, trying to piece together the story, that outside story that I hadn't witnessed. I remember, after hours of watching, stepping out onto my terrace to look south, to see the dust and smoke. Just to be sure it had really happened.

On the morning of September 12th, my phone rang. It was a parent from my class. She'd last seen me in the gym with a dozen children. She wanted to be sure we had made it out safely. I assured her that we had. And then I began to wonder and worry. What had happened to all those children after their parents picked them up? Where had they gone? Where were they now? Using my class list from the previous school year, I began to call. I called and called and called. Many numbers were not in service, but enough calls went through. Over the next few days I began to piece together our story. I picked up and passed on bits of news. I tracked families down in various parts of the city and state. I talked to grandmothers, godfathers, and neighbors. Colleagues and students called me. I spotted one mother on a local news program. I saw others at a community meeting. One family escorted me downtown to walk through the neighborhood and look at the school.

At the end of the week, the staff of my school met at our district office. It was an emotional meeting, marked by anxiety and tears. As we shared our stories, it became clear that despite being in the same school at the same time, we had experienced very different things and had responded in very different ways. We also learned one critical, and miraculous piece of news. Everyone in our school community, every child, every parent, every sibling, every teacher, everyone was safe.

We began making plans to reconvene school at P.S. 41 in a week's time. This meant shoehorning 600 children into an already crowded elementary school. The teachers and administrators at P.S. 41 cleared out all available space, but there simply wasn't enough room. Two of my colleagues and I—and our 75 third-grade students—were assigned to a room used by a team of speech and language specialists. There were five large teacher desks, eight filing cabinets, some bookshelves, about twelve student-sized chairs, and a few tables. We had a day and a half to get ready. We stripped the place down. We moved out the desks, covered over bulletin boards, turned around bookshelves, and turned filing cabinets into table-tops. Once the room was bare, we added some familiar props: attendance cards, a September calendar, a number line, a daily schedule, and a group photograph from the previous year. We carried in a few armloads of books, xeroxed stacks of writing paper and math recording sheets, collected as many pencils and crayons as we could find, and labeled a set of folders to store student work. We chose a spot to put the 75 lunch boxes, and hoped most kids would come without backpacks. Finally, we each found an easel and designated one corner of the room as our own. We knew we would have to function as a group of 75, but we also knew each class needed a home base. We had a lot to talk about; we'd need a place to meet.

I would describe myself as a confident, self-reliant teacher. I enjoy sharing ideas with colleagues, but I also like to think for myself and make informed decisions about what goes on in my room. In those first days at P.S. 41, however, I was hungry for advice and guidance. I did not trust my own instincts or my prior experience. I didn't want to "get it wrong." Our staff met daily, usually with Bruce Arnold, our school's consulting psychologist. Together we mapped out how we'd begin.

We all knew the first priority was to bring everyone together in one spot. We knew the children wouldn't believe everyone was safe until they saw one another, hugged one another, and counted noses. And we could predict that the children would grin and shout and jump up and down, while the adults would be on the verge of tears, worrying about the days and weeks ahead. But then what? What about when we went upstairs?

Bruce kept assuring us that we did know what to do. "You'll do what you usually do," he said. "You'll have a meeting, you'll ask a question, and you'll talk about it." As a staff, we settled on one open-ended question: "Does anyone want to say something about what happened?" After the meeting, we'd invite the children to write, draw, or talk some more.

The three teachers in my room planned to begin with a large group meeting, all 75 children together. The children, however, had no intention of becoming a class of 75 so easily. Once upstairs, they scoped out the room and then huddled around their own teacher's easel. They sat extra close together, waiting for their own meeting to begin. We teachers made a quick decision to follow their lead.

"Would anyone like to say something about what happened?" I asked my group. And they huddled closer still as two other meetings began across the room. Despite all the planning, I was not prepared for what I heard. A few children talked about how scared they'd felt or where they'd gone, but most began by sharing stories they'd overheard or been told by others. They told stories about people trapped in office buildings. They told stories about firemen and policemen. They told stories about international terrorists and American leaders. They told nearly everything except what had happened to them. Similarly, when they began to draw, they drew planes crashing into towers and people jumping to their deaths. They were reporting the news, as they'd heard it, and as they'd understood it. But what about their own stories? Were they too shaken to talk about their own experiences? Or did they think their own stories weren't the "real story," weren't newsworthy, weren't worth sharing even during a meeting at school?

And so, at the end of that long first day, when the staff met, we discussed how to help the children tell their own stories. We teachers would continue this discussion throughout the year, as the children continued to tell and retell and revise and revisit their stories.

The following day, we posed a question that we hoped would help the children focus on their personal experiences: "What did you do to stay safe?" Now the children talked and wrote and drew about heading north, running fast, sticking together, and trying not to panic. We learned who went home, who stayed with friends, and who left the city. We found out who watched the news, who avoided it, and who tried to play. Because this writing was about staying safe, we asked children to try to zoom in on themselves in their drawings, rather than on the crashing planes or burning buildings. Some children left the towers out of their drawings altogether; others pushed them as far into the background as they were able.

Two children's responses to the question, "What did you do to stay safe?"

"To stay safe we ran really fast. Our group split up at a fork but we got back together."

"We didn't panik or get crazy. All we did was walk and ran and walk some more."

Many of the children drew the World Trade Center over and over and over. As a staff, we decided that our students would not be discouraged from drawing these pictures, but that we would not display images of burning towers or crashing planes on classroom walls. And we began to wonder if and when we should begin helping children to *stop* drawing those images.

In those first days, the children also wrote a lot of letters. One girl wrote to an uncle who worked for the FBI to ask "Do you have any clues?" Others wrote to the president, to the mayor, to firemen.

Dear President Bush,

I live one block from the World Trade Center. My door is crashed open. My windows luckily aren't shattered. All my stuff smells very bad. I hate not being able to go home. I really hope we don't start a war. I hate hearing the crashing of planes, the booming of bombs, and the roaring of police cars. If there's anything I can do I will really try to help.

At that time, my husband was working on the Broadway show *Music Man*. After our first week at P.S. 41, he arranged tickets for our school's second and third graders to attend a Saturday matinee. After the show, a mother confided, "That was the first time I've seen my daughter laugh since all this happened." Another parent stopped me on the sidewalk and asked, "Is that what we should be doing? Because my wife can arrange something at Lincoln Center, I just hadn't thought of it." We adults didn't know what the children needed, and we didn't have much time to think it through. But the following day, as I watched my students drawing and writing about a Broadway musical, I concluded that they needed some relief from the 9/11 images on the news and in their heads. They needed opportunities to experience and think about something else at least some of the time.

One afternoon some supplies arrived from P.S. 234, including our crate of reading book bags and our writer's notebooks. The children were thrilled. They read, reread, and swapped the books inside their bags, and they began to write more ambitious accounts of their experiences in their notebooks:

Worst Day

This month is not a nice picture. I thought it would be a great month, no, I thought I would have a great birthday, no, I thought I would have a great school year without any stupid twin towers falling down, no.

This is how it all started. I went into school with everything I needed including my classmates. We just went into my class when we heard a eeeeeeeeeeer and in those few seconds all of us were standing by the windows looking out scared. Then we heard boom! A second later I sat down at the big table with some other classmates. W was one of them, N got picked up, then W's mom came and said calmly, a plane crashed into the twin towers. Then my mom went and got me. She held her hand out like wonder woman, I got out of my classroom with zero of my classmates, without my lunch box or note folder, just my backpack and jacket. We ran home, watched the news all day, next day we left.

By our 3rd week at P.S. 41, everyone in the city was talking about getting back to normal. Although school felt anything but normal to me, I decided to invite my students to join this citywide discussion. At our daily morning meeting I asked, "What are you doing to get back to normal?" Children talked and wrote about things they had already done, things they planned to do, and things they wished they could do.

The children voted to entitle the collection "What's Normal," and to send it to Mayor Giuliani. They wanted the mayor to know that they were doing everything they could to help themselves and help the city.

Dear Mayor Giuliani,

We are a third grade class from 234. Our school is 4 blocks away from the World Trade Center. Now we have to go to a school called P.S. 41.

We are trying to show that we can do things to help the city. We're trying to think about the good side of NYC. We're trying to get back to normal by doing what we used to do.

Three children's responses to the question, "What are you doing to get back to normal?"

"The way I got back to normal was that I went to the park and rode my bike my scooter my rollerblades and my skateboard and it was a lot of fun."

"What I would do to get back to normal is go back to my piano lessons, get back at P.S. 234, go to the movies and have fun."

"I feel normal already kind of, I mean I'm in school, but not in my own school and I really want to go back to my own school. Please let us go back to our school before the new year. I hate having 75 kids in my class."

The falling twin towers won't stop us from having fun.
Please read this book.

Sincerely, Class 318

I've shared a lot about our morning meetings. But what about
the rest of day? What about the curriculum? Shouldn't I be getting
my program back on track? Shouldn't I be concerned about these
third graders falling behind? Shouldn't I start insisting that they do
their best work? Perhaps I should have, but I didn't. None of us had
really gotten back to normal. None of us could handle a lot of pressure. None of us remembered what our best work looked like. Just
getting from temporary homes via a crippled subway system to a
temporary overcrowded school was a lot to manage. I did believe,
while we were in school, that it was important for the children to
be busy, it was important for them to work together, and it was important for all of us to accomplish something. It was also important
that they knew I was there to listen and respond to the ideas and
feelings they were expressing through writing, drawing, and talking. And it was essential that I be as kind and patient and honest as
possible, and that I help them to be the same.

So what did we do? I've never spent as much time on handwrit-
ing as I did in those first weeks. We took our time learning to make
beautiful cursive e's and l's and r's and w's. Soon we knew enough
letters to write "watermelon." That was a satisfying day.

We played a lot of math games, not because the games were just
what the children needed in their mathematical development, but
because they already knew the rules, the games were engaging, and
they needed to play together.

We read *Charlotte's Web*. I had planned to use this book to model
how to linger while reading, rather than gobbling up pages as many
third graders do. I'd planned to draw the book out, reading no more
than a chapter at a time. That's not what happened. Story time was
so comforting—the sound of good writing being read aloud, the intimate way we'd sit together—that whenever we managed to find a
quiet spot in the classroom, or hallway, or stairwell, we'd read and
read and read. Chapter after chapter. When we finished *Charlotte's
Web*, we started right in on *Stuart Little*.

We made self-portraits using the most gorgeous collage paper
we could buy. We didn't hurry. We set up two tables and six of

our precious chairs in the hallway, and invited children to work six at a time. We encouraged them to take as much time as they needed.

We sang. I had rarely sung with my students, but I knew a song or two about the city. One day, standing in the endless line on the clogged, single-file staircase that took 600 of us to our rooms, I taught them a song. We sang it nearly every day after that, often first thing in the morning. And we did the hokey pokey, and whispered through countless rounds of Telephone.

But it was hard being a class of 75. The crowding and noise were unbearable. It was difficult to hear during simultaneous meetings, and nearly impossible to concentrate during work times. The children were exhausted from lying on the floors, leaning papers on narrow shelves, and stepping over one another to move around the room. Arguments broke out over chairs and sharp pencils. Children began hoarding books and worrying that books from the three different classes were getting mixed up. One of my students wrote both her own name and my name on all of her work, as though afraid she'd get lost in the shuffle. There was an overwhelming feeling of confusion. Who was everyone? Where was everyone? What exactly were we doing? Much later in the year, a boy wrote about this time when we shared a room with the classes of my two colleagues, both of whom were named Kara:

> Our school went to another school, P.S. 41. We had to share a room with Kara's class, maybe it was Kara's class and the other Kara's class. It was a lot of kids.

Kara, Kara, and I decided to rotate our classes through the room. This meant finding places to go. We discovered that the auditorium stage was often empty, and began sneaking in for meetings and quiet reading. We lingered in the yard, and met in the cafeteria during off hours. We arranged visits to the local branch of the public library and its adjacent community garden. Two classes walked to a nearby Barnes & Noble for quiet reading. My class returned to the Neil Simon Theatre during a morning work call for *Music Man*, and were invited by the crew to walk on the treadmill, clamber up the scenery, ride a tricycle, wear headsets, and operate the midstage elevator.

A day later, I brought my class to a rehearsal at the Merce Cunningham Studio, where I had danced before becoming a teacher. I remember feeling awed by how vast and quiet the studio felt that day. At the end of the rehearsal, the children swarmed into the space, leaping, skipping, smiling, and racing about. One boy stood at the window and looked intently at the Empire State Building; he'd been drawing skyscrapers for days. The next day, some of the children wrote letters to their new friend Merce.

Dear Merce,

I really like how they would all stand still then break up and do all different movement. And I like how at the end Merce made them practice and practice and practice until they had it perfect and I mean perfect! When it ended we got to dance.

Dear Merce,

When I saw the dance it seemed like a dream. When I heard the tapping of the dancer's feet I was so happy that I had seen a grown up dance, all the mistakes didn't matter to me. All that I cared about was the show. When I saw the show I knew that it had to go on.

On these jaunts in the neighborhood, we found more than space and quiet; we found reasons to feel good about our city again.

Eventually, however, making the most of a tough situation wore thin. We adults—teachers, administrators, and parents—began discussing our next move. Some of us were eager, perhaps even desperate, to get back to P.S. 234. Others were just as determined to stay away. Emotions ran hot and high, options were fiercely debated, worry hung thick in the air. Following several days of tense negotiation, a compromise was reached. We would move to St. Bernard's, an empty parochial school in the West Village. We abruptly packed up everything we'd hauled into P.S. 41 and hauled it down the stairs and several blocks west to the new building. For the next 3 days we threw ourselves into what came to be known as a Tribeca Barn Raising. A small army of plasterers, painters, electricians, glaziers, architects, artists, teachers, administrators, parents, and friends transformed the building. Everything was new: new furniture, new carpets, new plants, new supplies, new books. The first-floor gym was stacked with gifts sent from all over the country and the world. We were encouraged to take whatever we needed.

We were also warned not to settle in, warned that this was only temporary. I ignored the warnings. Whether I stayed a week or a year, I was determined to move all the way in. I arranged and rearranged the furniture. I bought closet shelves, book baskets, pencil cans, and hanging files. I made a new door sign, a new attendance chart, an October calendar, and a new number line. I hung the collage self-portraits above the chalkboard, displayed the children's writing on the walls, and posted photographs on the bulletin board. It was October 9, the 14th day of school, and I had just set up my third classroom.

What did we talk about on that first day in our own room with our own meeting area? We began simply: What do you think of our new school? I don't recall what was said that day or the next, but I do remember closing the door, sitting in a circle, and leaning in toward one another. I remember feeling grateful for the quiet and the privacy, and I remember noticing how earnest and articulate the children sounded. I also remember that when an airplane flew overhead, we had to stop and wait for it to pass. I remember noting the new vocabulary that had crept into the children's talk: debris, rubble, terrorist, air quality, evacuation. I remember a conversation I had with a boy who had transferred to our school that year. "I'm nervous," he confided. "I'm afraid we might keep moving and moving. In my old school we didn't move around, we stayed in one place the whole year."

During that first week at St. Bernard's, the class responded to some letters they had received from schoolchildren in California. These letters suggest how things were going for my students.

Dear _____,

New York City is getting back to normal. Now we have our own school and we feel a lot better here than in 41 because we were smushed in one school with another 2 classes. Are you a boy or a girl? I am a girl. It feels kind of weird to be living 12 blocks away from one of the worst disasters in the world that is starting a war.

Dear _____,

Thanks a lot for the letter, and we heard about all the money you sent us. It really helped. I personally am not living at my regular house. Everyone really is helping. Things are getting a lot better. Thanks a lot.

Dear _____,

Hi my name is _____. My class moved to St. Bernards. I live in New York City. I have a lot of friends from last year. I like St. Bernards a lot. Its just like our school again. I wish we can go to our school again. I wish I can go back home again.

Soon after we settled in, I noticed a discrepancy between the number line we used to count school days and the number lines kept by other classes. Most teachers had counted September 11th as a school day, but a few, including myself, had not. We teachers weren't sure what to do. Should September 11th count or not? I decided to bring this question to my morning meeting. The children dug into the discussion. They knew they were responsible for making a good decision, and that their decision hinged on how they wanted to remember September 11th. What place did it hold? What place should it hold? Together, they began to weigh the significance of that day in their own lives:

We *should not* count September 11th as a school day because

- We were only in school for 5 or 10 minutes. And, it's a sad day, and people don't have their homes because of it.
- It wasn't really a school day because we were there less than half an hour. Parents were still in the school yard, and it wasn't close to lunch. We had just unpacked.
- A lot of people died that day. We were at school, but we weren't at school for a whole day. It wasn't a normal day. It was a sad day.
- We didn't have a meeting.

We *should* count September 11th as a school day because

- It was a regular school day, but we couldn't do that day. It was supposed to be a school day.
- We went to school for a little while. We learned a lot that day, that there are bad things in the world and we experienced one.
- We should count it. We should put a circle with eyes and a frown on the number line.
- We did go in the building, and we learned a lot. We pretended it was a normal day even after it happened. We read books.
- We went in school, and no other class had ever experienced the situation. No other class is going to experience this. We deserve to write it down because we made the best of it.
- It was sort of like a trip or adventure. We learned that every day is not a normal day. Anything can happen anytime.
- We should count it so we can remember what happened.

Toward the end of the discussion, a child said, "I feel like my head is split down the middle." The following day, the class agreed to count September 11th as a school day. How did they finally choose? It is a school tradition for second and third graders to go ice-skating on the 100th day of school. My class decided to count the day so that our numberline would match those of the other second and third grades. It was important, they insisted, that we all go ice-skating together.

About once a week, we used our meeting time to discuss something related to our 9/11 experiences. What did we miss about P.S. 234? What did the school or the neighborhood look like? How should we thank the people who had sent us supplies and gifts? Small group counseling was arranged for children who wished to discuss their feelings more deeply or regularly.

Meanwhile, expectations were on the rise. It was time to pick up the curriculum, to get back into the swing of things. Of course we all knew this year would be different. Anna Switzer, my principal, reminded us repeatedly that we needed to adapt our plans and our goals, that it wouldn't be business as usual. But what, then, would it be?

Our plan for the year had been very ambitious: a fall study of the Eastern Woodland Indians followed by a spring study of New Amsterdam. Both studies were big. The New Amsterdam study, which involved a series of walking trips in downtown Manhattan, was out of the question. But the Native American study seemed daunting, too. How would we marshal the energy to launch a study? How would we pull together the resources, most of which were still at P.S. 234? And how would I get through 8 more months of teaching every day, all day long? Should I admit how hard it was to focus on what the children were doing, to concentrate for a whole day?

Around this time, I wrote:

How do I comfort myself, when I comfort myself? Not with special treats or sips of luxury. I comfort myself by paring down. Seeking the company of those I love, and avoiding the rest. I am too worn, feel too fragile to maintain cordial interaction. I am wary of expending social energy. I might need it. Might need it to get through something big. Something else big.

I pared down my curriculum as well. We put off the study until later, and mapped out time for reading, writing, and math. Big chunks of time, with as few transitions as possible. I didn't want to hurry; I didn't want to push. I also wanted to be sure there was time to sing, and paint, and play, and talk.

During this time, some children began writing longer accounts of their 9/11 experiences. Others left that subject alone and wrote about vacations and hobbies and pets.

One boy spent much of his writing time reporting on his first-hand observations of the ongoing cleanup of downtown Manhattan. One morning he wrote a skyscraper-shaped poem about his neighborhood:

Downtown Manhattan

The
grounds
roar
the
streets
rumble
the wind moans
the river groans
the cars honk
the boats rock
the statues stare and stare
the flags blow
my toes get cold
the birds sing
the leaves fall
the buildings are bombed
the scaffoldings collapse
everything stays the same.

Although we couldn't manage a big social studies curriculum, my third-grade team decided to get started on an author study. We knew that Vera B. Williams, author of award-winning children's books *Cherries and Cherry Pits* and *A Chair for My Mother*, lived a block from St. Bernard's, so we wrote and invited her to our school. Once she confirmed that she was coming, we dove into her work. We spent weeks reading, rereading, and discussing her books. We wrote letters to her characters, and tried out aspects of her writing and artwork. Finally, in mid-November, she walked in the door, threw up her arms, and announced, "Here I am, your very own author!"

For many students, this author study was a chance to delve deeply into something unrelated to the traumatic events of the year. For others, however, the study provided another opportunity to reflect upon their changing lives. Several children, inspired by the special chair in Ms. Williams's books, wrote about their own special places. One child wrote about a bed in her home; another wrote about a favorite swing in Hudson River Park; a third wrote about a special spot in our new classroom. As this piece shows, many of us were putting down roots in our temporary school:

> I have a special place in the room. Under the dry erase board. You can read in there. It is dark, but you could still see. And you could poke your head out of the side. It is very cozy. It is so quiet. There is a bag in the corner. You can see the map. Sometimes people put books there. Then you have to move them. But no one can see you under there. And Trish's clipboard is sometimes there. It is like a tent in there. And you could put your knees to your chest and you can just read and read and read and read and read.

One child, inspired by Ms. Williams's acrostic poems, wrote a poem called "Terror." She wrote her own name vertically down the page. The *T* in her name became the line "Terror is happening." The *L* became "Lead me to a nice place."

We also celebrated our lives and our city with several short-term projects: personal time lines, elder interviews, and a 2002 calendar featuring a dozen of the class's favorite places in New York City. After a short debate, the children decided not to include the Twin Towers in the calendar, because they were no longer there.

With each passing week we felt more settled into St. Bernard's. Speculation began that we would stay the year, or at least until spring. Moving back to P.S. 234 seemed more and more remote. One child, who had joined the school that year, said in meeting, "Personally, I don't remember P.S. 234. This is *my* school."

Then, in early December, an announcement was made that the Board of Education might insist we reopen at P.S. 234 in early January. Suddenly the building seemed awash in conflict. Outrage, anger, fear, and exasperation thundered up and down the stairs.

Of course the children overheard this great debate. We spent one morning meeting talking about their views. Some students were adamant about staying or going, but many reported being "in the middle." "I'm sort of scared to go back," one girl began, "I have a weird feeling that something is going to happen if we go back." For many children, the long commute to school was a significant factor. "I want to go back because I don't like taking the subway all the

way to 14th Street," a boy explained, "I don't want to go back because it might be smelly and smoky and there's rubble." For many,
the issue seemed to be feeling out of place. "I really want to go back.
Here it's different. It feels like we're not supposed to be here. Our
other class felt normal." Several students followed up by writing
essays on this topic, which we posted in the hallway.

> I want to go back to our school. I miss my school, and really
> want to go to school. I think if we move back to school I will
> move back home too. I will feel a lot more comfortable. I think
> everyone will be more confidant about September 11th. I feel
> very sad about moving about everywhere and keep switching
> homes and then when I go to a strange school it makes me feel
> even worse. I'll buy 200 filters if it would make us move back
> to P.S. 234.

In retrospect, I questioned my decision to draw the children into
this debate. The decision was entirely out of their hands; the grown-
ups were going to decide. Meanwhile I was coming to terms with
the fact that the decision making was out of my hands as well. I
burrowed into my classroom, and tried not to listen.

Then a date was set. We would reopen at P.S. 234 in early February. Almost immediately, the moving was in full swing. There was
a great enthusiasm for packing, labeling, stripping bulletin boards,
saying good-bye. I couldn't share in this enthusiasm. I didn't want
to spend an entire month doing nothing but leaving. I was convinced I could pack up in 2 days, 2 exhausting days that weren't
nearly here yet. I closed my classroom door and carried on. We
made new self-portraits, we continued working on our projects, I
displayed new work on the walls, and we sang, "This Land Is Your
Land." Still, I felt swallowed up by grumpiness. Then one of my
students tossed off a poem that got all of us laughing:

Another Move

Pack up the bags!
Pack up the books!
Put away the packages,
Put away the hooks,

We're going for another move
and that is that.

We're bringing the closets,
the ceilings, the walls
We're bringing the storage rooms,
the bookcases, the halls!
We're going for another move
and that is that.

Move the windows!
Move the floors!
Bring them through the rooms
and out the doors!
We're going for another move
and that is that!

In our final weeks at St. Bernard's, each class took a trip down-town to see P.S. 234. Before going, I tried to prepare my students for how it would look. I had been shocked when I first visited. I had expected the room to be just as we'd left it that day, a kind of time capsule. But the room had been cleaned three or four times by three or four different crews. At one point the furniture and sup-plies were piled together in one massive mid-room jumble. Then, lots of the old furniture was moved out to make room for the new tables and shelves still at St. Bernard's. There wasn't much there. It looked like it had in August, but drearier. I tried to straighten up. The rug was gone, but I set up our benches in the meeting area next to the windows. As always, we'd need a place to meet.

The children were very quiet when we went inside. We all sat together in our rugless meeting area. "How does it feel to be here?" I asked. "It just feels good to sit on these benches again," one boy said. "It's better than I thought it would be," someone else added. But one girl shared, "It doesn't look anything like our classroom. It doesn't feel good to me." We did some exploring and drawing, and then went back for the last few days at St. Bernard's.

The 3 days spent setting up my classroom were the dreariest I remember. I was utterly exhausted, and I was tired of feeling tired. Parents offered to help, but I didn't know what to tell them to do. My mother came to town and spent an entire afternoon sharpening colored pencils and tossing out broken crayons. My new student teacher tried to weed out and reorganize our class library.

On February 4, we reopened school for the 4th time. Somehow, we were back. We began our Native American study the second day. A few weeks later we started playing in the yard. Soon we were allowed to open the windows again. The children looked happier and less disheveled. I felt my confidence returning. I felt like a teacher again. Learning subtraction seemed important again. Finding just the right book to read seemed possible. I found my-self smiling as we started building a longhouse model—I knew it would take a long time to finish, and that seemed just fine. We went ice-skating on the 100th day of school, all together. A minor homework assignment turned into a 2-week writing project about New York City. The children celebrated their city with gumption and gusto.

New York City

New York City is a great place to live.
Every day it is lively.
When you are on the street, remember don't get lost.

You have to know where you are going.
hour after hour people come and go.
in Rainy days people are rushing to go home.
Klacking and clinging shoes thumping the ground.

Cars rushing by.
I like living in New York. There are very tall buildings.
Try to live here just try.
You'd love to live here. I know it. Yes.

We planted corn, beans, and squash seeds, and watched in amazement as the first seedlings popped up. Before long the plants were a foot, then several feet tall. "Every day when the class comes in," a child wrote, "they run over to the plants. They don't even unpack. And every day the plants grow a little more."

We slugged through the standardized tests, and celebrated by eating ice cream at the coffee shop across the street.

And the children continued to write and write. One boy spent weeks writing his 6th account of September 11th. The piece, entitled "My Life," chronicled the important events in his young life: a death in the family, a new bicycle, a trip on an airplane, and "then a horrible month came, September. On 9/11 something scary happened." He described that day in detail, and tracked our year together from P.S. 41, onto St. Bernard's, and finally to P.S. 234. And then, most remarkable of all for me, he moved on. "Many months have passed since 9/11. It was weird that the date was 911 and also it was voting day for City Council. The baseball season is starting. It's May." He wrote a page about baseball, mentioned an upcoming trip, and closed with a question: "Who knows what will happen?"

There were difficulties, of course. But they seemed familiar. They seemed like the kind of difficulties that arise when 24 families share one classroom, when 500 families share one school. They seemed like problems we could work on, problems that just might have solutions.

One day in May, after a field trip, my class was eating lunch in the room. I overheard four girls retelling the events of 9/11. "Where were you when it happened?" one of them asked. And each in turn pointed to a spot in the room. "What did your mother do that day?" another prompted. And again they took turns telling: "My mother was screaming my name." "My mother held out her hand like Wonder Woman and said 'Come!'" "Why don't we each tell about that day, one by one." By then, I couldn't help myself. I edged over to the table, crouched down low, and listened. And I heard the story, the four stories, the stories we'd been working so hard all year to tell. They were telling them. It was going to be all right.

One warm afternoon in June we went to Washington Market Park to read and write. The park had been closed for much of the year due to fears of contamination from the World Trade Center collapse. While we were there, one of my students whipped together a poem that seemed to sing out, "We did it! We finally got back to normal!"

In the Park

I'm in the park
Where the birds are chirping
and the people are talking
Where the leaves are blowing
and the flowers are growing
Where the gazebo is standing
and the people are playing
Where the kids are reading
and where the kids are writing
and where the teens are laughing
Where the sitters are marching
and where the birds are pecking
Where the men are walking
and where the babies are playing
Where L____ is writing
In the park.

The end of the year came so fast. With just 5 days to go, the children presented me with a book of writing and drawing celebrating our class, our studies, and our shared experiences. They knew it was time to say goodbye.

I started planning my own good-byes. One afternoon the children wrote letters of introduction to their new fourth-grade teachers. Another day they wrote letters welcoming my incoming second graders. The second to last day we packed up the stuff and raffled off the group projects. I wanted all the packing out of the way. I invited the children to write a final entry in their writer's notebooks:

I Hope

I hope next year I will get a great teacher and a great education. I hope I will have a great summer. I hope I will graduate from college without getting held back. I hope that a lot of people know that I'm only going to school to be smart and free.

Last Day of School

Today is the last day of school. The classroom empty. Papers
packed up put away. Things being given away today. Kids
missing. Books missing. Kids packing up there [sic] work.
Raffles are going on for models and plants. Plants are growing,
being taken home. It is the last day of school.

Finally, there was only an hour or so left. We sat in our meeting
area, and each of us shared one thing we were proud of. One boy,
who had spoken very little about September 11th, said, "Well, I'm
proud I just made it through this year. It was such a hard year."
Then we each shared one thing we'd always remember. Children
mentioned funny stories, special projects, happy days. That same
boy looked me in the eye and said, "I'll never forget that on that
day you held my hand and you didn't let go."

Of course I held on. We all did, all year long. It was unthinkable
to do anything else. But that didn't make it easy. There were many
times when I felt too sad, angry, tired, uncertain, and resentful to
keep holding on. There were many days when I felt like I went to
school, made a bunch of mistakes, and came home even more tired.
There were days when I was exasperated by parents and children,
and days when they were angry or disappointed with me. There
were many days when I wished I could just stay home and look
after myself.

But there it was, the last day of school. We were sitting in meeting. We were safe. And everyone was telling a story.

I'd been telling my story all year, too. This last day I had a story
ready to share with my class. We got off the benches, we sat on the
rug, and I read my last story of the year.

Corn, Beans, and Squash

I've been thinking about our plants.
About the corn, beans, and squash.
About how they grew and grew.
About how they're growing still.

People keep asking about our plants.
What did we do?
What kinds of seeds?
What kind of soil?
What special this or that?

Nothing special, I say. *Everything* special, I think.

I've been thinking about our plants.
But what I've been thinking, I don't want to say.
Not to just anyone.
But just to you.

I know what's special.
It's not the seeds,
or the soil,
or the sun.

It's magic.

Plants don't grow as tall as children in little pots on a windowsill without some magic.

Are you surprised to hear that I believe in magic? I do. I believe in information, observation, and evidence. But I also believe in a special kind of magic. The teaching kind.

Our corn, beans, and squash grew, grew and grew so that we would learn something important. The hard part is figuring out what it is we're supposed to learn. Teaching magic doesn't give out answers. We need to work at it.

So I've been thinking about our plants. Thinking very hard. I'll tell you what I've learned so far. I know you'll help me puzzle out the rest.

Our corn, beans, and squash are teaching us something about our neighborhood.

Everyone has been worrying. Is it safe downtown? Is it healthy? Is it all right for people to live here, for children to go to school here? Our plants grew impossibly tall and impossibly hearty to reassure us that our neighborhood is safe. Safe enough for corn to race for the ceiling, safe enough for beans to wrap around window shades, safe enough for squash to splay out and bloom.

Our corn, beans, and squash are teaching us something about our school.

This year we shuttled from building to building, from classroom to classroom. We didn't spend as long as we should have in our own room. But still our roots have gone deep. Deep enough to wiggle through the bottom of pots. Deep enough to anchor us. Deep enough to keep us here.

Our corn, beans, and squash are teaching us something about children. About you.

The corn has grown tall and strong and proud, just like you have. The beans have wound around everything in sight, just like you have wound around everything we've studied, making it your own, reaching for the next and the next and the next good idea. And the squash has budded, budded, budded, and . . . *bloomed*! Smiling yellow blossoms out of tight green buds, yelping, "Life is good, life is marvelous!" Just like you.

And our corn, beans, and squash are teaching me something about saying good-bye.

The plants have outgrown their pots. They need more soil, more space, fresh air. They're leaving, a few each day. When we parade down the hall with our magical plants, I feel giddy with pride, overcome with sadness. It is so hard to watch them go.
It is the same with you. All of you.

>You've grown strong.
>You've grown curious.
>You've grown sure.
>You need bigger pots.

I am preparing to let you go. One by one by two by three, and soon all the rest.

Thank you for growing so well in my room.
Thank you for reaching high, wrapping tight, blooming bright.
Thank you for filling my year with hope.
Thank you for the magic.

Note

Portions of this chapter appeared in *Teaching Through a Crisis: September 11 and Beyond*. New York: Bank Street College of Education, Occasional paper #11.

Two

Questioning
the Answers
to 9/11

ISAAC BROOKS

And then my first cousin, who was working in the second tower,
the one that fell first, ran to the first tower which was still standing
and tried to rescue my step-brother and none of the cell phones
worked and the tower was going to fall down and there were
people screaming for help and running all over the place and
when I got home my mom said, "Come with me, we have to find
your cousin and step-brother," and we walked all the way down
to the World Trade Center from Harlem and we had to walk because there was no subway service, and the police pointed a gun
at my mother, my brother and me and told us to put our hands up
and my mother cried and she said, "Please, officer, don't shoot.
I'm only trying to find our cousin and Chyna's step-brother," and
that they were working at the World Trade Center and the police
fired at my mother anyway and she was bleeding and then they
let us go and we looked everywhere for them and no one knew
where they were and we didn't know if they were alive or not and
my mother cried and cried and we put up signs with their pictures
everywhere . . .

THURSDAY, SEPTEMBER 13th, 2001, 10:30 A.M. Meeting time
on the rug. Fourth grade in Manhattan School for Children,
located on the Upper West Side. Another achingly beautiful
day. A clear blue, cloudless sky, eerily like the sky 2 days before

when the Twin Towers fell. I had told myself that this was a day like any other day. Except it wasn't. We had started 2 hours later than usual. And, in addition to my 29 students, 8 parents and Lynne, my principal, were sitting on the periphery of our rug and on desks surrounding the meeting area.

As Chyna was speaking, I looked around and saw the same breathless, frightened looks on everyone in the classroom. The children were rapt with attention and worry, commiserating. The adults, by contrast, were looking at me. They wanted me to intervene or they might have to intervene themselves. Chyna had taken this meeting somewhere that they clearly didn't want it to go.

"Chyna, calm yourself. I don't think that telling this story in this way is helping anyone this morning. I'm sure that everyone is safe and sound, now." Chyna nodded. She ended her story. She was content now to be held and rocked by her friend, Charlotte. I knew Chyna's family. There was no cousin or step-brother. They had lost no one in this tragedy. The entire story was a fabrication, and we were Chyna's captive audience. Clearly, Chyna was hysterical about the events. We all were, to some extent. But Chyna had personalized it into a gripping, breathless tale that increased in feverishness with every sentence she launched into. She had a wild look in her eyes that almost begged someone to intervene, to help her find a way out.

It had always been a philosophy of mine that my students are my best teachers. Instinct told me to start with them. I knew that Lynne supported this, and she had in fact modeled it for me 2 days before when she broke the news of the "terrible accident" that had happened at the Twin Towers.

On that day, September 11th, she had gathered our class on the rug and told them that an airplane had flown into the World Trade Center and that there was a terrible fire. The firemen were there to put the fire out and try to save the people inside. I watched the class as she said all this and noticed that what Lynne was saying had no real meaning for my students. They were watching her and thinking that something bad has happened, that Lynne was concerned, but that they were safe and shouldn't worry. Throughout the remainder of that day, parents had come singly or in pairs, whispering gory details and rumors to me at my door as they collected their children. But it wasn't until my students went home to watch the video of the towers falling down that it probably hit them and invaded their dreams. Since our school occupied the 3rd, 4th and 5th floors of a former junior high school, they felt vulnerable about being in tall buildings. When they returned, for weeks afterward, when an airplane flew by they would move instinctively away from the windows or cower by their desks, holding their ears.

The parents who had chosen to stay today comprised an interesting cross-sampling of upper-middle-class parents: Among them there was a therapist who would go on to counsel anxious business professionals who worked in other tall buildings; the wife of one of the city officials who manned the Emergency Command Center; an academic publisher; a real estate agent; and a lawyer. Some had chosen to stay because they felt their child needed the reassurance that they were close by. Others stayed because they felt bewildered and wanted to know what tone to set with their child. I am sure that not every parent who wanted to stay could afford the luxury of going in late to work in order to do so. Half of my class's families were working class and several students were already taking public transportation or walking to school each day on their own.

That day I knew the class and I would be inextricably connected. A former teaching colleague of mine felt closer to one second-grade class of hers than any other class since. She had endured the assassination of John F. Kennedy with them in Dallas 38 years ago. I thought about the kindergarten teachers who were on the observation deck of the World Trade Towers during the first bomb attack years before. In the past I had wondered at their dedication as they stayed with their students, 5-year-old children, well beyond the stretch of a typical school day. Now I understood.

I already knew that Lynne and the staff had done an informal poll and determined that miraculously, of the 300 students in our school, no one had lost an immediate family member in this tragedy. This changed the dynamic of what I was to accomplish that morning. But what had happened 2 days before could not be simplified into what educators call a "teachable moment." That seemed like a trivialization of the events and of the lives lost. Public officials were urging us to go about life as usual, but that felt like a crass response to an event that was so horrifying, so large in scale, and so physically palpable. Beyond the training I gained at Teachers College, beyond my experiences as a business executive years before that,

beyond everything I learned and experienced up to this point, I still
had no idea how to help my students make sense of this event.

I took a breath and realized that it didn't make sense. Flying
two passenger jets and their passengers into skyscrapers is not
supposed to make sense. I had to go deeper than logic or human
nature to find something comforting to share with my students. I
had to mine the depths of my being to find what it was that gave
me hope. I knew I had to share that with my students: I had to
share hope.

I sat everyone around the easel with a fresh sheet of chart paper
and markers. I waited until almost everyone was there. I planned
to call on my students and to write down what they said. I wanted
them to feel heard. To see that their questions are taken seriously
and their comments are valued. I began:

> A lot has happened these past few days, and I'm sure you have
> a lot of questions. Sometimes it makes us feel better to talk
> about things that trouble us or when things don't make sense.
> I want you to know that there is a lot that happened that I still
> don't understand. A lot that doesn't make sense to me. But
> maybe together we can figure some of this stuff out.

Then Chyna raised her hand to speak and told her story—not a
good way to start this morning meeting. Boy, what an understate-
ment! What should I write down in response to Chyna's tale? I
pursed my lips and wrote "separation from those we love."

Amos raised his hand. His father is an architect. "Isaac, why
did the buildings fall? Weren't they fireproof?" I wrote down "designing buildings to be safe," and I talked for a while about the
central core of skyscrapers (actually, I found out later, the World
Trade Towers were supported by their exterior, not the core, meaning that the airplane impact and resultant fire affected the buildings where they were strongest, not weakest). I talked about the
programming of elevators to go to the ground level and how they
are controlled by fire and rescue personnel. We discussed the fire
towers and fireproof staircases. I talked about fireproofing and how
even fireproof materials can burn if the fire is hot enough. Finally,
I told them about the foresight of the designers of the World Trade
Towers: how they tested the building in the event of an impact by

a Boeing 707. Unfortunately, the planes that flew into the towers 2 days before were 747s and inflicted more damage.

Alex raised his hand and asked, "Why did the passengers let the terrorists take over the plane?" Alex was more attuned to current events than any of my other students. His mother informed me that since third grade he had read the *New York Times* and wanted to discuss what he learned. I looked at him and thought for a moment before I wrote "airplane security and hijacking." I told the class that until 2 days ago, our experience with hijackers was informed by the hijacking that used to happen when I was their age. I explained that it seemed that ideologically, or out of necessity, people back then were asking to be taken to Cuba. The parents in the classroom nodded in agreement. Typically, we were told by officials to obey the hijackers until others would come rescue us or until we landed and were sent home. It was not our place to resist, and we knew from experience that as long as everyone stayed calm, no one would get hurt. But this was different. These hijackers had no interest in saving their own lives, let alone the lives of their hijacked passengers. We couldn't make this assumption anymore.

I took a moment to generalize what we had just discussed. The safety of tall buildings and airplanes were now both suspect. For some of my students, flying by airplane to other places was an ordinary part of their lives. Formerly, occupying skyscrapers and flying in airplanes were benign activities. Now, both were recast in a sinister light. What before was seen as a birthright of New Yorkers now seemed to be an occupational hazard.

But among my less privileged students, the effects of this disaster had even more devastating effects. As usual in New York City history, times of crisis seem to be borne unequally by its citizens, with marginalized and at-risk individuals bearing more than their fair share. Chyna's story was evidence of her mindset, and we had experienced a bit of her cry for help a few moments earlier.

But Gabriel took the conversation in a new direction. "Isaac, those people who live in the desert; the dudes who wear those rags on their heads, why did they do this to us?" Gabriel asked.

"Whoa, Gabriel. Let's take your question and break it down into smaller parts, and then maybe we can try to answer it." I knew that I was buying time with this, but I was at a loss for what to do, what to teach, where to start. I had just come from 2 hours of comprehensive workshops hastily arranged to give me, the classroom teacher, the tools and frame of mind to help my students process the events of the previous 48 hours. Gabriel has boldly gone and asked the question that most of his classmates were itching to ask. Here it was, and what was my response?

"First of all, Gabriel, those rags are not rags. They are part of the dress of Arabic people. They are called keffiyehs. . . ." *Yeah, right*, I was thinking. Gabriel has shown bravery and asked a difficult question, and I responded with a lesson on semantics. By answering this way, was I sniffing out a "higher purpose"? There did seem to be a need for me to educate my students about the importance of stifling our appetite for revenge in order to protect our pluralistic values, especially in our extremely diverse New York City community. I knew that I myself had an aching hunger for getting even—with someone or something—a desire to fight the powerlessness we all felt. Yet Mark, a colleague of mine who teaches third grade at our school, had just told me about vigilante groups prowling all over his neighborhood in Brooklyn, looking for symbols of Arab culture to defile. Here we have endured the most blatant hate crime against the American people in anyone's recent memory, and I am chiding Gabriel on his caricature of Arabs. Was I bypassing this "teachable moment" and choosing to address the issue of a breach in political correctness? (I realized half a year later that when he said "rags" he was shortening "do-rags" and drawing a parallel between the seemingly exotic dress of Arabs and the dress of his friends and neighbors in South Harlem. So, who was less understanding of cultural difference, him or me?)

"Right, whatever. Why did those dudes do this to us?"

Good for you Gabriel! I thought. It was clear he recognized my dodge and wanted answers. After all, there were other grown-ups in our classroom today and they appeared to want answers, too. Gabriel was playing to the crowd and hoping the odds would bend me to give him what he wanted: the truth, whatever that is. My mind raced for an appropriate response. The parents were looking anxious. A few seemed to glower at what they might have characterized as the "defiant" tone that Gabriel was taking with his questions and responses.

Actually, I had imagined a question like this as I spent the previous day pondering what to tell my students. Where would I begin? Could I talk about terrorism? But I shouldn't begin there. It would be irresponsible to leave my lesson with just an assessment of terrorism. I needed to talk about safety. Was my job to reassure? To explain? My whole teaching career had been predicated on my desire to tell the truth and to give my rationale on any decision I made, if asked. I had gotten in trouble with my colleagues and my administrators in the past because I always erred on the side of my students. It was a risky strategy but one I embraced unflinchingly. If I took risks for my students, I reasoned, they would do the same for me.

But this had to do with events *outside* of my classroom. Were these parents asking me to help *them* explain what had happened? To help *them* reassure their children? To guide *them* on how to move forward? It certainly felt that way. Heck, I could use that guidance myself. My daughter was brought home early on September 11th, and cocooned herself sobbing in her room rereading her favorite books for comfort. It took her grandfather a couple of hours to calm her down. He talked to her about his recollections of New York right after the attack on Pearl Harbor. She was a fifth grader; these children are a year younger.

Should I reassure them on our common goals for public safety and the intentions of my city, my state, my nation to protect its citizens? This didn't make sense either. Intentions do not mean much to 9- and 10-year-old students. There are some hard facts about the disaster that had yet to be discovered. We still didn't know who had done this to us, and why.

I had more questions than answers. At Teachers College, we were told to model our perplexity at new problems if we didn't have the answers. This was to empower our students when they are baffled, to work through their confusion. So, I knew that pretending to have it all figured out and to try to explain this event was an unrealistic aim. I could model my confusion at the attacks and their aftermath. But I sensed when I saw my students and their parents that this would not do. They were assembled there for something more. Shrugging my shoulders and wondering aloud would not meet their needs. And, just as important, it wouldn't meet mine, either.

That previous day spent imagining the questions I would face from my students and the possible answers I would give could not possibly have prepared me for this morning meeting. The truth was that I had no clue about the true nature of the tragedy my class and classes across the country had experienced. I didn't know if any of my students had lost relatives (beyond their immediate family members) in the towers. I didn't know if there would be more bloodshed and devastation. True, there did seem to be a lull in the terror. We were exhorted to resume normal routines and not let a disruption signal our subservience to terrorist goals. Yet suddenly my job as a teacher had become onerous in its responsibilities to the children I was to teach. I hadn't been with the police or fire fighters who rushed into the Twin Towers, yet I was saddled with the clean up job—the repair of the psychic damage wrought upon our next generation of New Yorkers.

Sitting in a classroom on the third floor of a high-rise school with 29 students and a quarter as many parents, I was walking a tight-rope between helping and hurting them. I was hoping to say just the right thing, yet conscious of how unrealistic that hope might be. Everything seemed to be held in a precarious balance. I had a new appreciation for the importance to society of what I do for a living.

Here were my students and some of their parents. They had come to school looking for answers. I, the teacher, was supposed to have those answers. Yet even as I came to this awareness, it, too, had been tempered. Another layer above the expectations of behavior for a teacher from his or her classroom was also evident.

The chancellor of the New York City Board of Education forbade teachers from discussing anything with the press. Therefore, as a citizen of this city, was I to censure my feelings and beliefs in deference to my public service? It seemed unfair: Police and fire rescue workers were raising flags and talking to reporters. Yet I was denied this same right. Was it because I dealt with children? Because they were vulnerable? I was poignantly aware of the many strictures on what I was allowed to say. Yet I was given so little insight on what should be said. All I knew is that my city had been savagely attacked and that there was a gaping, smoking hole in its skyline and in its collective heart. My students were part of that collective heart.

This brought me back to Gabriel's question: "Why did those dudes do this to us?" "Sometimes, Gabriel, sometimes something *so* bad happens to us that when we try to figure out why, we can't come up with an answer. The danger is that when this happens, *we* can get angry. We can look back at ourselves over the past and try to come up with reasons, but . . . "

It seemed to me that a lot of history had to be taught to answer the question of what might have led to the attacks. Current events figured into it, too. Then, of course, an understanding of international law and comparative religion would be helpful. More important, the fractious nature of the Middle East and the Arab world had something to do with the attacks. I looked around my room and noticed that my classroom had no map of the region from which our attackers might have come. Our curriculum was focused on the first European settlements in North America. My colleague Kevin and I had just decided last week to redefine that to include an exploration of how a diverse population forges a successful community in the new world. It seemed like that lesson would be even harder to teach now.

Our American curriculum seemed woefully inadequate. Well, maybe not. As myopic as our social studies curriculum of European colonization seemed, all of a sudden, the Middle East figured into it in a crucial way. I saw now how we could discuss the Silk Road and Spice Route and why Muslim traders shut Christian merchants out of each. This was the impetus for European naval exploration. The very countries determined off-limits to Europeans 7 or 8 centuries ago were now hotbeds of Islamic fundamentalism. And what about the resurgence of the Wahabi interpretation of Islam? Born in the past millennium in response to the anti-Arab tactics and mindset of zealous crusaders, reborn now in what was left of Afghanistan under the Taliban?

"There's still so much we don't understand. Clearly, whoever did this to us is very angry. So much destruction and so many lives lost. And our getting angry back could make things worse." So, what was I left to teach? What was it in human nature that could produce such brazenly antihuman acts? What was it in the collective teachings of humanity that would help us see past this tragedy and assure us that we would survive—that a more positive force would prevail?

Here I was in the beginning days of my fourth-grade class, building community and trying to establish a safe space in which all of my students could take risks and grow. I was helping them find their writing voices and empowering them to become more resourceful outside of their parents' oversight. I was building my students' trust in each other and in me as their teacher. Most important of all, I was teaching them to trust themselves. "And, you know, the hardest thing to do when someone has hurt you is to keep cool while you try to sort things out. Something terribly bad has happened here. We are still trying to figure out why. It seems like a big mistake. . . ."

Each of them knew that day that something wrong had happened on September 11th. They could each judge it and come to the same conclusion. The numbers and the innocence of the victims alone helped anyone on this island agree that what was done, for whatever reason, was a crime.

> We have to try to understand why it happened and try to learn from it so that it will never happen again. Is there something we did in the past that made people angry? I don't know. Right now I can't think of anything that this country did in the past that would make the bombing of the Twin Towers make sense. I don't think I ever will. I am just as hurt and afraid as you are, Gabriel.

I looked at Gabriel. He wasn't satisfied. Something bad had happened and no one was doing anything about it as far as he could see.

> We'll have to wait and see how our country responds to this tragedy. We'll have to be patient. But, more important, Gabriel, we'll need to reach out and get to know each other better, whether we are classmates or foreign countries. One thing I can tell you for sure: no one would do this to someone they knew personally.

I sat back on my haunches and called on the next student. I listened and everyone else listened, too. I wrote down what my students said and began a conversation that I hoped would last for the rest of our lives.

Three

"By the Way, This Is Not in the Principal's Manual"

ADA DOLCH

T HE LAST DIRECTIONS to my secretary on September 10, 2001, were, "Don't forget to begin preparing the name placards for all teachers in preparation for the fire drill, scheduled for Thursday, September 13, 2001." As I entered my office on the morning of September 11, I noted name placards on Lisa's desk. I thought, "Gee, that was fast."

It was primary election day, and I was excited that our school building would be used, for the very first time, as a voting site. We expected Mayoral Candidate Mike Bloomberg (now our mayor), to cast his vote in our school building located just south of the World Trade Center. I had arrived at 6:15 A.M. to make sure that everything was in order and to observe the first members of our community who would enter our school building to cast their votes, on that beautiful, bright sunny Primary Election Day. As a high school with the name of Leadership & Public Service, we had dedicated much time in our public policy course to establishing the importance of voting and making a commitment to public service. Today would be a milestone.

In the lobby I placed a large cafeteria table as a barrier between the adults entering the building to vote and the students who would be arriving shortly. I ran upstairs to my computer and made two paper signs that would clearly direct traffic. When they were posted, the setup was complete.

I proceeded to my office on the seventh floor, to begin my morning routine. I looked at my watch and noted that it was not working. I went on with my work. Lisa walked in, the assistant principal (AP) walked in, we chatted, we prepared for the day. At 8:30 A.M. I said to Lisa, "I'm going down to the lobby to greet the kids, and then I'm running to the World Trade Center to get a battery for my watch." I put $5.00 in my pocket, picked up my keys and walkie-talkie, and proceeded down the stairs to the lobby.

I arrived at the lobby, did my usual shmoozing with my students as they entered the building, looked at the clock in the lobby, and said to School Safety Agent Moore, "Isn't this a most beautiful start to the day. It's 8:45 A.M. and there are only a handful of students waiting to get upstairs." And then the lights in the building went out. At first I thought it was just in the lobby. Surely it had to be a power surge thanks to the voting machines. I glanced around the entire lobby, looked toward the office of the custodian at the far end of the room, and noted that the door was locked. I exchanged a few more words with Agent Moore, and within 10 seconds the lights returned and with that came an extremely loud explosion. A police officer assigned to the building, supervising the election process, leaped out of the building. My two school safety agents ran out as well. I looked out through the large plate-glass windows in our lobby and noticed the reflection in the windows of One Liberty Plaza, diagonally across from our school building. There were large chunks of debris spewing down and lots of black smoke. I could see an inordinate amount of paper flying through the air, some of it on fire. We had experienced several ticker tape parades, and we knew what toilet paper flying in the air looked like, but this was no ticker tape. And no, it was not toilet paper.

I immediately picked up the intercom telephone on the security desk and called my secretary. I asked her to call the superintendent (it is the first call you always want to make), and asked her to inform him that there appears to be an explosion in a building nearby. I said to Lisa, "They are going to ask you for details so tell them that we don't have any details. Tell him we are all fine. Ask him if he knows anything and tell him that as soon as I know something we'll call him back." Using my walkie-talkie, I asked the assistant principal to go to the upper floors and let me know if he could see anything. He said, "I'm standing in Lisa's office [seventh floor], and I see a tremendous amount of debris falling from one of the Twin Towers. I'll go check upstairs and let you know what else I can see."

As I was talking to the AP via the walkie-talkie, the school lobby became engulfed with people. People were running in screaming, others were crying, some shaking, some praying. Some talking on their telephones. Someone asked me for a bathroom. Parents of students who worked nearby appeared to have arrived within seconds and were attempting to retrieve their children. A Hispanic 15-year-old student walked in, tears streaming down his face, and in a catatonic state. I asked him, "David, what is it?" He couldn't speak. I sat him down on the large granite bench in our lobby and asked him, "David, what did you see?" He couldn't speak. His tears just streamed down his face. A few seconds later, in a great hush he said, "A plane hit the building." Just at that moment, a female student, also 15, walked into the lobby and again in a whisper said, "Ms. Dolch, a plane hit the Twin Tower." I said to her, "You mean a little piper, or perhaps a helicopter?" And she said, "No, a big airplane." I asked her, "The Twin Towers?" She responded, "Yes." I asked her, "Do you know which building?" She replied, "The one further away from the school. I said, "The one with the antenna?" She responded, "Yes, the one with the antenna." I thought for a moment and then said, "Oh my God, that's my sister's building." (She worked on the 105th floor of Tower One.) Immediately I remembered that in 1993, when that same tower was bombed, her life was spared because she had taken off that day and spent the day shopping. I thought, "She's probably shopping again." But, just in case, I said a prayer, "God, please take care of Wendy. I can't, I must take care of my kids."

People continued to stream into the building. Some crying and many with a face of disbelief. The lobby was engulfed with strangers. People seeking refuge wanted to get upstairs. They asked for telephones, they asked for bathrooms. I thought, "What if there is a person with a bomb strapped to their body? I can't let anyone upstairs." More people streamed into the building screaming, many in a frenzy. All attempting to use cell phones that wouldn't work. People were crying. More parents arrived at a frantic pace. They wanted to get upstairs to pick up their children. One parent in hysteria tried to argue with me and made a move toward the elevator bank. I remember raising my voice at her and saying, "Do you know where your child is?" She said, "No," and I said, "Well, neither do I. Therefore, you will wait here until I can tell you where your child is." I was nervy. My secretary called down to the lobby to tell me that my husband had called, my sister in Texas had called, my sister in New Jersey had called, and my daughter who was studying in London had called. Each time Lisa was able to reassure them that I was fine, and everyone in the building was fine.

I spoke to the assistant principal via the walkie-talkie who said, "Ada, I am in the cafeteria [on the 14th floor of our school building]. The top of Tower One is on fire. There is lots of black smoke and a lot of debris is coming down from the top of the building. Students are in shock staring up at this sight. Some are crying. The teacher is shaking."

Immediately, I thought, what if something flies in through our windows. Every classroom has three 6-by-6 foot windows and if you are in a corner classroom you have five of them. I asked the AP to ask the teacher and the students on the 14th floor to move away from the cafeteria and into the corridor. I asked him to return to the seventh floor and make an announcement, that all teachers should escort their students into the corridor. We wanted no one in classrooms. (Obviously I had no clue as to what the students on the 10th through 14th floors had already experienced from their classroom windows.) I was able to maintain communication with the assistant principals, the deans, and the school safety agents via the walkie-talkies.

The principal from the school adjacent to ours arrived in my lobby in shock. He wanted to know what was my plan. Ha. A plan. What plan? Who ever planned for this? Oh sure, the year before we had written our school's safety plan, but we didn't plan for this. People were screaming, crying, shaking, praying. "Oh my God, what am I supposed to do?" I thought about the two students in wheelchairs, the blind student, and the student who had just returned from open-heart surgery. I said to the assistant principal, "While we still have electricity and the elevators are working, let's get the girls out of the building." He put that into motion. Within 2 minutes, though it seemed to be an eternity, three of the girls were in the lobby with two paraprofessionals. The blind girl remained with her teacher in the classroom. I asked them to exit the building and walk toward Battery Park, which is the southernmost tip of Lower Manhattan. I said to them, "Just wait there. We'll come and get you."

I asked the AP to make an announcement asking all non-teaching personnel to report to the seventh floor, where he was. I then asked him to send down to the lobby the guidance counselors and the social worker. When they arrived in the lobby, I asked the social worker to report to the basement to see how the students in the gym classes were doing. I asked two of the counselors to watch the doors to make sure no adult would attempt to get into the stairwells. Remember, now I'm thinking, "What if someone has a bomb strapped to their body?" Our building is on Trinity Place, right next door to the American Stock Exchange and across the street from Trinity Church. If someone wanted to cause greater chaos, we were right in the middle of it all. I asked the other guidance counselor to offer emotional assistance to anyone in the lobby who might need it.

My secretary called me to say that the superintendent wanted to know what was going on. I asked her to tell him, "I don't know." Ask him, "What can you tell me?" At that moment, there was another horrific explosion, and the entire building shook. The screams in the lobby were deafening. Now the parents that had congregated were hysterical, people were shaking, there was lots of praying. Someone ran into the building screaming, "Another plane has hit. There are eight planes on their way to New York City, Washington, and California." Now I start to pray. What else could I do? I said, "God, you promised you wouldn't leave me or forsake me. I need to know what to do. I need to know now."

With that, I got up on top of a table in the lobby, and in a loud voice I said, "This is a school. I am the principal. Right now you are in my building. If you want to be in this building, you must follow my instructions." (Oh, I was sounding so tough. All right, so what are my instructions?) I said, "We are going to evacuate the building. We will proceed south to Battery Park." Using my walkie-talkie I called the AP and said, "Get on the loudspeaker. Tell everyone that we are going to evacuate. Everyone is to remain calm and most importantly, everyone must listen to directions. Tell them that no one is to leave their floor until you personally deliver the instruction." I directed him, "Go to the 14th floor and begin evacuating the floors one by one."

Just as I finished talking, Captain Kam of the School Safety Squad walked into the building. He was covered in soot. He said, "Ada, I think you have to leave." My angel had arrived to deliver the confirmation to the decision I had already made. It was time to go. I got up on top of the table and said to those in the lobby, "We are evacuating this building. Everyone must leave the building now. Please proceed south, toward Battery Park. Parents, if you want to meet your children, please do so at the corner of Trinity and Rector, by the food store."

I emptied out the lobby and proceeded to the outdoor exit closest to the American Stock Exchange. There I met the head of security who asked me if everyone was okay. I said we were, but we were evacuating to the park. He immediately called some of his security personnel to assist with my evacuation. I greeted each student, teacher, and other personnel as they exited the building. I asked them to stay together, to take the hand of a friend, to comfort each other and that I would meet them at the entrance to the park. Evacuation of the building lasted for about 10 minutes. (I lost all track of time. Remember, my watch was not working.)

Parents reunited with their children on the corner, and we continued to walk toward Battery Park. Halfway there I turned around looked up and said to the AP, "Do you see what I see?" I was in disbelief. This couldn't be. The tops of the towers were engulfed in flames and black smoke billowing. Two towers on fire. Actually, it looked like two big matchsticks lit up with smoke billowing up into the sky. The top of the North Tower was engulfed in black smoke, while the South Tower had red flames and black smoke streaming upward into the sky. The flames appeared to roll, over and over again. As noisy as it was, there appeared to be a silence enveloping the atmosphere, almost like in reverence to what was unfolding right before our eyes.

I turned around and walked faster toward my destination, Battery Park. Accompanied by several teachers, secretaries, and other non-teaching personnel, I asked them to quickly block the oncoming traffic on Battery Place, to make sure that all of the students would get across the street safely and into Battery Park. They needed to find their teachers in the park. Cars honked their horns, and I with my walkie-talkie in hand simply stood in front of the traffic making sure that all of the students would get across.

All of a sudden there came the sound of popping, cracking, snapping; a silence, screaming. I looked up and saw people running in every direction, most of them coming toward me. I was pushed. I looked behind me in the direction of the popping and snapping sound. It was a tsunami wave of darkness. It was moving quickly in our direction. I was pushed. I was shoved. I looked back again. There was the black wave. Now much closer. I looked into the park and cried out, "Oh my God, where are my kids? Please take care of the kids." I was pushed. I looked back and the cloud appeared to be approaching the next corner. It was as tall as the buildings. I was pushed. I almost fell. I said, "I can't die trampled to death." I started to run. I was wearing heels. I was wearing a skirt. I jumped on a park bench, over a fence, and onto the foot of a tree. I fell to the ground just as the cloud hit me on my back. It turned black in an instant. It hit my neck. It felt like pins and needles on my neck. It was cold. It was hard. I screamed to God, "Mercy! Please, mercy!" I thought I would die. I wasn't alone. Others were praying alongside me.

Then it, the cloud, ran away. I opened my eyes. It was gray. It was light gray. There was white ash falling. It looked like snow. Snow in September? I saw a sharp ray of bright sun breaking through the gray haze. I saw a large cloud of smoke overhead. It appeared to dissipate over the river.

What just happened? I tried to speak. I couldn't. It hurt. Someone said, "We've been attacked. There are eight planes coming toward New York City. They hit the White House. They hit Pennsylvania. In silence I cried out, "Mercy, God! Have mercy!" I couldn't speak. It hurt. It felt like chips of broken glass were embedded in my throat. It hurt. I attempted to stand. Someone helped me. Someone gave me a bottle of water. A man said, "You have to take water and spit." I said to myself, "Spit. I can't spit. That's gross." I realized I couldn't swallow. I realized I couldn't speak. It hurt. I put water in my mouth, gargled, and spit. There, I did it. Not lady-like. Where did the man go? Where did the water come from?

I stayed surrounded by the people at the tree and found others crying out to God for mercy. Planes were flying overhead. Surely the other eight attack planes had arrived. "Oh my God! What is going on?" I looked up through the falling white ash and noted, in the reflection of the glass of a semiround building along the park, a plane fly by. I screamed, "Get down!" I said, "Lord have Mercy."

I got up and started to walk. I thought, *Where are the kids? Oh my God, where are the kids?* My throat hurt. I gargled with the water and spit some more. I knew no one. I saw a man standing by a water fountain with his finger on the spigot (imagine water pouring out of a water fountain in a New York City park). He asked people to find tissues or take pieces of their clothing to wet and place over their faces. Men and women were ripping their jackets, their shirts, to give strangers something wet to place over their faces. The man said, "You can't let this get into your lungs. It's toxic. You'll die. Cover your faces." I looked in my pocketbook and found tissues. I wet them and placed them over my face. Oh my! Did my face hurt. It was glass. I started to wash it off. I washed my tongue. It was dry. Cutting. My neck hurt.

What's that noise? Cracking, crashing, popping. I looked back. "Oh no, not again?" Another tsunami wave. What was it? What had happened? I fell to the ground again, this time at the foot of another tree. I began to pray loud. I found others who joined me. We held hands. We put our faces to the ground as the wave hit us again. It was hard on the back. A heavy wind. It turned black. It turned dark gray. It turned light gray. I opened my eyes. I saw a ray of sunshine streaming through the grayness. I heard planes overhead. I thought, *Oh my God. Am I going to die now? Please forgive me. I'm sorry. Oh my God. Where are my kids?* The planes flew overhead. Was it the enemy? "Oh, my! The Statue of Liberty. They will bomb the Statue of Liberty. I must run away from the water. Where can I go?"

I walked fast away from the water and saw some of my kids. I asked, "Where is everybody?" One girl grabbed me and said, "Mrs. Dolch, many of the students are in the restaurant." (What restaurant? How sad, I didn't even know there was a restaurant in Battery Park.) I used my walkie-talkie and said, "Can anyone hear me?" Immediately I heard a response, "Where are you?" It was my precious Sergeant Crockett. I said, "I'm fine. Where are you? Is everybody okay? Who are you with?" One girl said, "Look Ms. Dolch, the kids are getting on the ferries." I thought, *What? Oh my God. Now what will I do? Who is with the kids? Is everyone safe? Is anyone hurt?* I saw my teacher, Heather. I hugged her. She said, "Conrad [another teacher] told the kids to start getting on the boats. He went with them. Several other teachers got on the boats as well." I asked, "Has anyone seen Becky or Stephanie [they were my two wheelchair students]? Heather said, "Yes, they are right around the wall." I ran to find them while speaking into my walkie-talkie and attempting to connect with the others who had radios as well.

I looked toward the water, and I saw some of my students jumping on ferries that would carry them to Staten Island and New Jersey, where they would spend the night sleeping on the gym floor of a school, a church, or a local YMCA. Over the walkie-talkie I heard a call from one of the deans who said, "Ada, come into the restaurant. Many of the kids have congregated in here." I walked into the restaurant to hundreds of eyes staring at me in a catatonic state. Some kids were crying. I heard babies crying. An ambulance was assisting a woman. What was wrong? One of my students said, "We think she's in labor." Several adults were sitting at the bar ordering drinks. Imagine, sitting down to have a drink. One of my students said to me, "Mrs. Dolch, you have to wash your face and you need lipstick." She wanted me to put on my lipstick! We've just been through hell and she's worried about my lipstick.

I walked from table to table. Touched my kids. Some were crying. Some said, "Mrs. Dolch, I'm so scared. I have to call my mother. There are no telephones." Once again, the kids were depending on me, but I had no answers for them. I asked the kids to direct me to a bathroom. I entered. Oh, my God. What the hell do I look like? White ash all over me. My hair is white. A ghost. Ashen. What a mess. I splashed water on my face. It just wouldn't come off. Someone gave me what looked like a dish towel. Oh yes, people were using the dish towels, the cloth napkins, and the tablecloths to wash themselves. I washed my face with the dish towel. It hurt to scrub. It felt like I was removing glass. It felt good. Clean. I put on my lipstick. I used the toilet. I left and walked into the kitchen. We started filling the pots and pans with water and handing them to the kids so they could wash their faces. That felt good. I felt useful. Once again, I felt in control. Kids expressed their joy to see me. Kids cried.

A call came on the walkie-talkie. It was the principal from next door. I ran outside. I ran and hugged him. He was a basket case. He had delayed leaving his building and found himself running into a parking lot, seeking safety when the tower fell. He said it was dark. It was scary. There was no way out. He thought he would surely die. No, there he was, talking to me. He found some of his students and teachers. We walked around, finding more. The sun was shining. It felt warm. We saw many students and staff jumping on the ferries headed toward Staten Island. We found more people.

Everyone was fine. A little shaken, scared, but happy, so happy to see everyone. We would immediately hug. Every time I met a teacher I would ask, "Have you connected with your students?" My blind student was with her teacher. One boy was having an asthma attack. I placed my hands on him, and I prayed that he would be okay. A police officer came by and gave him oxygen. How crazy is that? Every time a helicopter or an airplane few overhead we would jump. Many ducked. Everyone's head would turn up to the sky to see whether it was friend or foe. What else could we expect?

Three and a half hours later, I reconnected with my neighboring principal, over the walkie-talkie, and with the help of the other staff members that had gathered, we started making plans to leave the park. We asked, "Who lives in Queens, the Bronx, Upper Manhattan, East Side, West Side?" We deployed groups of people led by teachers and other staff members. I volunteered to take charge of the Brooklyn group. Using the walkie-talkies we managed to inform as many people as we could that we were leaving the park. We gathered the students and staff. We waved good-bye. We said, "Be careful. Stay together."

I started my journey home to Brooklyn. My goal was to make it across the Brooklyn Bridge. So we started our mile-long walk toward the bridge. Along the way people gave us water. Others handed us dust masks. Others gave food. So many people helping. Who were they? Where did they get all of this stuff? The crowds of people leaving Lower Manhattan appeared to get larger as we got closer to the bridge. They wouldn't let us get on the Brooklyn Bridge because there were too many people so we had to walk another three quarters of a mile north to the Manhattan Bridge.

I noticed a little Muslim girl following me. Who was she? I asked her. How embarrassing. This was the 4th day of school and I didn't know that she was one of my new freshman students. Ugh! I always know my kids. She was wearing a head covering, which identified her as Muslim. I never had a student who wore a head covering. This was different, and of all days. She said, "Mrs. Dolch, I'm scared." I said, "Of what?" She said, "Of what happened." I said to her, "You just hang onto me, and together we will cross the bridge." She locked her arm into mine, and we started the journey. It was hot. It was sunny. It was long. We walked and walked. We sang songs. I said to her, "Don't look back." (What did I think . . . I'd turn into a pillar of salt?) We didn't look back. I wouldn't look down, either. Scary up on top of the bridge. We walked. She said, "My legs are tired." I said, "What about me, I'm wearing heels. Come on, if I can do this you can do this." And so, arm in arm, we walked across the Manhattan Bridge. We did it. We made it across the bridge. I had walked the bridge with an angel. Yes, my own special angel.

For a couple of hours on that September day, I along with many others faced the reality of a possible violent death. What if there were more airplanes? What if other buildings would collapse? What if the debris we were ingesting had a chemical that would kill us shortly after breathing it in? I began to think about the life of others around the world. What about the Israelis and the Palestinians? What about the people of Bosnia or Sarajevo? Is this what they experience every day? For the first time I was speaking the same language of so many others around the globe. I didn't like it. I hated it. I was beginning to accept the fate of death. There was fear and despair on everyone's face. I didn't want to die. I wasn't ready to die. I had much work to do. What about my students? What about my family? What about my daughter far away in England? What about my parents in Florida? I was experiencing the common language of many around the world, the language of hatred and rejection, nails and spears, bombs and air strikes, terror attacks and the bleeding bodies of children in places like Ireland, Baghdad, Jerusalem, and now New York. No, this couldn't be the end. The Rev. Dr. Martin Luther King, Jr. said in his 1963 "Strength to Love" speech,

> The ultimate weakness of violence is that it is a descending spiral, begetting the very thing it seeks to destroy. Instead of diminishing evil, it multiples it. . . . Through violence you may murder the hater, but you do not murder hate. In fact, violence merely increases hate. . . . Returning violence for violence multiplies violence, adding deeper darkness to a night already devoid of stars. Darkness cannot drive out hate; only love can do that.

For the next 3 days, I attempted to locate every teacher. I couldn't reach those who lived in Manhattan, for telephones weren't working. Somehow I didn't worry about the kids. I knew all had left the building and they were safe. Five school days later, I met with the superintendent. He wanted me to start making plans for a move to another school building, for we would not be able to return for some time. I cried. What else was I to do? I cried some more. For the next couple of days we fought to secure the best possible learning environment. Oh, by the way, this is not in the "principal's manual." We had to figure it out step by step.

One thing I was sure of; I didn't have to make these decisions on my own. Establishing a learning environment that truly embodied the concept of collaboration was the work that we had completed years before. Our school culture was set; we are a school of leadership and public service. Gathering the teachers and staff, we sat and cried, held hands, and planned, and cried and planned. We cried some more. Through the tears we managed to get school started all over again. There were no pretty offices, no pretty paper, no scissors, no paper clips, no telephones, no computers, but we had each other. That was enough to get us through. The questions that we had to respond to had no answers, so we learned to live with the questions and create a tightly knit web of support that would ensure our own safety and welfare during this time. You see, everyone else was "moving on." Imagine, 2 weeks later people were saying, "Move on." Oh, we were moving, all right. Backward and sideways, but never "moving on."

We sought the means to provide as much assistance and guidance to the staff and to the students. We put in place mechanisms that allowed for breakdowns and for pick-me-ups. We took nothing for granted. We listened to everything and responded to everything. We didn't say things like, "get over it" or "move on" or "enough already." Although there are many who are distant from the emotional trauma that we endured, we live it every day. School is no longer just about reading, writing, arithmetic, and preparing for college. No, it also includes self-help, emotional healing, caring, support, finding strength, and searching for purpose and destiny. We listen more. We listen carefully. We react quickly. We take nothing for granted. We have walked "through the valley of the shadow of death" (Psalm 23), and we seek the means to get to the mountaintop.

Dedicated to the memory of my sister, **Wendy Alice Rosario Wakeford,** *who along with thousands of others, gave her life for our freedom on that beautiful September morn.*

Four

Playing Through Adversity

TOM GOODRIDGE

MY CLASSROOM WAS a mess. Five-year-old Jared had just hit 7-year-old Taquesha. Taquesha was whining in such a way as to ensure another hit. Rodney, who was just coming into language, kept singing, "You deserve a break today." It was today's advertisement; he would repeat it, at random interevals, throughout the day. Cory, sent to my class for the day, was knocking over puzzles in the rear of the classroom. He did not stop when I told him to, and he was too fast to chase. Shavone, who had been actually listening to me read the picture book *The Very Busy Spider*, gave up on the book and yelled at Cory, "Stop it!"

Ms. Jenkins, who was assigned to assist in my classroom but was called to help in the office (because she could do payroll), dashed into the classroom long enough to tell me, "The World Trade Towers have been attacked and they have collapsed. The Pentagon was also hit. The White House will be next!" And then she was gone, like some latter-day Paul Revere.

My first thought, I am ashamed to say, was, *Will they cancel school tomorrow?* It's not that I hated school, but I was becoming overwhelmed by days like this. I loved being with these kids, but I was losing my equilibrium in trying to meet the needs of these wild little ones under the conditions of this school in Harlem. When I learned that the world at large was violent and chaotic like my classroom was that day, I felt a strange relief.

The apocalyptic news certainly gave me direction. There were no further instructions from the Public Address System. Usually teaching was regularly interrupted by a voice from the P.A.—to learn of cars about to be towed or children gone astray. Today, when our country was under attack, we heard nothing. "Stay calm," I told myself, "Await further developments." I knew the focusing power of chaos from 11 years of teaching this class.

I rarely knew what would happen next in this Special Ed class. This was different, though; this time it was the outside world's tumult that was rocking our classroom boat. The next wave delivered Josie's mother to the classroom. Ms. Gonzales was a recent immigrant from Mexico. She was hysterical, and she just needed to hold her daughter. She announced (as far as I understood her Spanish), "I'm taking her home now to safety." It was interesting that Josie, the most volatile and aggressive child in my self-contained classroom for developmentally disabled children, would be the first one to get home safely.

I figured that getting children home that day could be a difficulty. As a single man, without a family to worry about, I knew I could remain at school until each of my students was picked up by a bus or by their family. I had entered teaching so as to have children in my life. I especially value these profoundly original children who come with their obvious developmental disabilities; the ones who can so easily "fall between the cracks." These kids put me in touch with raw and essential humanity; they also make it clear that I am needed. Along with their cognitive impediments I discover a warmth and a curious wholeness within most of them. That makes the travail of teaching worthwhile. I am a gay man, and this little community of my classroom has become like my family.

The bus came an hour late and picked up four of my students. I delivered Lacia home to her mother; they lived across the street. Her mother, who was under treatment for cancer, had three other children at home so it was difficult for her to come get Lacia. At 5:00, the last parent to arrive came for Sophie, a 5-year-old girl with Down Syndrome. The school's two other special ed teachers were also still at school. Special ed students who can't travel independently, which included all of my students, are generally picked up by bus. Knowing that my students were safe, I could now go home and encounter this changed world on my own. . . .

*   *   *

More than 100 blocks north of the World Trade Center, the sky over Harlem was deep blue as I emerged from the school's neon-lit corridors. The air was sweet, cool, and dry—how could such a day hold disaster? The prevailing wind must have been from the North, as no ash, smoke, or smell made its way Uptown.

Walking home that day, I felt safer to be in Harlem. I figured that whoever had aimed their attack so precisely at the World Trade Center, the Pentagon, and the White House (my understanding at the time) would probably not go after us here. Their target appeared to be the jugular of the military industrial complex; Harlem didn't qualify.

My apartment is about 12 blocks from the school; the streets were unusually empty as I returned home. I imagined that folks were huddled around their TV sets gathered in family clusters. Usually I got to meet the regular stoop sitters on my walk home. They would call to me, "Hey, teach, wuz up?" and we'd chew on some bit of news. But today's news was too much; it must have knocked even the hardiest stoop sitters from their posts.

Walking home, I thought that this crisis might help me define just who my family were. . . . I made a mental note to call my brother, who works in Lower Manhattan—and then I'd call my boyfriend, who lives on Staten Island. Fortunately, I knew no one who worked in the immediate vicinity of the Twin Towers.

As a white man living and working in Harlem, I wondered how this disaster would impact differently upon people of color. One of the neighborhood men had recently said to me, "When you whites get a cold, we blacks get pneumonia." The goodies aren't distributed fairly in this world; I wondered how this disaster's impact would get divided up.

My home is a nice-sized one-bedroom apartment, with a balcony, in a moderate-income, 50s-era co-op, filled with old-time liberals. I'm active in my building and feel like I'm a part of its community. I figured these times would provide a test for our community. I'm a Luddite who lives without a TV or a computer, and my toaster and stove are from the 50s, like me. I see my home as a sanctuary from the tumult of the school and the city. I've filled my place with reminders of the natural world: pine floors and a natural birch totem pole, and large windows to view the trees on our grounds. Would I miss having a TV, now that this news had broken? Or was I fortunate to be able to protect myself from being bludgeoned by this day's horrific imagery?

I don't trust the mainline media anyway; they just manipulate us in order to sell the goods they advertise. That's in the best of times—in these times—the Pentagon, or what was left of it, would probably shape the news. So I turned to the most radically "alternative" radio station I know, WBAI, which I trusted would give me a critical view to balance the government-sanctioned media. I heard enough in one half hour to ponder for that evening. I baked a sweet potato and had a watercress salad. I made the promised phone calls before going to bed. I figured I needed sleep the most—in order to prepare for a rapidly changing world.

Before going to sleep I wrote in my journal; I understood these times to be significant—I wanted to be able to remember my responses. My preferred learning style (teachers are always helping kids determine their learning style) is to listen for my inner story and confide it to my journal instead of barraging myself with the "outside" news. I don't generally read too much of my students' files until I meet them—I like to discover my own response to people and events first.

I got my wish—there was no school the next day. I stayed pretty close to home and saw some neighbors. I received phone calls from concerned friends, some far away. I was glad to hear from John in Ireland, a music therapist who worked with deeply disabled children in an intentional, residential community. It was good to know that my first love still cared.

The next day, school was in session. I wanted to learn how this horrific attack, and its consequences, had played out in the lives of my students. Had whoever masterminded this tragedy considered the increased suffering upon the most burdened of lives? Many of my children struggled to win the attention of their parents, who are consumed by their battle for survival. Now, how would they fare? I cringed to think.

School had a delayed opening for students. Teachers were to gather first in order to prepare to receive the children of this wounded city. Special Ed teachers are generally as concerned with how their students feel as how they think, and they understand that both are connected. I actually felt better prepared for the issues that confronted us this day than with the pressures that have been created by the standards that drive today's schools. Our schools have become increasingly programmed (from the top down) in order to raise reading scores on standardized tests. Today's educational policy makers largely ignore the emotional and spiritual lives of children. Most of our students, regular and special ed, struggle to meet the demands of urban living—yet I find our schools unable to offer them much support.

The school's part-time psychologist spoke to the assembled staff about the fear and grief that would arise in children. He suggested that we make space in our classroom for whatever a child might need to feel and express. Yes, I agreed, wholeheartedly. Why is this not always so? I'll never forget the last words of this meeting as spoken by our principal: "Today the standards don't matter, just be there for your kids." She had just given me permission to do what I do best; it is why I teach.

My class was smaller that day. Ms. Sanchez had told the bus driver she wasn't going to send Arias to school for a while. Lacia's mom wasn't up to bringing her in. I did want to make contact with my children. But children, especially the young 5- to 7-year-olds I teach, need lots of time with their parents. Maybe this crisis would prove a boon for these children, if families were able to huddle together and remember that they were still a family. No matter how disabled the children are, they know when they are loved.

I knew my children would sense that something was different since 9/11, and I knew the politics of this global crisis was beyond their understanding (as well as my own). However, my students could read fluently the hearts of the adults who mattered most to them. My students could always find my emotional buttons; every day they taught me something about myself. A cataclysmic event had happened which would have an impact on them. How was I to convey it to them?

Play is the best way I know to teach my students. I often need to convince parents, administrators, and other teachers how children learn through playing. Play is the genius of children. Let a child loose in a safe community, with a few basic props, and they will show you what they most need to learn. Play provides the purest form of assessment as well as the most natural context for learning. Play, for my students, is as necessary as food. Most of them have limited speech and social skills, play is how they communicate. I believe in play's importance for all of us, including adults. But the child is clearly built for play. The heart of a child is revealed through their play.

What do I mean by play? In our culture the word is often used to mean "goofing off." Our children, when provoked, will often say "I'm not playing with you" as a warning that they mean business. I mean just the opposite, for play is what you do—when it's up to you.

My classroom is divided into play spaces: the drama center, the block/building center, the art center, and the game center. When it's play time, the children choose their center. I ask them, "What is your plan?" It is so engaging to hear them attempt to communicate their plans. If Tyisha wants to play restaurant in the drama center, she may hold up an imaginary bowl and stir it with an imaginary spoon. I may challenge her further, "What do you want to cook?" If she is at a loss, I will make suggestions: "Are you going to cook pizza or chicken?" If the next child should choose the drama center, I ask him, "What will you do in the restaurant?" Finding a role in ever-changing social contexts is how children learn to be competent and cooperative. I encourage collaboration. I don't expect them to follow through on all these plans. Play is a mutable land where adapting to change becomes the only constant.

I contend that we all play roles—I'm playing teacher. The trouble with adults is that we get stuck in our roles. We take our roles so seriously, we forget that with each evolving minute it is possible to change roles. We could ask ourselves instead, "What role best fits my inner state to the outward situation?" Children understand this grease and grace of play—it is how they explore the complex surface of reality. Play is not an escape from the real world; it is a direct encounter with it. If school is about preparing for a *changing* world—then let's get playing!

Discovering the parts my students play best and fitting those parts into the community's whole is the primary goal of my teaching. It's hard to master this with worksheets or to divide it into subject areas. When my class can find effective individual roles to play within the context of an imaginary restaurant, they are co-creating a world in which 9/11 will no longer be necessary.

On the 13th day of September we began the day with our regular "welcome back" circle on the carpet, where we share personal news. I had them each get a block from the building center. We went around the circle, each child contributing his or her block to (what I named as) a tower. Then we built another one, just the same, and I called them the Twin Towers. When I asked them what had happened to New York City's Twin Towers, Tyisha said, "A plane hit them and they fell down."

In play it is helpful for children to construct their own props. "What can we use for a plane?" I asked, since we had a limited arsenal in the classroom. Play is as much about creating a symbolic reality as it is about the mastery of that reality. Julio said "Look," as he grabbed a long Duplo, the large-sized version of Legos, and intersected it with a short one to make a cruciform shape, "An airplane!" he said. We approved. Julio taught us how to make it and stood a bit taller.

"What happened downtown?" I asked. "I'll show you," Tyisha volunteered as she made her plane crash into one of the towers, knocking it down. There was great applause from her audience. I asked her to rebuild the tower. Then we each took turns flying a plane we each assembled into a tower, watched them fall, and then rebuilt the tower. The repetition was important for comprehension.

Was I teaching my students how to become terrorists? Children need to imagine themselves as possessing the power and skills necessary to shape their lives. When we first taste power, we often exploit it. The 2-year-old asserts his power by saying "NO." In play, dolls are often spanked and sometimes killed. In play children are able to act out their impulses. Playing with others, with occasional interventions from a teacher, children can learn about the consequences of their actions. Had the men who were responsible for the 9/11 attack (and I don't think women could have done this) known this power of play to explore their impulses and learn the consequences of their actions, I don't believe they would have chosen that path.

The therapeutic power of play is all about giving children a chance to exert an imagined sense of control over situations they do not actually control. Making a tower and then knocking it down enabled children to grasp and re-create the drama of an event that had engulfed our collective lives. They were bringing what was happening in the larger world into the world of our classroom—to understand it better.

"What happens when a building falls down" I asked.

Julio said, "Things get broke, and people can get hurt, and they can die."

"What can we do to help?" I asked.

Ricardo said, "Get the police."

I asked who wanted to go to the block center and find a police person. I tried to get consensus upon what we will use to represent the police. Humans are symbol makers; that is the power that language grants us in co-constructing our reality. Someone got the carpenter (since our police figure was missing), and we all agreed he would become our policeman. "What do we need to help those who were hurt?" I asked. They gathered nurses and doctors. Tyisha added that animals were hurt, too. So I introduced the term *veterinarian*, and we selected the figures who would help wounded animals. We enacted rescues using these symbolic figures. I asked children to work together on their rescues, but some were still most interested in the knock-down phase. We also carried this theme to the drama and art centers. Children need various open-ended materials (paint, clay, sand, and blocks) from which to select a medium in which to translate their own story. In play, children show us what they most need to do and do it. I trust this human "instinct" for healing.

An event with such profound consequences as 9/11 can be approached through many divergent paths in the attempt to "bring it home" to each individual. My primary goal in these first days was to help the children understand what had happened at the most practical level. Then I tried to assure them that their own world need not collapse as a result of it. I didn't attempt to address what might have motivated the attack, for I judged it to be beyond their understanding. However, while Ricardo was flying planes into the towers he observed that, "Maybe the towers were too high—so the planes knocked them over."

In his simple, yet symbolic understanding of the event, he may have revealed a portion of the truth. Maybe the towers were too high. Had our arrogance and greed inflated their height? Had our endless quest for material growth gone too far? In our lust for world trade, were we losing our souls? These children, for all their innocence and lack of experience, regularly taught me what was essential and what made life worth living. In the troubling times that lay ahead, my life would be balanced by their simple, pure wisdom. Maybe the children of this generation will choose never to build such tall towers again.

Five

Commandeering the Phones: The District Office

CLAUDIA DiSALVO

WHILE GETTING READY for work on September 11th, I was unusually struck by the rays of dazzling sunlight beaming through my Upper West Side apartment windows. I paused a moment to take in and reflect on the many architectural cityscape views looking back at me from my southerly New York view. The sky was an incredible blue; the clouds were white, billowy, and plentiful. They were performing a breathtaking dance as they caught the draft, rolling upward and then floating down until another wind draft gently caught their tips lifting them skyward again. The rays of the sun bounced off the Empire State Building, transporting its radiant and glowing reflections to all of the surrounding buildings. It was just a glorious morning, and I couldn't wait to venture out to listen to the day. I can recall saying to myself that this was one of those days that you could really see forever.

I continued to be captivated by the beauty, warmth, and clarity of the morning as I left my building. It was evident that this beautiful morning had a profound effect on many of the doormen and friends that I see and greet each day. Folks were smiling, waving, and sending good wishes for a wonderful day. I glanced at my watch. Yikes, seeing 8:38 A.M. brought me back to the day and the work I had before me. I dashed down West 79th Street to Broadway, skipped down the subway steps, paid the fare at the turnstile, and waited on the platform. I anticipated that the #1 local downtown train would be there within the next minute or so because there were so many passengers already waiting on the platform. The trains at that time of the morning arrive every few minutes. So why wasn't my train there when I needed it? Thank goodness I was only traveling seven subway stops downtown to West 28th Street.

While looking down the long, dark, subway tunnel, I found myself organizing, managing, and prioritizing the work at hand for the day when suddenly the train emerged from the tunnel. Great, it was 8:42. The subway doors opened and happily I jumped aboard, found a seat, pulled out the *New York Times* and settled into the rhythm of the train on the tracks. Just barely past 34th Street (Penn Station), the train came to a screeching stop. I glanced again at my watch. It was approximately 8:49 A.M. We sat in the dark, holding our breath and waited, as all good New Yorkers do, for some explanation. Those moments underground (even before the WTC attack) trigger a wide range of thoughts, and unfortunately my mind always conjured up the worst possible ones. I reminded myself to focus on the emergency signs on the trains. Just then, I heard a voice from the public announcement system, "There has been a gas explosion somewhere around 14th Street. West 28th Street will be our last stop." Just then the train began to move slowly. I was elated as it began to pick up speed. I had less than one stop. The train came to a stop at 8:51! I was up off my seat and at the door. I remember saying to myself, "Thank you God, thank you God." I had so much to do and so little time to get it done. Thoughts of sitting underground in a subway car were just not part of my plan for today.

As special assistant to a district director of Pupil Personnel Services, my job involved supporting the director, who is responsible for developing, coordinating, implementing, administering, and delivering a wide range of programs to approximately 26,000 plus students in 41 schools. I had scheduled a series of student-parent meetings from 10:00 A.M. to 4:00 P.M. today. My goal for September 11th, 2001, was to finalize the district's high school admission process and ensure that every graduating eighth grader was registered in a high school. But finding a high school seat for students at this time of the year was like trying to find a needle in a haystack. Our high schools were always crowded at best. As a former high school principal, I knew what principals were going through to finalize school schedules and make their schools operational, efficient, and safe so that they could focus on the rigorous work ahead. An additional student or two could potentially change and shift schedules and present challenges for principals, teachers, and the rest of the staff. But little did I know then just what was in store for all of us that day. What I did know at the time was that there would be a host of families and students who would arrive well before their 10:00 A.M. appointments. I anticipated finding our reception room full of families.

I ran up the subway stairs to Seventh Avenue and W. 28th Street. It was 8:53 A.M. As I stood waiting for the traffic light, I realized that there was little or no car traffic. I looked uptown (north) on Seventh Avenue and it was unusually empty for that time of the morning. I could clearly see Madison Square Garden and Macy's. I looked downtown (south) in the direction of Greenwich Village and again Seventh Avenue was nearly empty. Mentally scratching my head I thought, *This is very strange. What's going on? West 28th Street is the cross street of Seventh Avenue and is the center of the flower district and the street is practically empty? No taxis, flower vans, UPS or Fed-Ex trucks, and no cars.* I reflected back to the subway conductor's comments that there was an underground gas explosion in the 14th Street area and figured that drivers paid attention to traffic reports and they were simply staying away from the area or finding alternate travel routes. The light changed, and I crossed the street and made my way into the lobby of our building. It was close to 9, and the lobby was virtually empty.

Our district offices were located on the seventh floor. We shared this huge building with a wide range of advertising agencies, fur manufacturers, not-for-profit organizations like the YMCA, and others. There was always a whole host of people in the lobby, and we would informally set up lines at the elevators so that we could get upstairs in an efficient fashion. All of the elevator cars were down in the lobby. One elevator door was open and waiting. Entering, I pressed seven and traveled up alone.

The elevator door opened. I slowly walked through the foyer into our reception area. It was not only empty but the office was

jarringly still. There were no parents or students, and our receptionist was not at her desk. As I walked in the direction of my desk, I
peered into offices of colleagues, and they, too, were empty. I said
to myself, What am I missing? I knew that I had a full day of meetings scheduled. I found myself feeling very uneasy. While walking
down the corridor to my office, I scanned the floor. There was no
movement, not even our playful mice. I say that literally because we
were dealing with some very aggressive mice who enjoyed playing
hide and seek in our corridors.

I dropped my bags, hung up my coat, and from that vantage
point saw light and movement but little sound from the superintendent's office. I walked quickly over to the door that was slightly
ajar. I knocked while opening at the same time and found my colleagues either huddled around the two television sets or on the
telephones. The room was filled. Everyone's eyes were glued to the
television sets. I saw the superintendent, deputy superintendent,
director of Pupil Personnel Services, the director of Health Education, special assistant to the superintendent, and other staff. One of
my colleagues finally looked up and said, "Claudia, you're never
going to believe this," as I walked toward him. No one else spoke,
but we all at some point made eye contact. I didn't know what was
happening, but I recall seeing anguish and fear in everyone's eyes.
My eyes followed theirs to the surreal images on the television
screens. Out of all of the emotion in that room, I somehow realized that I was watching one of the World Trade Towers burning,
and it was all I could do to not be overcome by the horror reflected
from those scenes. At that point my colleague said to me, "A plane
hit the World Trade Tower." I was stunned. Those words literally
scrambled my brain. I remember while looking at the television set,
that I had a clash of two reactions—I started praying, while trying to reconcile the emotion of how the plane could possibly have
crashed into the building.

Then all of a sudden, out of the blue sky we saw another plane
heading toward the second Tower. We started pointing at the sets
and shouting. Everyone in the room was screaming and shouting, "No, No, No!" The plane didn't listen; it flew right into the
building, exploded, sending up huge plumes of smoke. The tower
started to burn. Smoke was spewing out of the building. There
was an unbelievable silence and stillness in the room. The images

from the television set confirmed that the first plane crash was not accidental. We were being attacked, but why? Who was attacking us? The office erupted into a management crisis mode. I am very proud to say that I work with the most professional, caring, skilled, knowledgeable, and loving colleagues in the world.

Over the years, our staff had experienced and managed a wide range of crises in our schools, but obviously never of this magnitude, and one that was so unimaginable. For those readers who are not familiar with New York City schools, every principal is responsible for designing a thoughtful crisis management plan that provides for the health and safety of every member of the school community. These plans are reviewed and approved annually. Every school district designs a crisis management plan that in essence is an overarching school plan to provide every available support and service to the school or schools in crisis. The plan focuses on the logistics and coordination of the delivery of services while allocating district office staff to specific schools to support and assist schools in the event that a crisis occurs.

Many of our district's schools are located in the downtown area that includes Chinatown, Greenwich Village, and the Financial District that lives in the shadow of the towers. After the second tower was hit at 9:03 A.M., our phones began ringing off the hook. We received information that our downtown schools were evacuating to other schools. We knew that these receiving school sites would need as much direct assistance as possible. Public School 89 and Middle School 289, which are located on Warren Street and the Hudson River, were evacuating to P.S. 3 on Hudson and Bleecker Street. P.S. 234, located on Greenwich Street, was evacuating to P.S. 41 on W. 11th Street and Sixth Avenue (see Chapter 1). Several of my colleagues and I left the office with a clear destination. We were going directly to P.S. 3 and P.S. 41 to meet the students walking north.

As we exited the door on Seventh Avenue, we all stopped short at the same time. It was as if we walked into a brick wall. We realized that Seventh Avenue was empty. There was an eerie silence on the streets. And there was a new and strange scent. There were very few people around. They appeared to be walking in a fog. We headed quickly downtown passing W. 23rd Street, a large cross street. There was no street traffic. Continuing downtown on Seventh Avenue to W. 14th Street, we could see lines of people standing in front of St. Vincent's hospital in the Village.

I glimpsed my watch, and it was about 9:25. Getting closer, we saw lines of people disappearing all away around the block. Hundreds of young people stood very quietly. It was a remarkable and memorable scene. I will never forget it. We stopped to talk to some of them. They shared that when they heard about the tower crash they decided the only constructive thing they could do to help was to give blood. It was obvious that hundreds of people recognized that there would be many injured people from that building who would need emergency care. This was a remarkable tribute to our young people and how they responded to this crisis. I don't believe I can find the words to express my thoughts, feelings, and gratitude to their resolve to helping others in this time of crisis. In my eyes, they were all heroes!

We said good-bye to our colleague who was heading farther down Seventh Avenue to P.S. 41 to provide support. We walked past the hospital swinging further west over onto Hudson Street. Throngs of people were walking out of Greenwich Village crying and covered in black soot. We observed people walking aimlessly in the streets. Their eyes were blank. They were in shock! We stopped to console men and women who collapsed onto chairs in front of coffeehouses. They were crying and sobbing. All we could do was what came naturally. We wrapped our arms around them, held them for a moment, and reminded them that they were safe. It was distressing, but we knew we had a specific job to do so we couldn't linger. As we walked faster, I could almost feel my heart in my throat. The air quality had deteriorated as we pressed farther downtown, breathing was difficult, and the smell, acrid and obnoxious.

Upon seeing P.S. 3, we started to walk faster. There was a large crowd of people in front of it. We walked through the crowds, entered the building, and ran up the stairs to the principal's office. We wanted to alert the staff to our presence and that we would be working with the P.S. 89 school community. Additionally, if there was anything that they needed, we would be there to assist. They ensured us that everything was under control and that we could find the P.S. 89 community in the gymnasium area.

We went back downstairs, entered into the side corridor, which was actually a small gymnasium, where we found the principals, children, and staff. They were all safe. We observed teachers doing what they do best, consoling "little ones" while consoling each other. Principals were consoling children, teachers, and aides. We observed older students sitting down in organized groups, talking. Some were actually doing schoolwork. I was astonished by the incredible calmness in the room, given the enormity of this catastrophic event. And it was apparent that this environment would never have existed without the leadership of these two fine principals and staff. Although they were celebrated and honored later in the year, they are still unsung heroes in my mind.

I do not want to minimize the fact that there were signs that the community was still in shock. This school had endured the ghastly and gruesome events that led them to evacuate their building that beautiful September 11th morning in full view of the WTC. All of the "little people" with their principals, teachers, and staff walked nearly two miles north to get to a safe environment at P.S. 3. The children and staff had to endure the fiery views, the explosions, the smells, the sirens, the agonies of passersby's faces, and lord knows what else during this trek to safety.

It was difficult at that moment in time to deal with the magnitude of the catastrophic events that happened that morning. Nonetheless, we were crystal clear about our mission and the job ahead, which were to support the schools in any way we could and to ensure the health, safety, and security of every child and person in that building. In retrospect, we would never have been able to manage our enormous job if we had stopped to think about the details of the events. We were all like that mom whose adrenaline was supercharged when she found her child under a car. That adrenaline rush enabled her to pick up the car and pull her child free to safety.

The school was in a "lockdown" mode. This meant that no child could be released to anyone other than his or her parent or parent designee. Children could not leave even if they lived across the street from the building. After speaking with the principals of P.S. 89 it was decided that we would manage the parent contact for them. The principals had brought the student information contact cards with them. It was time for us to contact every family to pick up and get their children in the new school location. Families needed to be together this day so that the healing could begin. Even though there were some cell phones among the principals and staff, we needed an office with a landline telephone. The cell phones were needed for emergency use. Since I had spent some time working in the building I knew that the custodian's office was in close proximity. We headed to the office hoping that he was there, because I didn't have a master key. Just then, as if my prayer was answered from God, I saw a man coming out of the office. He was not the regular custodian. I told him that we needed the office and the telephones so that we could make contact with parents. He wasn't quite sure whether or not we could use his office or telephones. We told him he could forget about that notion. We told him that we were using the office and the telephones and if there was a problem he could call the superintendent's office. We were not budging. P.S. 3 and Greenwich Village Middle School were using their phones to contact their school community. The custodian's office was the only game in town for us!

The office was very old and small. My colleague and I needed to set up phone stations quickly so that we could process the calls efficiently and as quickly as possible. Additionally, we devised an informal telephone script ensuring that if we had to leave a message, we would be able to provide pertinent pickup information for the families. As we were writing this script, it dawned on us that we could be calling an office in or around the towers. It was an emotionally charged experience not knowing if a family member actually worked in the building. It was truly distressful.

We were now getting ready for the trenches, and we had hoped that our plan would establish a smooth, efficient, and safe result for every one of our children. The first group lined up at the door with their emergency information cards. As each child approached the desk, we warmly welcomed and comforted him or her and proceeded to start making a phone call. As the first child read aloud his telephone parent contact number to me, I quickly realized that the telephone keypad and its contacts were not working properly. After much prayer and some practice, I finally developed a touch rhythm on the keypad and was able to make outgoing calls. On average it took me at least three to four tries to make each outgoing call. Needless to say, I was quietly frantic because of the manner in which I had to make these calls, and I must admit a bit angry about these circumstances. Here we were having to "make nice" to a who-knows-how-old telephone. I knew that carpal tunnel was now in my future. We were truly operating on a wing and a prayer.

We made hundreds of calls. We listened to hundreds of voice messages from family members. We held and comforted many children during the course of those 10 plus hours. In the middle of all of these calls, the telephone rang. It was someone who had worked in one of the city agencies. He briskly said to me that they would have to take over the school and convert it to a morgue. Don't ask me why, but I told him that he would have to do it over my dead body. I don't know where that came from, but I said under no circumstances was I able to move hundreds of children out of this building. I informed him (and by the way, I never got his name) that he would have the wrath of the entire school community and the New York press to deal with if he dared step one foot into this school. He said, after listening to my tirade, that "he would get back to me." Well, I never heard from him again. How dare he? I was furious at that point. But I had to get over the conversation and get back on to what was really important.

We finally made the last call and dealt with every conceivable problem, and suddenly it was profoundly quiet. We had worked for so many hours in a sea of noise, tears, and commotion that the stillness was deafening. It was so still that when my colleague and I finally looked at each other, we said, "Let's see who's left in the building and figure out how we are going to get home" We knew that transportation was not available in any form. We walked around the building and found several colleagues who also lived on the Upper West Side. We had agreed that we would walk each other home. As we started to walk out the door and down the stairs, one of my colleagues slipped and quickly went down, hitting her head on the concrete steps. Our breath was taken away, but we all moved quickly to assist her. To this day, I still do not know how she got up, rubbed her head, and said that she was all right. She went down so quickly that no one had a chance to break the fall. We insisted that she sit still because we were all very concerned for her. This incident was just unbelievable and not needed given the circumstances of the day.

We walked slowly up to West 14th Street, quietly reviewing the day. We couldn't find the words. As we got to the intersection, we saw a bus, ran to it, and asked the bus driver if we could travel uptown with him. The driver said yes because he was moving triage teams from hospital to hospital. We thankfully jumped on and took our seats near a team of physicians who were still dressed in their "greenies." We asked them to give us some account of their day. They reflected quietly that they had spent their day running from hospital to hospital, but that there were no patients. And as all of us sat looking at each other, someone said, "And we thought we had a bad day."

Six

Hopeful Visions: The Faces of Children

MARYGRACE BERBERIAN

HOT, CHARRED FRAGMENTS fell from the sky as I looked up, trying to figure out what was going on. It didn't make sense to see the parade of white papers falling against the clear sky. "What's going on?" I asked naively as I waited to get fruit from the Green Market set up right in front of the towers.

The Asian couple who ran the fruit stand handed me my bag of a large fresh fruit salad basket to be shared at an early morning meeting. I overheard an Au Bon Pain delivery man tell someone that there was a fire in the World Trade Center. I thought it was best to get to my consultant work at the Partnership for After School Education (PASE) on the 30th floor at 120 Broadway, directly across from the towers. PASE, a nonprofit organization dedicated to improving education beyond school hours, provides educational resources through collaborations among community agencies and schools.

As I walked into the PASE office carrying my bags with a fast-beating heart, I was eager to tell my coworkers that there was a fire. The receptionist began picking charred fragments out of my hair. "There's a fire, a fire in the World Trade Center," I kept saying as I replayed my morning. At 7:45 I had arrived in the lower concourse of the World Trade Center to buy a present for my brother, a New York City Police Officer. Where was the fire? It could not have been on the lower levels. I would have smelled the smoke. It must have happened after I left around 8:45 A.M.

"Are you okay?" another coworker asked, because my eyes must have been glazed over. Seeing the charred fragments being pulled out of my hair confronted me with my own vulnerability and, far worse, my own mortality, as I replayed the morning like a video that was taped through my camera eyes. I had begun to drift to a different place. My mind responded to the surge of hormones that had begun to put my body in crisis mode.

The conference room television broadcasted CNN, showing live footage of the towers with smoke bellowing out of one side. Soon, the CNN coverage skipped a blink. Our building, a historical building, was no longer seemingly invincible in its grand marble and limestone construction. The building, more commonly known as "The Equitable Building," suddenly rumbled. I heard windows crashing. CNN reported a second plane had hit the towers.

The emergency broadcast system came on in the building with directions for complete evacuation. I walked with a coworker down the 30 flights of stairs. The shudder inside my body had increased. One older woman was found sobbing around floor 24, blocking the stairwell and huddled in a fetal position on the floor. As she held her head in the palms of her hands of her shuddering body, she was crying, "Those poor people! Those poor people!" I told her, "People are on the way to save them, but you now need to save yourself. We'll go down with you." We walked slowly as my boss had a bad knee and hobbled down in pain.

At the bottom of the building, a sea of horrified and pale faces were outside, looking up and checking with others to see if cell phones were working. My colleagues began to collect at the corner of Broadway and Cedar Streets, just across from the towers. I looked up to see the building cut with a red glow as if a bloody incision had been made in its side. "They're going to bomb the bridges!" people were heard shouting. I suddenly thought of my father, a Port Authority detective who spent most of his 27-year career responding to the rescue operations at local airports. "You never stand around looking at an accident, Marygrace, you need to get out of the way." I heard his strong voice in my heart and told my colleagues affirmatively, "We need to get out of here." One woman told us we should take the train. We would be safe underground. The Wall Street train station gates were open. The token clerk was gone. The train was about to pull out when we got on. My inside tremble had stabilized, knowing I was going to be home soon. The train moved slowly. People were sharing eyewitness accounts.

Every salesperson I encountered earlier flashed in my mind. Was the older woman in the Hallmark card store safe? She had wrapped my purchases with such care. Was the nasty cashier who rang up my shoes in the Nine West store safe? She had stared at me blankly when I offered my "good morning" smile. How about the Asian couple at the market? They would certainly have not abandoned their cart, their livelihood.

The train finally slowed to a complete stop. You could hear the slow, drawn pitch of the train losing power. There were no lights, no ventilation, no announcements. I tried to look forward to the next car and saw only darkness. In a moment, I thought of my grandmother, my namesake. She was victimized during the Armenian genocide and was forced to flee through the mountains to escape the religious persecution of the Muslim Turks. If she survived, so would I. I am *not* scared. We are *not* going to die. Other passengers had begun to cry out, "We are going to die!" One woman sitting in front of me began to faint, leaning heavily into my legs. I quickly reached in the bag and offered her my fruit, as I figured the sugar would help her. I kept telling myself I was not scared. I was in rescue mode. This time in the darkness seemed eternal while the floods of faces I saw in the World Trade Center that morning passed at lightning speed before my eyes.

Slowly, a whining sound of the power being restored was heard. The lights were on but dimmed, and we slowly moved into the first station in Brooklyn. Still far from home, we took this opportunity to get above ground and climbed to the street level. Realizing we could not go far with my boss's condition, I found a cab to drive us farther into Brooklyn. On the radio in the cab, we heard that while we were trapped underground, between Brooklyn and Manhattan, the first tower had collapsed. In silence, we all then knew that we must have lost power when the tower fell. When I finally got home, I collapsed into my bed.

I spent the 2 days that followed much like every other New Yorker—I was glued to CNN reports, retelling my story with loved ones, unsuccessfully trying to give blood. While countless friends and colleagues were consumed in the clouds of debris that day, no one I knew personally perished. I remained in shock—a shock that numbed every functioning part of my spirit and body.

Since PASE had been displaced from our building, I returned to my other part-time work on Friday. I was also working as the art therapist for a school-based pilot program led by New York University in a public school in Hell's Kitchen, a New York City neighborhood in the West 30s and 40s. As an art therapist, I worked with students struggling with a host of emotional and social difficulties. The primary intervention of mental health treatment was offered through the nonthreatening and gratifying experiences of art making. As mental health practitioners were limited in the school, I spent the day wandering aimlessly through classrooms to assess students who were in need of intervention. I myself was disorientated and felt quite fragmented in my ability to care for the mental health needs of others, but I felt committed. Schools had instructed students to write letters to police officers and firefighters. As I observed the students, almost all had spontaneously drawn the Twin Towers in their letters. As an art therapist, their spontaneous drawings made complete sense.

Young people needed to rebuild the Twin Towers; they needed to rebuild what had been destroyed. The capacity to express through line, color, and form is a birth process. Art is a creation; a recreation of past representations significant to the artist in the moment. Creativity allows for describing, building, and reconfiguring an injured object so that mourning can begin.

On that Friday, I also spoke to teachers at the school. They felt relieved to be working with students once more. The school closings had interrupted routine and left many feeling uncertain about how to proceed. I also spoke to parents who shared that they needed to be strong and persevere for their children. Children provided a sense of hope and encouraged adults to mobilize resources for survival.

At the end of the day, I went home exhausted and slept hard. My brother served 12-hour shifts with NYPD at Ground Zero, guarding remains that were pulled out of the rubble. Friends who were displaced from their homes in Battery Park City, the area right beside the towers, were staying in my apartment in Brooklyn, three miles from Ground Zero. The days immediately following September 11th felt like a warp of time and space. I felt similarly when my grandmother died. It is that disturbing cycle of mourning, exhaustion, and lapses of consciousness. The faces of the missing were the most difficult for me to endure. It was hard to accept that the victims were people just like me. I experienced continued flashes of seeing people in the debris—images that had not actually been recorded by my eyes but had been horrifically ingrained in my mind. I continually became consumed by remembering all the people that I had crossed paths with in that concourse on that busy morning—forcing myself to remember their faces as if their existence was relying solely on my engraving them into my visual memory. September 11th was loss, a loss that fragmented every aspect of my core sense of security and being in this world that had suddenly become a lot larger and frighteningly more consuming.

I woke up on Saturday and replayed my observations from the day at the school. It has been my ritual since I began as a therapist to take a shower at the end of the day to symbolically cleanse myself from the hardship and pain that I routinely encountered in my work. I began Saturday with a long, meditative shower. During my shower, I felt compelled to do something. I decided to rebuild. In my mind's eye, I imagined providing young people with the opportunity to symbolically rebuild the towers like they had tried to do in their drawings at school. I wanted to provide an opportunity for them to gain mastery amidst profound feelings of helplessness. I did not want to engage young people in a process that would create added vulnerability. I decided to focus on their strengths.

I conceived of children drawing self-portraits. The face is what fascinates even infants early in development as they stare intrigued at the faces of their caretakers. The face, the most expressive part of the body and center of communication, is often depicted in drawings as the whole image of the person, even without any other appendages noted.[1] The face is an image all children have mastered early on, and it authentically represents cultural attributes. Drawing a face validates the person, serving as a document of that person's identity. Cultural awareness needed to be emphasized, since anti-Arab sentiments were emerging. I envisioned mounting the faces together on a large mural of a new cityscape for New York.

---

1. Machover, Karen. (1949). *Personality projection in the drawing of the human figure.* Springfield, IL: C.C. Thomas.

My earlier vision in the subway car to simply survive had been transformed into a vision of healing. In my vision, the children's faces of all colors and ethnic backgrounds wishing to rebuild would inspire adults. In my shower robe, I immediately began to draft facilitator's guidelines so that teachers and youth workers would have exact directives, including all the specific verbiage to present the project to children. I knew my idea would need the backing of a larger, more reputable institution. I contacted the director of the New York University Graduate Art Therapy Program and shared my idea. She agreed immediately to serve as the reception point for the images that would be sent in. If teachers and parents knew their children's images were being submitted to a large institution, they might be more inclined to participate. Over the future development of the initiative, three additional partners were added to provide greater exposure and validity to the work being done. While I would ultimately name myself as the director, the university was named a partner in the project.

On that same Saturday afternoon, a local printing store donated 800 copies of my flyer addressed to adults outlining the objective of the initiative and providing guidelines for creating artwork with children and a consent form for including the image in the project. I walked through my neighborhood and passed out flyers to every parent I encountered. I knew adults needed to be actively involved in promoting strengths in their families, most specifically in their children. Flyers were posted at groceries, libraries, and laundromats. Informational packets were also sent to schools and community-based organizations. In a short time, the response was overwhelming. Adults seemed eager to offer young people the opportunity to process what had happened. Many were apprehensive about approaching the subject with young people and needed hands-on guidelines to do so.

In its simplicity, the World Trade Center Children's Mural Project, as my idea came to be called, was designed so it could be easily facilitated. Since the amount of materials often varied from school to school, the supplies that were required were modest: 8½" × 11" or 9" × 12" paper and any type of drawing materials—pencils, crayons, paint, markers, and so on.

The directives were intended to be completed in sequence; all activities could be done in one to two classes in which a facilitated discussion preceded the children's work on their self portraits. The groups first shared what they knew about the events so adults could dispel any false perceptions about what had happened. As described by Beverly James,[2] erroneous information often attaches to actual circumstances. Since the television footage was being shown repeatedly, some young people believed many buildings in New York City were attacked. Children became hypervigilant about the cracks in the older school buildings, wondering if the building had been hit. It was critical to explain the situation clearly and in a manner in which children could understand. Of course, children's concerns extended to buildings beyond their own school. They named Central Park and McDonald's as their favorite places in New York City. Facilitators confirmed that these places were indeed still safe in the city.

Facilitators anticipated that cultural and racial differences might contribute to the children's anxieties. Children were asked to compare hands to examine skin colors and share countries of origin. Since New York is such a diverse city, it was important to acknowledge cultural differences during this period of international conflict. Facilitators then organized a vote of the children to determine whether or not the group wanted New York City to be a peaceful place. (The votes were always unanimously positive). Project facilitators emphasized that the community's wishes for peace were not dependent solely on the basis of color or culture. As a community, we all wished for peace.

Each young person then shared ideas about what we should do to respond to the terrorist attack. Sometimes their answers presented important teaching opportunities. I had the privilege of working with classes at the school in Hell's Kitchen and quickly modified the directives to more effectively respond to what I was observing from the children. One second-grade student boldly stated in a group I facilitated, "We need to get rid of the rabbits." When I asked why he thought we needed to get rid of the rabbits, he said they killed people in the Twin Towers. I tried to clarify by asking, "*Rabbits* killed people in the Twin Towers?" He answered, "Yeah, the rabbits, the people who wear their hair like this" (motioning to a turban-like wrap on his head). I quickly realized that he must have heard about

---

2. James, Beverly. (1989). *Treating traumatized children: New insights and creative interventions*. Lexington, MA: Lexington Books.

Arabs but understood this seemingly unfamiliar word to be *rabbits*. I asked why he thought that would be the solution. He responded, "They are all bad people. They killed many people." Sensitive to his developmental level and what he might be hearing from adults in his environment, while noticing he was wearing red sneakers, I explained, "not all people who wear their hair in turbans are bad. If there was a bank robber and he was wearing red sneakers, would that mean that all people who wear red sneakers are bad and are bank robbers?" The young student was able to understand my example and understood that we cannot stereotype others based simply on their appearance. He smiled, slowly nodding his head positively as this new concept was penetrating his young, impressionable mind in a way that challenged earlier thinking.

Children shared ideas about what they could do as children to respond to the attacks. Communities around the world had gathered to offer support. Adults were sending resources and donating blood, yet there were no venues for children to become involved in community action. The events of September 11 had created almost insurmountable isolation and helplessness. Individuals felt compelled to join with others. The mural project gave children that opportunity.

This prescribed series of activities was first conducted throughout New York City. The activity's simplicity and emphasis on strengths enabled other educators and professionals to conduct the exercises. In this capacity, educators and other professionals have served as healers for the wounded children by promoting artistic expression and offering validation and nurturance. Across the city, children began working on the mural that would become a collection of over 3,000 portraits.

Two different cultural institutions were excited by the initial response for this project and committed exhibition space. Along with a growing group of committed volunteers that were immediately mobilized, the project was off and running, fueled simply on the spirit of New Yorkers. When the project was later promoted on America Online, drawings were received from 14 other states. The Christian Children's Fund (CCF) arrived in New York to provide assistance and partnered with the project. CCF has historically responded to countries devastated by war and poverty. CCF supported the World Trade Center Children's Mural Project by translating the project into 12 different languages. They also provided a small amount of funding to cover assembly costs, and most important, distributed the information to 30 territories exposed to war and terrorism around the world. Children in 22 countries, such as Uganda, Kosovo, and Colombia, sent portraits and messages of hope to encourage the survival of New York City's children. The portraits of these international faces symbolize profound resiliency and offer solidarity for world peace. It was incredibly poignant for a child who was living in the harsh conditions of Kosovo to send a message of hope to a child living in New York City.

Volunteers for the project came willingly and abundantly. At New York Univeristy, every Saturday and Sunday, a team of 70 volunteers assembled the mural in a very methodical way so that each child's contribution was tracked and recorded. We were committed to include every portrait that was submitted with parental consent, despite our gross underestimation of project numbers. It took 4 months to build the mural as more images arrived each day.

Exhibition space was challenging. We were essentially a grassroots organization, and all the early promises made to give the project exhibition space were compromised when other arts initiatives developed by well-known institutions emerged. The two cultural institutions that had earlier promised us space subsequently declined. We had begun the task of assembling the mural in pieces, unsure of the dimensions of our yet-undefined exhibition space. The efforts to locate exhibition space in New York City and the later efforts to produce a printed catalogue of the exhibit were the most discouraging. The project had been assembled with hours of commitment and less than $7,000 worth of funding. Many other funders and publishers were eager to see children's drawings of bloody faces and burning towers. They were not eager to support what was healthy and hopeful in our next generation.

Resolution came in April 2002. Larry Silverstein, the lease holder of the World Trade Center, arrived at the NYU Studio Art Building in the East Village to see the work being completed. He was moved to see young people committed to rebuilding New York. He offered space across from Ground Zero emphatically and generously. On March 19, 2002, the montage mural, comprised of over 3,100 portraits, was unveiled across from Ground Zero in the lobby of the

The Children's Mural Project displayed near Ground Zero.

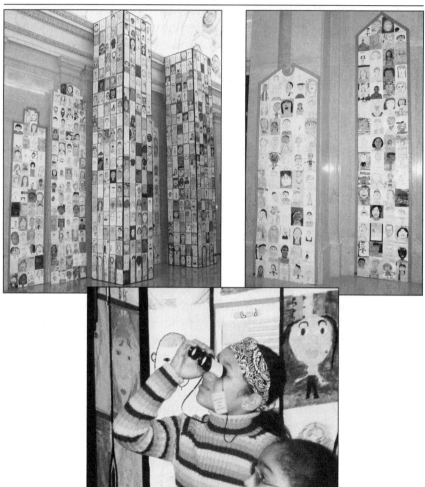

Equitable Building at 120 Broadway in New York City. The mural, a collaboration of hope and strength, stood strong across from the pain and devastation that fragmented the community of New York. Adults who viewed the exhibition were deeply moved by the tremendous message that had been delivered by children throughout the world. Many just stood in silence examining the features of each face and reading the messages. Adults seemed to respond with a reverence similar to that observed at the sites established for missing persons flyers at major crossings in the city, namely bus and train terminals and Ground Zero. The loss of September 11th was more than a number over 3,000—it was a cascade of perished faces, perished lives. The number of children who participated in the Children's Mural Project was close to the number of those lives lost. The children had filled the city with hope by paying homage to each life lost in the attacks of September 11th. Hopeful visions of children around the world collectively attempted to restore the charred, pained, and fragmented spirits of New Yorkers following the September 11th attacks.

As a victim of September 11th, I have examined the resources that were summoned in my own recovery. My motivation was to become involved and create positive change. I know now, 5 years later, that I was motivated to attest to the life that still existed and would help resurrect this city. After September 11th, people wanted to join with others and somehow be involved in the recovery efforts. I knew how to enable children to create art. That is what I chose to do because that is what I could offer. Subsequently, the conceptual framework of the World Trade Center Children's Mural Project was credited to my knowledge and experience as an art therapist and art educator. However, simply stated, the response was a humane response to an inhumane act. As a person, a wounded person educated in children's artistic expression, I responded.

I am grateful for the opportunity to write about my experience on the morning of September 11th. My survival was influenced by multiple sources. On that morning, I had heard the internalized voice of my father. I learned of his heroic efforts only when I was old enough to understand. After he was exposed to horrific carnage and destruction at work, my father would come home and just watch my brother and me sleep. He needed to be reassured, just as I did, that family and life were intact after being confronted with such great devastation. As I fled the Downtown area, I heard my father's lessons, which had become internalized. My love and respect for my father had never grown so great. Each shared moment with him was now embraced so tightly.

I look at the land that I stand on today and also see the pieces of my grandmother's painful journey. Despite the great violence she experienced, my grandmother summoned the energy to flee. I was never fearful in that stalled subway car. I had inherited her resilience.

Countless schoolchildren visited and used the binoculars provided to find their drawings on the mural that was displayed at 20 feet high and 160 feet wide. In a small group discussion prior to a class visit of the exhibition, one 7-year-old girl shared: "I'm very sorry for the people that lost their children and parents. The mural might help them gather hope. I made a difference."

I knew then that the World Trade Center Children's Mural Project was a positive response to aid in our healing and recovery by recreating life after the destruction. Since that time, the mural has been distributed to agencies and schools throughout New York City. Many have taken pieces from this collaborative venture. The soil of this city will slowly integrate the painful debris of what has fallen, just as I continue to process and respond to my experiences as a member of this community, walking on this wounded, yet very richly composed, land.

Seven

Hominid Development: On Being a Social Studies Teacher During September 11th

DALIA HOCHMAN

ESCRIBE YOUR EXPERIENCES teaching during September 11th. My assignment is clear; the instructions, well-defined. Yet I sit at my computer and the screen is blank; I do not know how to begin. Such paralysis is uncommon for me. I have always excelled in my studies and completed written assignments with ease. As a lifelong student, I have been trained to believe that the answer to most things in life comes from reading, experimenting, and observing. I have been dutifully taught to collect my evidence, step back and unemotionally analyze and criticize, compare and contrast, and always, no matter what, make sense of the world within the neat confines of a five-paragraph essay.

Yet as I sit down a few years later to recount my experiences teaching history at a New York City public high school during September 11th, my confidence dissipates. The rationality, empiricism, and emotional distance of the academy cannot begin to express the experience of teaching history and explaining the world to young people, at a moment that was inexplicable: when all logic, equations, and theories on human behavior went down in the rubble of the Twin Towers.

How do I attempt to tell my own personal, subjective story in an analytical, scholarly manner? I begin by recording my most vivid memories of those perverse days, and the faces, sounds, and sights flood out onto paper. As I am writing, I realize that the events of September 11th unearthed certain latent issues in education, teaching, and history; that I can both tell my own personal story and link my experiences to larger, universal themes.

The first of such themes is the loneliness of being a new, young, idealistic teacher in a system that suffers from low morale and disempowerment. The second theme is the split that has become common in high schools between teachers as conveyors of subject matter and teachers as nurturers and counselors. A third tension that the events of September 11th forced me to confront is the nature of curriculum, especially high school history curriculum. Teaching history during and after September 11th provoked a fourth issue: How do we teach morality and ethics in public schools? Finally, September 11th, at base, challenged me to consider the fundamental nature of human beings, a large question that was answered primarily with the help of my students.

What follows is my attempt to explain my experiences teaching history during September 11th in the best way I know how.

"Just Chalk and Talk, Honey, Chalk and Talk"

Both Tower One and Tower Two were hit during second period. In the world of high schools, time is measured in 40-minute intervals, internal clocks recalibrated to match the harsh ringing of the bell. Because classrooms are the most isolated places in the world, bereft of any outside contact (turn off your cell phones kids, get rid of that CD player, stop talking in the hall), there was no way any of us in our class—neither the 34 incoming freshmen nor I, the 23-year-old incoming teacher—could have known what was happening. It was a typical morning at the large, imposing Upper West Side high school, a beige, cinderblock rectangle that houses over 2,500 students. Our children hail from all five boroughs of New York, but more accurately from all corners of the world. The mix of languages—from patois to Ukrainian—and spices—from curry to coriander—fills the building, creating both a literal and figurative soup amidst the typically crowded, noisy hallway.

After second period ended at 9:34, I walked into what we called "the office," the small room that served as the command center of the Social Studies department, still exhaling from the intensity of teaching. The sunlight was always especially bright at that time of day, but today the sun's rays were so strong they appeared fluorescent; the tiny copy room felt like it was on fire. The only person in the office that morning was Enid, the most formidable, intimidating woman I had met in the school to date.

A thin, wiry woman who subsisted on coffee and cigarettes, Enid was the reigning queen of the overhead projectors, who, having taught for 30 years in the New York Public School System, had developed a caustic, bitter attitude about teaching; most of her anger was always directed at the ubiquitous evil—"the system." She treated the new teachers with disdain, barking out orders and gruffly criticizing our work. She abhorred new, fluffy teaching methods and often chastised me when I attempted to be too creative: "Honey, just chalk and talk, chalk and talk." As I later found out, Enid had managed to retain a sensitive, inner core, keeping in touch with former students and sending care packages to those who went away to college.

But that day, the 4th day of the school year, I knew none of this yet, and there was Enid, who had fished out an antique transistor radio from storage, and brusquely told me that there had been an attack on the World Trade Center, that the towers had collapsed, and that there were thousands dead. I was immediately suspicious of the veracity of this news, coming from Enid and from an antiquated transistor radio. I am not sure if my incredulity stemmed from the human or technological source, so I, the recent college grad, sprinted to the one computer in the office, which belonged to the chairwoman of the department, and turned to the sources that *I* most trusted—cnn.com, nytimes.com—to confirm Enid's fatal news. We stood there, Enid and I, in silence, confronting each other as much as what had happened.

Enid was the last person in the world I wanted to be with when I learned of such news. Like duelers before the duel, we sized each other up, top to bottom. We were a complete opposite pair. I was the optimistic, idealistic newcomer, fresh out of the Ivy League, who saw my role as an educator as nothing less than a transformer, not only of my students but of society. I viewed myself in professorial terms, wanting to be an "expert" in my field, and staying up late each night to read about the topic of my next day's lesson. Here was Enid, bitter, angry, skeptical, and disempowered. She copied the notes from the textbook and probably hadn't read an academic book in many years.

The loneliness and disempowerment of being a teacher is often not discussed in larger political debates. In order to survive and work in a school system, is it necessary to lose a certain level of high expectations, standards, and creativity? For those of us who enter the field because we love learning, does the profession offer us sufficient intellectual stimulation and discourse? Is academic mediocrity among students and teachers the result of a system that rewards years of experience over performance?

Enid and I looked at each other in silence, both realizing that we needed to subsume our selves—our fears, our hopes, and our concerns for our own family members—because the bell was about to ring, and we had to be teachers.

The Affective versus the Cognitive Domains of Teaching

In education training courses, teachers-to-be are taught about the important distinction between the cognitive and affective domains of learning. The cognitive involves the more scientific method that the brain uses to decode and integrate new information. The affective domain relates to the subjective feelings and associations that surround such information. The duality between the cognitive and affective domains reflects a larger dichotomy in the role of teachers, especially in high schools. In the traditional, compartmentalized high school, the function of the teacher is to deliver a certain subject matter, whether history, chemistry, or French. Like an efficient conveyor belt, large groups of students arrive for 40 minutes at a time, the teacher fills the empty vessels with information, and the students dutifully file out of the room. The interaction between teachers and students often becomes professional, formal, and distant. The schedule and structure of the comprehensive high school precludes teachers from serving as mentors, advisors, and generally counseling students on personal and academic matters.

The events of September 11th sharpened the strong dichotomy between the cognitive and affective domains of teaching. In the days and weeks after the event, I was the consummate subject-matter teacher. I called on raised hands only. I employed the Socratic method and posed questions back to the students, as I had been taught to do in my training. I assigned quizzes on current events. I pulled down the overhanging map, and integrated geography and spatial skills into my instruction, showing the Middle East and other relevant places. I drew charts and time lines and Venn diagrams on the board. (For some reason, teachers, I have found, simply adore the overlapping circles of Venn diagrams.) If anyone had been watching, they might have seen me playing out the archetypal role of the schoolteacher because I was removed from myself, and in many ways, from the internal lives of the children—and because I pretended to have all the answers.

Yet certain events in the aftermath of September 11th forced me to step outside my prescribed role, to "smile before Christmas," and to help my students cope with their trauma, confusion, and grieving. I'll never forget the parent-teacher conferences of the fall of 2002. A year had passed since September 11th, and most of us had returned to our routine, rarely acknowledging the attack. One of my students, Joan, was failing all of the exams and had not handed in any homework, a situation that would not have been out of the ordinary except that Joan was in the center of a highly academic, studious peer group. It is rare for students to deviate so extremely from their peers, and I knew something out of the ordinary was going on. I was therefore looking forward to getting a chance to meet Joan's mother. A petite, shy immigrant from China, Joan's mother sat down at my desk, and before we could even begin our discussion, began to let out deep, mournful sobs, crying uncontrollably in front of me, as well as the other 20 parents in the room who were waiting their turn for the conferences. Between sobs, Joan's mother managed to tell me that she knew her daughter was failing and that there was nothing she could do about it. Her oldest daughter, a successful 24-year-old investment banker, had died in the Twin Towers, and Joan was suffering immeasurably from the loss of her beloved older sister.

I sat in shock, clutching my grade book, not knowing exactly how to respond to this information. Here was a 15-year-old child sitting in my classroom for months, suffering in silence and I, I had responded with red X marks, chastisement, and assumptions about her skill level. My first response was anger. I could not believe that the school administration had not informed me of a critical piece of information about one of my students. Then I blamed the school system: How was I supposed to keep tabs on 170 human beings? It is inhuman to give a high school teacher five classes of 35 kids. Yet anger at extrinsic factors soon subsided, and I was forced to consider my own culpability: How had I managed to become so out of touch with my students? Why didn't they share anything about their lives with me? In my effort to create a serious classroom environment, in my rush to teach one more fact or date or war, I had, at least in Joan's case, failed to meet the complete needs of the child.

The intensity and trauma of September 11th forced me to confront the multiple roles involved in being a teacher. I somehow had to attempt to bridge the gap between the affective and cognitive domains of teaching, domains that are, I have found, inextricably linked.

Breadth versus Depth

After September 11th, we social studies teachers used to perversely joke that the terrorist attack had only one positive effect—it increased student interest in history and currents events. In the weeks and months after the attacks, our previously apathetic students, who often found no personal relevance in studying the history and culture of foreign societies, were noticeably more engaged and interested in the material. For many teenagers, classrooms are one of the few safe spaces where they can let down their cool facades and clarify what they have heard on the news or on the street. When we talked about terrorism, about September 11th, and ultimately, about Iraq, I never saw a single student slouch in her seat or look at his watch. September 11th was not only the ultimate "teachable moment" but also confirmed that students learn best when material is made most relevant to them.

Increased student interest in current events, specifically in learning about Middle East history and Islam, posed several new obstacles and dilemmas for me as an instructional leader. In New York State, as in many states across the country, the curriculum for high school social studies is tightly proscribed in preparation for a cumulative final exam. Beginning in ninth grade, students enroll in

Global Studies, which includes a chronological history of the world across every continent and culture. This means that we spend 3 to 5 days on each empire, dynasty, civilization, and war. Questions on the test require students to compare the Roman Empire, the Han dynasty in China, and the Inca Empire in South America. (They share the development of advanced road systems.) Students needed to be able to drop obscure names, make associations, and thematically organize cultures, without really knowing any one society in depth. For many of us teachers, the greatest challenge in teaching the curriculum is learning about the ancient kingdom of Songhai or about the difference between the Mughal and the Mogul empires. Even for those of us who had studied history, keeping up with the vast array of material is a challenge.

Language can be powerful, especially in a field as political as education. In my own training, my favorite professor had drilled into our heads that the word *cover* should be an anathema for teachers. For her, as a progressive educator, education was a journey and a process that involved developing critical thinking skills and in-depth student learning. Therefore, I instinctively flinched when colleagues and supervisors compared how far they had "covered" in a given week and lamented who was ahead of whom in some sort of existential "race" to the Regents exam. The tension between depth and breadth is one of the most important dialectics in social studies education and in education in general, especially as the standards movements seeks to formalize what students should know by the end of high school. On one hand, having taught in a large urban high school where teachers were able to engage students through in-depth topics, creative projects, and intense discussions, I realize how powerful depth can be, especially as a motivating tactic for those students who are disengaged from the entire learning process. On the other hand, I believe that especially in social studies, it is important to have a bare-bones framework and time line of major events to contextualize student understanding and further study. As a colleague once said, it is hard to debunk history if students never learned the "bunk" in the first place.

The question of breadth versus depth, while omnipresent, became especially relevant in the weeks after September 11th. Because we were on a tight schedule, in an attempt to "cover" (that word still gives me chills) all the material for the exam, I constantly had to make executive decisions about whether to follow the curriculum or take breaks and answer my students' questions, and teach material that I deemed was more important. One of the problems with such a prescribed curriculum is that its prescription obviates one of the central tasks of teachers, which is to make executive decisions on what is more and less important. The skill of prioritizing significance, one that we try to instill in our students, becomes lost in a cookie-cutter curriculum.

So I decided to forge ahead on my own. I extended the 3 days in February that the curriculum called for teaching about Islam to 3 weeks, choosing specific aspects of Islam that I thought were particularly relevant, such as the original story of Mohammad's revelation in the cave, the five pillars, the role of calligraphy and religious art, the concept of *jihad*, and the role of women.

In those cold winter days, I remember the intensity and focus that I brought to my task; in a way, creating meaningful, well-informed lessons on Islam was my own personal method of healing after the events of the fall. I would often spend my weekends in the cozy bookstores of New York City, devouring books about Islam, and then at the end of the Sunday (and several cappuccinos later), carefully returning the unbought books to their shelves, satisfied that I had gleaned just enough information for the next morning.

That year, a few of the mandated topics went uncovered. However, I believe that an in-depth, critical approach to teaching history was ultimately worth the sacrifice.

Moral Equivalency and Teaching History

"But why do they hate us, Ms.?" my students kept on insisting, regurgitating the clichés they had heard in the media. This question, for all of us, was most difficult to answer, and I tried as best as I could to give the students a satisfying answer, problematizing all of the popular theories on "civilizational clashes," antiglobalization, Western imperialism, and reviewing the history of American involvement in the Middle East. But my students and I, along with most Americans, were not satisfied with the answers, and the question on the motive for the terrorist attack continued to plague our discussions.

Toward the end of our unit on Islam, I received a letter from a parent, also a parent of a U.S. solider, who was concerned that my goal in teaching about Islam was to provide an apology for the events of 9/11. The parent was worried that schools' attempt to contextualize every culture, and in her words "understand where they are coming from" would blur the lines between right and wrong, important boundaries in a child's development.

The letter from the parent deeply affected me, even though I did not agree with its premise. I thought back to my own education in the liberal public schools outside of Boston and at Yale University and realized that the conscientious educators of the 1970s and 1980s had stressed the postmodern theories of multiple perspectives on truth and the supremacy of subjectivity. Unlike perhaps our parents' generation, who were taught that such phenomena as fascism and communism were clear "evils," I had learned, and subsequently taught, every historical event and movement from multiple perspectives, and stressed the importance of understanding each actor's own reality and truth. Did this way of teaching, and of thinking, absolve students and teachers of certain moral responsibilities to clearly differentiate a good act from an evil act? Was it important for educators to help nurture such moral capacities in students? Or is it the role of the family to teach students to have a moral barometer, while we, as educators, are simply supposed to present as many sides of the issue, as objectively as possible? In my response letter to the concerned parent, I posed many of these questions back to her, without, I admit, any confident answers. The issue of moral education was another unexpected question that the September 11th events unearthed for me as an educator.

Hominid Development

As I recount the experience of teaching during September 11th, my memories inevitably make their way back to where I was when the planes hit the towers—in Room 559, busy teaching second period Global Studies. Our topic that morning was prehistoric society and the evolution of the first hominids or early human beings; a topic that, in retrospect, was quite ironic. We were discussing the difference between Homo sapiens and Homo erectus (a name that provoked the usual giggles from the back row), trying to draw the line between human and animal. We analyzed the evolution of hunt-ing tools, prehistoric cave art, and kinship patterns. We discussed whether killing and violence is, as a result of the evolutionary pro-cess, inherent to human beings. The irony was great. Here we were trying to draw some type of concrete, essentialist boundary between what is human and what is animalistic, when unbeknownst to us, these two categories were being blurred even as we debated.

The class was split. Half the students, perhaps fatalistic for their young age, examined the sharp flints and daggers of each succes-sive species of early humans and concluded that the killer instinct is an evolutionary adaptation. Humans are coded to kill. The other half of the class disagreed. Pointing to evidence of cave art, remains of a Neanderthal flute, and other artistic and religious devices, the students asserted that human beings are essentially good, evolved to make music just as readily as to make war. Little did we realize the significance of our debate and its relevance to the world outside our classroom.

Three weeks after September 11th, I administered the final essay test for our unit on the development of hominids; "'When I look at history,' wrote Jan Smuts, 'I am a pessimist but when I look at prehistory, I am an optimist.' Do you agree or disagree with this statement?" As I made my way through the stack of essays, I was astounded by the thoughtful responses of my students. One fresh-men wrote:

> In prehistory, life was more peaceful and harmonious than it is now, when people are divided by social classes and competi-tion. Some people argue that since the Neolithic (Agricultural) Revolution, there is security and a sense of certainty about life that the hunter-gatherers never had. But what type of security and certainty can you really have when there is war, terrorism, and so much hatred in the world?"

Five miles south of my social studies classroom lies a mass grave that pushes the limits of human rationality and calls into question all concepts of certainty. For those of us who are used to having an-swers for everything, who see reason and intellect as a panacea, my students' questions cause us to pause. What is the ultimate adapta-tion in evolution? What are human beings ultimately seeking? Is it the certainty and security that proved so elusive for early hunter-gatherers? What are these basic elements common to all human beings? How do we draw the boundaries and set the limits of human nature?

Conclusion

New Yorkers and Americans have each made meaning out of the events of 9/11 in their own personal ways, and the tragedy has triggered a variety of thought processes and changes in lifestyles. For me, teaching social studies in the aftermath of September 11th put into focus and sharpened many underlying tensions and questions on the nature of teaching, curriculum, and even on human nature.

I also felt a great sense of responsibility not only to care for the physical and psychological well-being of my students, but to help explain to them the "why" that tends to be the favorite question word of children. Such a responsibility also heightened the burdens of teaching—the isolation, the lack of resources, and the overcrowded classrooms. Yet alongside the burden came the honor that I could play such an important role in the healing process. As a teacher in the New York City Public Schools, I do not share Smuts's pessimism about historic humans. After witnessing the thoughtful questions, raw humanity, and willingness to learn of my students, I retain my idealism on the nature of Homo sapiens and the future of civilization.

Eight

Equal and Opposite Reactions

ABIGAIL DEUTSCH

W HAT DRIVES A WITTY, bright-eyed, middle-aged physics teacher to bang his head against a wall during class? It
started with the girl who sat behind me: Tracy Mulligan.
"Mr. Stein," she said, early in the class.

He looked up, blinked, registered Tracy: smart, outspoken, red-
haired, D on last quiz. "Yes?"

"Mr. Stein," she said cautiously, "did you read the homework
questions before you assigned them?"

"Of course."

"Would you mind reading them again?!"

He raised his wild eyebrows. "Sure."

Only nothing seemed wrong. And he told her so.

"Um," she said, glancing around the room.

He read them again. "Look, Tracy, I really don't—"

"Mr. Stein!" she said. "Read *number 57.*"

He read it. And reread it. And finally something clicked. We
knew something clicked because he walked to the door, and stared
at it as though pondering whether to leave. But instead he banged
his head against the door for a full minute.

The question wasn't particularly demanding. It required the
application of constants y and g to the equation that links time,
location, and acceleration of a falling object. The arithmetic was

simple—the numbers multiplied to produce a square. We didn't even need a calculator.

There was only one problem. The equation demanded that we consider the time, location, and acceleration of an object dropped off the top of the World Trade Center.

At any other time or place, the demand would be reasonable. But this was just weeks after September 11, 2001, and just blocks away from the World Trade Center site. The windows of Stuyvesant High School had offered prime views of the planes plowing into the towers—"What an interesting trajectory," a biology teacher remarked of the first plane's path, before sputtering, "Dear God!" We saw both buildings smolder like candles. We saw the top floors shed debris as candles drip wax, saw one tower, then the other, seem to melt to the ground. Some of us saw what looked like debris falling from the tops of the buildings. But upon closer inspection, it turned out not to be debris: "He had a tie on," recalled a classmate. Once outside, we squinted in the ashy sunlight. Had the towers actually fallen? Wasn't one still standing? "I can see 70 stories," I told my friend before she steered me uptown. Confusion ran deep. Several of my classmates mistook the popping floors of the collapsing second tower for gunshots, heard cries to "Run!", and sped up the avenue from which, minutes later, I would claim to see a nonexistent building. I walked up that avenue for around an hour, still vaguely convinced that the buildings were standing. In the apartment of a friend's grandmother, I took off my sneakers and realized my ankles were bloody, but I couldn't feel any pain. It was only after I saw the towers fall on television in that apartment that I realized what had happened.

Mr. Stein and I were both confused, though in different ways: just as I saw towers where none stood, so did Mr. Stein fail to see them when they appeared in problem 57. September 11 taught me you can't always see well, even—especially—from up close.

Confusion did not end on September 11th. After the towers fell, my classmates and I had no school for a week and a half. Just as we weren't sure the towers had fallen, just as we weren't sure of the identity of the debris that fell from the upper floors, we weren't sure our school building was okay—rumors circulated that its windows had blown out, that its floors were dusted with lead and asbestos. We didn't know if we would return to Stuyvesant or relocate. If we relocated, would we attend one school or divide among several? We didn't know our new school hours. We didn't know if we would keep our original schedules or lose "luxury" classes like gym and band. Another rumor informed us that two different schools would host us, and warned that one had a history of violence. We could only wonder how its muscled community would receive the skinny, bespectacled students of Stuyvesant High School.

Even after we learned our fate and relocated to Brooklyn Tech, the world felt hazy. I rose strangely late, at 11:30 A.M., to get to the school, that Stuyvesant students attended between 1:00 and 6:00 P.M. (Brooklyn Tech's actual students were in class between 7:00 A.M. and 12:00 P.M.) When we were dismissed, the sun was already sinking behind Manhattan. Then I took an hourlong subway ride down dark and rattling tracks. By the time I resurfaced, night had fallen on the city. I bought a latte every evening, as though it were morning and cold out, some other season during some other year. The caffeine kept me blurrily awake till 3:00 or 4:00 A.M., and after deep sleep empty of dreams, I woke again, and headed to Brooklyn for another day at a school I didn't attend.

Relocation thoroughly disoriented me! I didn't know Brooklyn, didn't know this new high school; oddest of all, I suddenly felt I didn't know my teachers either. My Spanish teacher, who originally seemed simple enough—a solidly built woman with dark skin and hair yanked into a tight ponytail—became a puzzle. On our first day of class in Brooklyn, she was chipper despite the unfamiliar surroundings, despite the labyrinthine structure of our new school, despite the despair that filled the streets and air. She seemed, in fact, unaware that anything was wrong. Not that she failed to mention our week and a half off. She asked, "¿Que hicieron ustedes en sus vacaciones?" or "What did you do on your vacation?", as though we had just returned from rollicking spring breaks in Bermuda!

Other teachers approached the topic subtly. One asked how we were handling everything, and I perked up, hoping we would finally discuss our experience of September 11th. But the teacher quickly added, "This school is built like a maze. You guys finding your way around?" The school's makeup was not nearly as confusing as the shifting makeup of our world and minds, but the teacher seemed reluctant to address the greater issues. Another discussed college that first day. "You guys are lucky," he said. "Your greatest trauma, is, like, not getting into Wesleyan." The other trauma went unmentioned. Still another addressed September 11th indirectly but sensitively: She distributed a packet of poems, each of which handles grief in a different way. We read Adam Zagajewski's "Try to Praise the Mutilated World," Emily Dickinson's "[After great pain, a formal feeling comes]," Mark Strand's "When the Vacation Was Over for Good." Last of all, there was W.H. Auden's "Musée des Beaux-Arts," which chronicles the world's failure to notice Icarus's fatal plunge into water. It describes a ship so near the disaster that it certainly saw "something amazing, a boy falling out of the sky," but that nonetheless "had somewhere to get to and sailed calmly on." My high school community seemed to me to be the ship; the thousands who died on September 11th seemed Icarus. Had my classmates and teachers seen nothing? Had they heard nothing? They must have—and was it not "amazing"? No matter what the answers to these questions, my school community "had somewhere to get to and sailed calmly on." My class had college to get to and sailed calmly through exams and papers and applications; my teachers had teaching to get to and placidly delivered lessons and homework assignments and grades.

In retrospect, my English teacher's decision to share these poems seems to bear almost as much meaning as the poems themselves. Broadly summarized, the pieces appeared to represent different responses to grief: the Zagajewski, hope; the Dickinson, shock; the Strand, regret; the Auden, at once indifference and indignation due to this indifference. Each poet described different reactions, and likewise each student and teacher harbored different reactions. There were as many ways to respond to grief as there were differences in childhoods, in goals, in opinions. Each individual responded differently, and each wished his surrounding community to respond in a different way. Some desired discussion of politics; others, discussion of the Yankees. Some, like me, wanted discussion of the event itself, and of its emotional ramifications. But others would have rolled their eyes at such a discussion: Why is everyone still thinking about that? It's so *last month*. We have more pertinent issues to consider: "Are you applying anywhere early?" "Do you think he meant anything when he used the word *date*?" "How is your foot feeling?" I'll never forget a conversation I shared with a friend a couple of weeks after we had returned to Stuyvesant. She said she felt miserable. I asked why, though I already knew why: Smoke was rising from Ground Zero; the air stank; we weren't allowed to leave the building for lunch because the air wasn't considered safe; but was the air inside the building safer than the air outside, given our famously flawed filtering system? If so, why were we all getting headaches?

"I hate my math teacher," was all she said.

But that wasn't why she was upset. She was upset because of everything else, and I know this because for months she bit her nails and hardly smiled; because she jumped at any unexpected noise; because finally one day she burst out: "They were like two *big teeth*, and Manahattan is like a mouth that's had its teeth knocked out."

Yet this friend and I hardly discussed September 11th. She never brought it up, and after a few days I ceased mentioning it to any of my classmates. No one seemed interested in discussing it. In fact, no one seemed to have *noticed* it. After a time I even began to doubt the gravity of the tragedy. Maybe it wasn't such a big deal. Maybe this kind of thing happened all the time. Why was I so troubled by it? Why did I alone feel the need to analyze it, understand it, work through it? Which led to the inevitable question: What was wrong with *me*? I wonder sometimes which I found more psychologically unsettling: September 11th, or the fact that my school community seemed set on the notion that September 11th had not occurred. Suspecting I was either perceiving things wrong or so fundamentally different from my classmates that no conversation was feasible, I ceased bringing it up.

Not that I never had outbursts. Once in my history class, a boy argued that for us, war was always theoretical; it never touched us directly: "It's not as though our cities are attacked," he said. "It's not as though we walk by ruined buildings every day." I yelped, "*What?*" The class looked at me. "Never mind," I said, and slumped into my seat.

My freshman year at Yale, I was reluctant to mention the previous year's experience, assuming I would meet with the same apathy I had encountered at Stuyvesant. To my surprise, a single mention of my high school's proximity to the World Trade Center prompted shock and concern among college classmates. "Do you still think about it a lot?" asked one friend. "Oh, my God," said another, and again, "Oh, my God." At Yale, 80 miles from the World Trade Center, I found more solace among Midwesterners and Californians than I had among my Stuyvesant classmates—those who had shared my experience, but not my reaction. I had been so conditioned not to discuss the situation that, sophomore year, one of my closest friends told me she had no idea *what* had happened to me on September 11th. I had never told her my story. Stuyvesant's silence had taught me to keep silent.

The comparison between Stuyvesant and Yale students may be unfair. Yalies were not exposed to the trauma, and had no cause for the denial and silence that Stuyvesant adopted. Less affected, they could risk feeling its effects—from the safe distance of New Haven, Connecticut. Stuyvesant students and teachers were so close to tragedy that acknowledging it threatened their psyches. To acknowledge September 11th meant, for us, to acknowledge that the world was not safe; that we were not safe; that, had the pilots miscalculated and crashed a few blocks north of the towers, we would have died; that, had the towers been more carelessly constructed and fallen on their sides rather than imploded, we could have died beneath their weight. What is more threatening than these acknowledgments? My friends at Yale did not have to consider such ideas. Hailing from Texas, Florida, and Maine, they managed to maintain their older conception of safety—one I lost forever on September 11th. Thus, their empathy sprang from the fact that they had not been where I had been, that they could not quite understand. And conversely, the denial of the Stuyvesant community affirmed the commonality of our experience.

It was only later, when we ourselves had achieved both physical and temporal distance from the tragedy, that my Stuyvesant friends and I became able to discuss it. One friend, from whom I had felt particularly distanced because of her silence on the topic, observed 2 years later that she had understood me perfectly in 2001; I had verbalized what she was thinking but could not say herself. And now, inspired by a fiction seminar, she writes story after story about September 11th, and says she could publish endless books on the topic. Whenever we see each other, we discuss September 11th, and she is the one to bring it up. We must seem a bit like old war buddies, leaning back in our chairs, draining coffee cups, recalling harder times. Except—as I sometimes need to remind myself—we're 20 years old. In the same conversation we discuss acne treatment, the pros and cons of being premed—and September 11th. These conversations show how far we've come: September 11th has become just another fact of life, and in discussing it we work it further into our lives.

The solace of these conversations is continuously necessary, because September 11th is a continuous event. It recurs in small ways, and will for the rest of our lives. No day is free from its flashes. Construction workers hacking at concrete and raising dust clouds become workers at Ground Zero; masked doctors striding outside Yale-New Haven Hospital become Downtown residents who fear the air; the two steaming towers of a power plant become the World Trade Center. September 11th did not end on September 11th. It happens over and over. But so do conversations that help us make sense of it.

Yet before solace came solitude, and memories of my bewildered isolation continue to haunt me. In a school intent on pretending nothing was wrong, I wondered what was wrong with me. More than once I left classrooms mid-lesson to stare at my reflection in the bathroom, questioning the calm of my classmates, the cool command of my teacher. *Who cares about Joyce?* I, the future English major, wondered. How do the mating habits of praying mantises figure into the fact that the World Trade Center fell? Why are we trying to understand poetry and geometry and physics when we, steeped in denial, can't seem to understand that two buildings crumbled right next to us? But if September 11th taught me you can't see well from up close, the distance of time has given me a fuller perspective of what the experience—including its more painful aspects—has meant.

I wish my teachers had responded differently to September 11th. I wish they had normalized my feelings of shock and sadness. I wish they had eased my feelings of isolation by anticipating and articulating what I felt, by speaking of the variety of reactions we might be feeling, even by sharing some of their own. But in their failure to act the way I wanted, they taught me more than they could in the classroom.

I learned that just as I had reasons for reacting as I did, they had reasons for reacting as they did. Just as I saw towers rather than debris within the dust cloud, just as my friends heard gunshots rather than popping floors, our teachers saw within their students what was not necessarily there. We were shocked and grief-stricken and grave and happy and numb and raw and unbothered. We were a mess of contradictory reactions, and our teachers were, too. So they saw in us what they needed to see. They saw what would help them believe their world still made sense, despite overwhelming evidence to the contrary. Perhaps this need for coherence explains our teachers' insistence that we students were "resilient," despite evidence to the contrary—skyrocketing drug and alcohol abuse, symptoms of post-traumatic stress disorder, and, of course, silence. Some teachers, fortunately, saw through the silence and the ever-exemplary test scores; some faced and handled the distress of their students. To these teachers I am forever grateful. But the overwhelming tenor was one of wishful thinking—or wishful vision—on the parts of students and teachers alike. Unwilling or unable to take on the threatening truths of our experience, many of us closed our eyes to the facts of September 11th, to the devastation of our city and neighborhood and psyches, to the troubling behavior of our fellow students or colleagues. It is in this spirit, I believe, that my physics teacher was unable to see the reference to the World Trade Center in the problem he had assigned, even after a distressed student pointed it out to him several times.

Our teachers needed coherence about as much as we did, and never was this commonality clearer than during my own episode of banging. The classroom was full of the noise of second-term seniors preparing for a lesson. Outside it was snowing, and the snow—as it does to this day—reminded me of the ash that fell from dust clouds on September 11th. The teacher was talking uneasily with a colleague, who always popped in at the beginning of lessons in what appeared to be attempts to woo him. I was holding a ruler. And that's when the urge to bang overcame me. What drives a curly-haired, wild-eyed, physics-loathing student to bang a ruler against her desk until the nervous giggles of classmates shame her to silence? The same force that drove her witty, bright-eyed, middle-aged physics teacher to bang his head against a wall just weeks earlier. It was the sudden, overwhelming feeling that nothing made sense any longer.

We were joined in this feeling, if not in our reactions to it. And in this evolved world, this post-September 11th world, the functions of teachers and students had changed, and emotional reactions mattered. Teachers taught not just by textbook, but by outburst. For it was this error of his—the thoughtless selection of a textbook problem—that I remember from his class, rather than his thoughts on h and g and, God help us, dx/dy. Perhaps the biggest lesson September 11th offered was in this commonality—in the painful, puzzling process we all endure as we try to make sense of what seems senseless, and in the equally puzzling process of observing others endure this process. When Mr. Stein banged his head on the door and I banged my ruler on my desk, we were both banging at the perimeters of our own limitations. Neither of us felt capable of understanding a world in which September 11th happened; neither of us felt in tune with the reactions of those surrounding us; both were astounded by the horror and proximity of what had happened. I assume his astonishment because selecting such a clearly offensive question suggests a defense mechanism as sturdy as the basin that prevents the Hudson from washing over Lower Manhattan, suggests his own complex inner operations, suggests a mental process with which I can wholly empathize. To my great shock, 5 years after the fact, I am grateful for his insensitivity, for it suggests commonality between us; it suggests an emotional struggle we shared. And I am grateful because the complex and varied reactions of my classmates and teachers put my own sensitivity to the test. Comprehending September 11th continues to be a challenge, and comprehending the response of the Stuyvesant community is nearly as difficult. The best thing a school can do is grant students lessons that bear continuous analysis. This is not to say I am wholly glad Stuyvesant responded—or failed to respond—as it did. But its reaction, like September 11th itself, taught lessons all the more indelible for its devastating effects.

Nine

Building Inner Preparedness

LINDA LANTIERI
WITH MADHAVI NAMBIAR
AND MICHAEL CHAVEZ-REILLY

That Morning

AT 8 A.M. ON SEPTEMBER 11, 2001, over 8,700 children and 400 teachers showed up for school in Downtown Manhattan as they did every morning. Nobody could have predicted that within 2 hours, more than 5,000 students and nearly 200 teachers would be running for their lives; 9,000 more students would be evacuated in the following days; and 8,000 students would be asked to shelter other teachers and students as refugees from disaster. In the end, over 20,000 students would be directly impacted by the events of that day. Miraculously, due to quick thinking, deep caring, and the inner resourcefulness of educators in the area, not a single student life was lost.

One interesting question remains: On that day, what skills and behaviors did school leaders, teachers, and students draw upon? Certainly in that moment it was less important to know the capital of France than it was to know how to establish a sense of safety in the midst of profound uncertainty. In that moment, a school's performance on standardized test scores became less important than its ability to reflect and regroup as a community. That day, facing the deepest test of life, the question of academic preparedness took a backseat to the question of inner preparedness—what were the skills and resources that each individual and school community had to access in order to connect to their deeper wisdom, and remain calm and balanced?

At P.S. 89, four blocks north of the World Trade Center, it was only the 4th day of school, as elsewhere in the city. Around 8:45 A.M., when the first plane flew overhead, many parents were still in the schoolyard, saying good-bye to their children and mingling with teachers and the principal, Veronica Najjar. She vividly recalls the events of that morning.

> We witnessed, at close range, the impact to the North Tower.
> Parents were shocked—screaming and crying in the yard.
> Everyone was encouraged to come inside the school building
> until we could assess what was happening. . . . The parents
> started arriving in a panic trying to get their kids out of school.

Furthermore, the classrooms on the south side of P.S. 89 had a full view of the World Trade Center. Teachers on the south side of the building remember hearing a "kaboom." In focus groups, they later recalled looking out the window and then suddenly thinking, "We shouldn't be looking at this. The children shouldn't be looking at this." Some teachers drew their blinds and took the younger children to the activity rugs and reassured them that they and their parents were going to be safe.

Teachers and administrators at P.S. 89 gathered the children into the auditorium and gymnasium—windowless spaces in the middle of the building. Najjar and her staff understood intuitively that a sense of safety and calm was the first thing their students needed. From that moment on, Najjar and other school leaders in the area would have to start making life-and-death decisions in a split second. They had to make decisions about how to respond to on-the-spot questions, such as who would be allowed to pick up the children and whether older children could be dismissed on their own. Later that day other questions would arise, including whether teachers should be allowed to take children to their homes if parents could not be contacted. These are not the type of questions most educators are trained to answer at administration courses in schools of education.

As panicked adults were flooding the building, school leaders contacted the District Office to try and figure out what was going on. Marjorie Robbins, at the time head of Pupil Personnel Services in Community School District 2, recalls what it was like for those desperately trying to coordinate escape routes for students and teachers. Despite their best efforts, she admits,

> It was chaos. . . . We thought vans would get there to help evacuate students. We didn't know what trains were running, if any were running at all. . . . In the end, we provided the information we received from the City, but the principals themselves ultimately had to make the most difficult decision of all—when was the time to evacuate.

For the students and faculty of the High School for Leadership and Public Service, located two blocks south of the towers, the experience of evacuation was particularly terrifying. As Principal Ada Dolch vividly describes in Chapter 3, she had to walk south with faculty and students, watching some of them board ferries leaving Manhattan Island and eventually organizing the others into groups to walk to safety in other boroughs. In these moments, educators had to draw on an inner reserve of courage and unconditional service—qualities that are seldom discussed within the context of professional development. In a focus group with teachers, Helene Jackson of the Columbia School of Social Work takes note of this special quality. "Some of them talk about when they realized what was happening, saying to themselves, 'I'm a teacher, I'm responsible, I have to take care of these children.'"[1] Unlike in many other professions, to be a teacher during and after an event such as 9/11 opened one's personal thoughts, feelings, and life to public scrutiny.

The Lingering Impact

Unfortunately, for many downtown teachers and students, the sense of crisis did not end with that terrifying day. In the wake of September 11th, over 5,200 students from seven different schools

---

1. Helene Jackson, Ezra Susser, & Christina Hoven. *Terrorism and Mental Health in School: The Effects of September 11, 2001, on New York City School Children.* Fathom, the source for online learning: www.fathom.com/feature/190150, p. 3.

found themselves displaced and temporarily housed in other schools for several months. Not surprisingly, this situation created a tremendous strain on teachers and students throughout Lower Manhattan.

P.S. 150, The Tribeca Learning Center, remained housed at P.S. 3 for 4½ months while the air was being tested and the buildings cleaned at and around Ground Zero. Students had minimal supplies, and either shared classrooms or held class on the floor in the hallways. The entire administration and support services operated out of one room. Helene Jackson describes this experience for teachers as "a kind of re-traumatization."[2]

In the weeks following September 11th, Marjorie Robbins visited many of the dislocated schools. She described how teachers attempted to cope:

> In the aftermath, teachers tried to re-establish who they were as a class and as a classroom. They got books, they found space, they took care of their own and their children's immediate needs first. They felt they had to establish a sense of safety and normalcy. It was only later that they could talk about their feelings.

In the quest to maintain normalcy, months elapsed before some teachers realized they had not spoken about these issues with their peers and colleagues. As Helene Jackson noted based on the focus group she led with P.S. 150 teachers:

> They didn't talk about it. . . . They didn't know that they needed that space until they had the focus group many months later. It was just mind-boggling to them and to us that they hadn't talked about it. They had no idea what each other's experiences had been.[3]

In fact, it was not uncommon to meet school personnel who had not shared their personal story of that day with anyone, even 2 years later.

While avoiding discussion of a traumatic event may be necessary to survive in the initial aftermath, this strategy can become

2. Ibid.
3. Ibid.

counterproductive over the long term. As time passed, tensions between teachers, parents, and students surfaced. Increased incidents of physically and verbally aggressive behavior between students were reported. Teachers began to voice their frustration about the way events were handled in the immediate aftermath. Tensions were visible as the anniversary of the attacks approached. Principals and the district office did everything they could to help staff cope, but the frustration tolerance among teachers was very low.

When teachers, guidance counselors, and administrators came together for various meetings and trainings, they described experiencing symptoms consistent with post-traumatic stress disorder, including exhaustion and a loss of creativity. Some of them talked about having nightmares. When asked what they did to take care of themselves, many said, "Sleep and eat." It was clear that teachers and administrators paid a terribly high price for taking care of others that day. The effects of the caring were slow to surface in the midst of the great need of the young people in their charge. They were only just beginning to feel.

Within the schools around Ground Zero, there remained much debate among teachers, administrators, and parents about how often and how openly to talk about the events of September 11th. Some parents requested workshops on how to identify signs of stress and trauma in their children, while other parents actively resisted them. A year later Robbins reported:

> There remains a lot of desire to get back to normal. A lot of
> these teachers feel they've lost time in their curriculum, and
> with the pressure of standardized tests upon them, some teach-
> ers feel that they do not have time to address these issues.

Nonetheless, everyone acknowledged that the ongoing psychological effects of 9/11 will continue to be seen in the schools for years to come. Evidence of the long-lasting effects of 9/11 can be found throughout schools in lower Manhattan. Two years later elementary schools reported that they were treating "incoming students of Pre-K and Kindergarten who were 2 or 3 years old at the time of the attack and who suffer from residual unmet trauma-related difficulties." Ada Rosario-Dolch observes, "Though the blackout of 2003 occurred during the summer months, the many e-mails and phone calls we received from our students expressing their fears served as a reminder that time does heal, but healing is coming slowly."

Clearly, there was a need to address the long-term recovery of both youth and adults in Lower Manhattan. However, it also seemed clear that different people were healing at different rates, and in different ways. As a result, the challenge was to create long-term preventive programs of inner resilience. These efforts had to be flexible and inclusive enough to address differing needs in a subtle and respectful, yet profound, manner.

From Crisis to Opportunity: The Development of Project Renewal

Project Renewal was formed in spring 2002 in direct response to the diverse needs of the teachers and students who had been affected by the September 11th attacks. Linda Lantieri, whose experience includes serving as director of the Resolving Conflict Creatively Program of Educators for Social Responsibility, became the director of the new program.

"Throughout my career, I have always felt that the education of young people involved not only their intellectual development, but their emotional, social, and spiritual growth as well," says Lantieri, who has served as a teacher, school administrator, education activist and college faculty member.

In taking on her new role, Lantieri drew on her 3-year experience as a senior scholar at the Fetzer Institute in Kalamazoo, Michigan, which she had completed just before September 11th. The institute is a privately endowed foundation whose mission is to help people make a deeper connection between "their inner life of mind and spirit and their outer life of action and service."

During her time at the institute, Lantieri was part of a group of 18 individuals from all walks of life who had been brought together to reflect with each other about how to bring a more holistic perspective to their various fields of work. Lantieri also used her time at the Institute to edit the book *Schools with Spirit: Nurturing the Inner Lives of Children and Teachers*, which was published in August 2001.[4]

---

4. Boston: Beacon Press.

As Lantieri visited schools in the aftermath of the September 11 attack, she saw educators struggling to cope with their own sense of helplessness and feelings of despair without any personal support. As a result of the attack, countless educators were transformed overnight into grief counselors, recovery coordinators, and crisis intervention experts for their students. "I saw how much listening they had to do—to experts, to students, to parents, and to administrators. But who was listening to their stories?" Lantieri asks. "Many displayed the classic signs of 'compassion fatigue.' In all the listening, they had not yet had the chance to check in with their own feelings and tell their own stories. It was clear to me that teachers were running out of the personal and emotional support they needed to sustain those they were serving."

Research confirms that the prolonged psychological stress these educators were experiencing could lead to burnout, which in turn leads to a wide range of physical disorders. Unfortunately, "giving one's all" is sometimes seen as a status symbol in our society, proof that we are capable of overwhelming workloads. New York City's educators needed help in gaining control over their circumstances, strengthening their inner resources, and supporting one another in contexts where they would be able to formally debrief their experiences. How could these educators be protected from the possibility of what author Wayne Muller describes in his book, *Sabbath: Restoring the Sacred Rhythm of Rest,* as "doing good badly"?[5] Who was taking care of the caregivers? Where would they get the time and space to renew, rejuvenate and rekindle their own spirits and resiliency?

To help answer these questions, The September 11th Fund provided a seed grant for Lantieri to establish Project Renewal, which was initially sponsored by Educators for Social Responsibility National. Soon after, Project Renewal became a project of the Tides Center whose mission is to enable people to create and sustain a healthy, just, and vibrant world. The center accomplishes this by providing organizations like Project Renewal with the needed infrastructure to support their many activities. "It was clear that the need for action was immediate, and if I wanted to create this program, I'd have to start now and hit the ground running," Lantieri remembers.

---

5. New York: Bantam, 1999.

Project Renewal's philosophy of focusing on addressing the inner lives of students and educators grew out of the work that Lantieri had done at the Fetzer Institute and in editing *Schools with Spirit*. "When I speak about inner lives, I do not just mean our emotional lives, but that which gives our life meaning, direction, and purpose," she explains. "Trauma experts will tell you that experiencing trauma 'rends the fabric of meaning' in our lives, and that to recover from trauma, you have to build that sense of meaning back up again."

Whenever someone experiences either a catastrophic event or chronic adversity, it is rarely the presence of this single event or circumstance that determines whether a person will break down or break through. The research on resiliency shows that the outcome is actually a balancing act between risk factors and protective opportunities.

Breakdowns occur when several harmful risk factors build up without being counteracted by an equal number of inner and outer resources, or protective opportunities. This is true for both young people and the adults who serve them. Individuals' own internal resources and external assets can and do make all the difference in how they are able to cope with traumatic circumstances. Although they may have little control over the adversity that comes their way, people can increase their protective opportunities. They can prevent their coping capacity from being overwhelmed; they can bounce back and avoid long-term negative effects from traumatic circumstances. That is the concept that Project Renewal was created to explore. As Lantieri recalls:

> During that spring I met with many close friends and advisors inside and outside of Community School District 2 [the district that encompasses Ground Zero] to discuss what was most needed. It struck us that as the first summer after September 11th approached, and teachers finally got a chance to reflect on the most intense year of their professional lives, many suppressed feelings would emerge. We again asked ourselves the question, "So during the summer, who will nurture the caregivers who have so faithfully served?"

Out of these conversations, Cheri Lovre, of the Crisis Management Institute, and Lantieri developed *A Summer of Renewal—A*

Guide for Reflection for New York City School Personnel—Integrating the Events of September 11th. It provided educators with a self-guided set of activities to enable them to reflect weekly throughout the summer on the events of the previous year and what it meant for them. The activities were designed to help them find ways to restore a positive sense of meaning and vitality to their lives and their careers. The guide reflected the goal articulated by Parker Palmer, author of *The Courage to Teach,* of "learning as many ways as we can of talking to ourselves." As Parker says, "We need to find every possible way to listen to that voice and take its counsel seriously, not only for the sake of our work, but for the sake of our own health."[6]

In June and July 2002, 3,000 print copies of the guide were distributed to New York City educators. Project Renewal followed up the publication of the guide by coordinating and assisting with training sessions for administrators, guidance counselors, school psychologists, and social workers in the affected schools to help them create individual school plans to commemorate the anniversary of September 11th. In addition, site visits to specific schools were conducted in preparation for the anniversary.

As the first anniversary passed, it was clear that the effects of September 11th were going to be long-lasting. An advisory team for Project Renewal was formed, including Yeou-Cheng Ma, Carlos Monteagudo, Robin Stern, Lynne Hurdle-Price, Martha Eddy, Carmella B'Hahn, Lindamichellebaron, and many others. With the help of an initial grant from the Surdna Foundation, the group worked together to begin to develop a wide range of renewal activities for school personnel.

"At that point, what I refer to as 'divine synchronicity' seemed to play a role, when I connected with Madhavi Nambiar, a young woman who had gravitated back to New York City in the wake of September 11th," Lantieri says. "Madhavi's experience as a teacher whose own inner reservoir was running out and who was well-versed in holistic modes of healing and renewal created a sense of purpose that met and matched my vision. She was really the last piece of the puzzle I needed to launch the program."

Lantieri and Nambiar joined together with the advisory team to begin to work toward the vision of creating a safe and loving community as well as a body of knowledge and skills to help educators

---

6. San Francisco: Jossey Bass, 1998.

stay the course and build their inner resilience during uncertain and fearful times. "From my experience at the Fetzer Institute, I knew one of the most important ways to recover from 'compassion fatigue' was to physically distance one's self from the workplace," Lantieri notes.

> This distance allows for a greater sense of safety and a deeper degree of perspective that ultimately allows a person to reflect on their work in a deeper way. I realized that many of the ceremonies and rituals I had experienced at the Fetzer Institute could now be shared with a larger community of educators. I wanted to offer this type of an off-site experience to teachers who needed a deeper level of calm.

Out of this idea, the Seasonal Retreat for Educators for Renewal and Restoration was born.

The first retreat was held an hour outside of New York City at Stony Point Center, one of three national retreat centers owned and operated by the Presbyterian Church USA. The retreat took place over a weekend in mid-December 2002. A group of 20 educators who were previously strangers gathered and, through the course of the retreat, formed a network of support for each other. One participant, a teacher from the High School of Leadership and Public Service (the high school closest to Ground Zero), described her experience on the retreat in these words:

> I learned more about myself in that weekend than what I had known my entire life. For the first time in my life, I saw qualities within me that others had always observed, but I was unaware of. I felt comfortable enough to open myself up to a room of total strangers and left knowing that I had gained a new family. I was able to let go and be free. This was truly one of the best experiences of my life, and I will treasure it always.

Soon thereafter, Presbyterian Disaster Assistance (PDA) gave Project Renewal a $145,000 grant to help teachers and counselors build personal reserves during ongoing retreats at Stony Point Center. PDA has since renewed the grant to continue these retreats.

Since the first retreat, Project Renewal has conducted 20 more residential retreats at Stony Point Center and has scheduled many more for the future. To date, over 5,000 school personnel have benefited from Project Renewal's various offerings. "We were nurtured, attended to, and now we can do the same with our children," one teacher wrote after a retreat in April 2003. Another participant, writing after a retreat in October 2004, declared, "I can't wait to teach again! Courage. Love. Faith. These are values that *are* our curriculum, however we may teach. I want to strengthen my conviction, take the challenge on of really keeping those things at the forefront of my work."

As a result of the success of the seasonal retreats, Project Renewal began to explore other modes and venues that could be used to offer restorative services to teachers. The idea of holding after-school workshops in the schools seemed a natural one, because that was the quickest way to get to busy teachers. The after-school workshops focused on the connection between the mind and the body and the individual as part of the community. Research shows that the more modalities people work in, the more opportunities and ways they get to heal. Talk therapy was being offered free of charge for those deeply affected by this tragedy, but many educators come from cultures where individual talk therapy may not be the most effective way to access emotions. Project Renewal's programs were designed to introduce teachers to as many different ways to heal as possible, including indigenous, alternative, and complementary ways to integrate mind, body, and spirit.

In studying many indigenous cultures of the world, anthropologist Angeles Arrien notices that there are four "healing salves" present in all cultures that nurture the inner life—silence, music, dance/ movement, and storytelling. The work at Project Renewal began to reflect this awareness. Participants had many experiences of silence and contemplation and were provided with some concrete tools to control their physiology and to identify and manage intrusive emotions. They learned various ways to relax both the body and the mind through progressive muscle relaxation exercises, simple meditation practices, and guided imagery.

Educators were also invited to collectively explore the "healing salves" through workshops covering topics such as: Using Poetry for Inner Reflection; Energizing Ourselves Through Creative

Dramatics; Emotional Intelligence: Using the Emotional Competence Inventory; Gentle Stretching/Movement for Peace; and the Role of Music in Nurturing Our Inner Lives. Project Renewal's initial plan was to pay teachers per session for attending these workshops, but it soon became clear that there was no need for this, because the teachers were grateful for workshops that helped them explore their own possibilities around self-care and renewal.

Having witnessed the powerful effects of massage and healing touch on firefighters and rescue workers at Ground Zero, Lantieri contacted Martha Eddy, who at the time was the coordinator of the Wellness Program at Riverside Church, to discuss the possibility of offering similar services to teachers and school personnel. Eddy agreed to use part of a small grant she had received to offer bodywork and healing-touch services to educators in a few schools near Ground Zero.

The 20- to 30-minute body-work sessions were easily incorporated into the school day during teachers' free periods. Typically, during one of its "stress-reduction days," Project Renewal arranges for one to three body-work practitioners to work within the school setting during the school day. Depending on the circumstances and the clients' preference, bodywork may occur seated on a chair or lying on a table or mat fully clothed.

Project Renewal has delivered over 2,000 such sessions to school personnel in more than 30 different schools in New York City since 2002, and hopes to find funding to do more. Teachers, security guards, and administrative personnel have all participated, learning about where they store stress and how they can reduce that stress. "I felt empowered and was treated with the utmost gentleness and care," one participant wrote after an October 2004 stress-reduction session. Another participant described the work as an "extremely healing, generative" experience.

In addition, Project Renewal has addressed the mind-body connection to releasing trauma and stress through weekly yoga classes. Attention to the body and somatic therapies brings heightened awareness to traumatized individuals and allows them to reconnect with themselves, their community, and the world at large. These approaches can facilitate integration of the traumatic experience, which allows the individual to move beyond the past and embrace the present.

Another important aspect of the group's work was the need to address bias and discrimination, which was heightened after September 11th and which continues to persist throughout society. As world issues became more complex, educators were faced with the challenge of presenting avenues for meaningful dialogue that allowed diverse viewpoints to surface. Educators needed concrete strategies to be able to help young people develop skills for understanding and discussing complex world issues in an informed way.

Project Renewal offered selected trainings for educators that approached a range of world issues with the objective of broadening their knowledge base and encouraging dialogue. One such offering was a Teacher Institute in collaboration with the Asia Society and Educators for Social Responsibility Metro in October 2003, which was entitled "Teaching about Contemporary World Conflicts: Case Studies and Classroom Strategies to Promote International Understanding." In being able to look deeply and honestly at various issues, educators experienced profoundly meaningful dialogue about different values and experiences.

Project Renewal also began to realize the importance of working with youth leaders in high schools around some of these concepts. The group designed workshops that took the young people away to cultivate their resiliency and coping skills and prepare them to go back to their schools, empowered to create a positive peer climate for learning. Since then, this has become a powerful and significant part of Project Renewal's work as well. Project Renewal also hosted 14-day-long retreats for graduating seniors who began their high school careers on September 11, 2001. These retreats gave students an opportunity to fully integrate this tragedy into their psyche. They were able to acknowledge their pain, identify the lessons learned, and look optimistically toward the future.

Future Plans

At this writing, Project Renewal moves into its 4th year, the program is at an exciting juncture in its young history. Project Renewal continues to be engaged in an ongoing dialogue with the schools in and around Ground Zero about how to make a lasting impact on the educators, students and parents affected by the events of

September 11th. Based on these conversations, the group is exploring ways to continue to expand and deepen its core program, and in so doing, test and refine a long-term holistic approach to strengthening inner resilience in schools in New York City and eventually nationwide. As Lantieri points out:

> Our biggest realization has been that this work has broader
> implications for the field of education. It is not about wait-
> ing for another disaster to take place. Teachers are leaving
> the teaching profession in record numbers, mostly because of
> compassion fatigue and burnout. This is work that needs to be
> introduced into the very fabric of professional development for
> teachers.

As a result, Project Renewal has received funding to develop a project to recruit and select a cohort of 15 K–12 schools (eight elementary and three middle schools in which the group has already been working) that are willing to serve as demonstration sites over a 2-year project period and become models of deepening and sustaining this work in "inner preparedness." Over the next 2 years, Project Renewal hopes to develop a series of curriculum modules for students in grades K–12, provide workshops to equip parents and caregivers with the knowledge and skills needed to increase their own resiliency, and develop materials to enable school leaders to facilitate the work at a "whole school" level.

Another important step is to find concrete ways to determine whether Project Renewal's work is producing positive outcomes that are measurable. The group is in the process of engaging in a rigorous and comprehensive evaluation of its work to assess its impact on both adult and youth participants in a more systematic way, as well as replicate those aspects that educators have found especially valuable.

One major challenge faced by Project Renewal is how to sustain its work as the institutional memories and services attached to September 11th begin to fade. The group first aims to secure enough resources through June 2007 to leave school communities in Lower Manhattan with the know-how to continue the work on their own as September 11th monies cease. At the same time, Project Renewal hopes to make inroads in both the foundation and education communities to advocate for this heart-to-heart resuscitation to be integral to what we offer school staff before we lose them.

Challenges and Lessons Learned

"People often tell me they are surprised that we are able to do this kind of work in New York City public schools," Lantieri acknowledges.

> We have actually found teachers and school leaders in the Ground Zero area incredibly open to trying new activities that are not on the traditional list of professional-development topics. We have made many allies among people who were former skeptics of this approach. Initially, in some schools, there may have been such a desperate need that they were willing to try anything if it came from a person they knew and trusted. But as they tried our offerings, the vast majority of school leaders found that helping their staff and colleagues reconnect to what gives their lives and jobs true meaning and purpose was about as important a topic as they could address.

For example, one participant in a recent teacher retreat admitted that his signed letter of resignation was sitting on his desk at home. After the retreat, he decided to rip it up because the retreat helped him remember why he was in this profession in the first place.

To introduce new and different offerings to the school system, a program must be both efficient and effective. Organizers must understand the needs of those they are serving. "At Project Renewal we know that if we want to get New York City schoolteachers to a retreat outside the city, we have to hire a bus to take them there, since most of our teachers don't have cars," Lantieri notes. "We also know that if we want to conduct a training with teachers off-site, we may have to pay for the substitutes in their classroom, to make sure it can happen." Only by running an effective and efficient program can organizers gain the necessary trust that both gets them in the door and gets them invited back to develop and sustain a relationship over years.

Of course, implementing innovative programs in traditional institutions is never without its challenges. Some guidelines around mental health services continue to be narrowly culturally defined. Some people are more open to new ideas than others. However, what is most important is to develop reciprocal, respectful relationships with the people in large, mainstream institutions who are open to new ideas and approaches. If you cultivate these relationships, and respect the limits and pace of what people can do when, they will be able to help you move things forward when the time for change arrives.

As the world continues to be chaotic and uncertain, we will need more and more educators who are ready to make schools places where children are prepared for life's tests. The recent focus on academic competence must not let us lose sight of the skills, understanding, and awareness both teachers and children will need to be prepared to live a life that matters. Project Renewal and other organizations must continue to work to create safe spaces and nurture trusting relationships where honesty and healing can occur for students, as well as for the teachers, administrators, and school staff who work so hard to serve them.

Ten

Testifying to Our Existence: Exploring Religions and Cultures Through Mural Painting

DEBBIE ALMONTASER

ON JUNE 3RD, STUDENTS and their families began arriving bright and early at P.S. 230 in the Kensington area of Brooklyn, where there is a large population of South Asians as well as people from various other cultures. They were there to create a mural on one of the school's outer walls that would stand as a testament to the friendship and understanding that endured across cultures in spite of the September 11th attacks and their aftermath. As the paint and brushes were distributed, there was an energetic charge in the air. Everyone was excited about the idea of painting what was near and dear to them on a wall that would testify to their existence.

It was an exciting day for me, as well, because the mural-making session represented a culmination of all the work I had done since the September 11th attacks to help build cross-cultural understanding. It was a day for the children and their loved ones to tap into the healing power of art, and it was also a day for me to reflect on the long road I had traveled since that tragic day when the Twin Towers fell.

*   *   *

September 11, 2001, will forever remain etched in my mind. I remember that morning when I walked out of my house; I looked up into the sky and took a deep breath. The sky was so blue and clear, and the air was fresh and clean. By 8:00, I got to the school where I was teaching then, in Cobble Hill, which is quite diverse and has a large Arab-American community, as it is a couple of blocks away from Atlantic Avenue, or "Little Syria." At 8:30, I skipped down the stairs into the schoolyard to pick up my fifth-grade class. They were happy to see that I was the first teacher to come out, and they all started to clap and cheer. As I was waiting for them to line up, I looked up and noticed the blue sky that stretched from Midwood to Cobble Hill and into Manhattan, where the skyline shared this beautiful blue backdrop. Little did I know it would be the last time I would ever lay my eyes on the Twin Towers. My class was ready to go. We went up and started our 3rd day of school.

At about 9:15, a parent from the PTA came to my door and asked to speak to me. I walked over from the carpet where we were solving the math problem of the day. Her request made me feel very uneasy and concerned about what she might have to tell me. As I stood in front of her, she pulled me nearby, grabbing my arm, and she said, "I don't want the children to hear this. We are going around to all the classrooms to tell teachers of what has happened; please don't be alarmed when I tell you."

I said to her, "What is it?"

She said, "One of the Twin Towers was hit by a plane minutes ago. We believe it's an accident."

My stomach twisted and then dropped like a water-balloon that almost busted but instead bounced and rolled. I was speechless for a moment, with my jaw hanging. I looked over my shoulder and saw my 10- and 11-year-old students waiting patiently for me. "Go about your day as if it was any other day, try to keep the kids in the room, and we will get back to you with further news," the parent said.

As I was walking back to the carpet to join the kids, a million thoughts raced through my mind. How could a plane crash into a building in daylight, in a cloudless sky? How could a plane not see a high-rise that was endless in height? I took a deep breath, and asked the children to close their math journals and get ready for the reading mini-lesson. I quickly taught the mini-lesson, had a few kids share their process, and sent them all off to do paired and independent reading. I have no idea how I was able to focus and concentrate on the lesson. The disbelief continued to race through my head.

Moments later, the parent came back to share more bad news. She whispered, "Debbie, the second tower has just been hit. What has happened is no longer an accident, but an attack." I felt the world spinning out of control around me, my heart dropping in the pit of my stomach. She grabbed me by the arms and shook me for a few seconds. She asked me if I was okay. I nodded my head in disbelief.

Horrible thoughts and images flooded my mind, as well as suspicions as I speculated that the attack might have been carried out by people who call themselves Muslims. I said to myself, "Please, God, don't let this be true. Don't disgrace us or burden us with such a crime you know true Muslims would not commit." I thought about the last catastrophe on American soil, the Oklahoma bombing, and prayed it was that group again. I just wanted to run as far as I could and scream as loud as I could to God to take all this back, to rewind my day, to let me find myself in bed having a nightmare, so that I could wake up and realize that it was just a horrible dream. I thought about my husband and two sons, who at that time were in Manhattan. Inside, I started to panic about my family's safety, but on the outside, I remained calm, especially after looking at my students, who were reading peacefully on the carpet. Where and how I got the strength to keep calm remains a mystery.

One of my students, Steven, a delightful young Latino who connected with me the first day, asked to go to the bathroom. He came back a changed child, subdued and speechless. He walked over to me and whispered in my ear that the Twin Towers were covered with a large ball of smoke. I asked him to keep this information to himself, but his classmates started to ask why five of the children had been picked up by their parents and why there was so much noise outside. I could no longer go on with the charade. I asked the children to sit in a circle in the meeting area. I broke the news to them gently, so as not to frighten them. I started by assuring them that while they are in school, they are as safe as when they are at home with their families, and then I told them the horrible news. I explained to them that they would remain in school unless their parents came to pick them up. Most of the children were calm; a couple started to cry, and I comforted them. My worst fear was that their parents or another family member worked in one of the towers. To my relief, they didn't.

At lunchtime, I called home. My husband answered the phone, relieved that I had called. I, too, was relieved to hear his voice. I asked him about our kids. He answered by saying, "Yousif just got home, Shifa is on her way, a classmate's parent is dropping her off, and—"

I impatiently interrupted by yelling, "Where is Mohammed? Where is he?" There was a long pause. My eyes started to swell with tears. He finally spoke. "Mohammed hasn't called yet. I'm sure he's okay."

My husband urged me not to go home alone. He said I should find someone to take me home and, if I couldn't, I should call him back and wait for him. His last words were, "It's not safe out there. I don't want anyone to identify you as Arab and Muslim. They might want to hurt you since there is some suspicion that the attacks may have been planned by Muslim extremists."

As I was pulling myself together, I heard a parent crying hysterically. I ran out to see what had happened. It was an Arab-American Muslim mother who had been verbally abused by a group of people standing in front of the school. She was terrified to leave the building with her kids. I called for a car, but there were none available for at least an hour. A parent helping in the office offered to take her and her children home.

When I went to pick up my class after lunch, a few of my students had already come to the conclusion that it was "those dumb Arabs" who had attacked the towers, based on what they had heard in the lunchroom from the adults. I was truly dumbfounded that such conversations took place. In addition, I was deeply hurt and saddened that only a few hours after the planes had struck, people were already looking for a scapegoat.

I let the children share everything they had to share. When we got to the classroom, I asked everyone to join me at the meeting area. This was a teachable moment I could not avoid delving into. I explained to them that we would be hearing a lot of stories for weeks to come about this tragedy, and that we mustn't say things that we later might regret. I mentioned to my students that I was an Arab-American and that my feelings were hurt to hear these accusations when no one in the government knew anything yet. A few of them yelled, "We don't mean you! We know you wouldn't do anything like that!"

I responded by saying, "There are a lot of Arabs and Muslims like me who would never do anything like this."We had a conversation that helped them to understand that we can't make generalizations about all people of a particular race. I gave them examples such as, "All youth are lazy" and "All Spanish people only eat rice and beans," and they started to understand what I meant. One student said, "Can we say, we have reason to believe that those who are involved in the attacks are terrorists who may be of Arab descent?"

I asked the other children what they thought. They replied, "When you say it that way, you are not blaming all Arabs or saying that this is a proven fact." I also mentioned how Arabs were initially blamed for the Oklahoma bombing, when in fact the culprit was an American native. Some students wanted to change the statement to, "We have reason to believe that those who are involved in the attacks are terrorists."

Besides blame and speculation, we also discussed safety issues: Is our school safe? Will this happen again in a few hours? Is our country under attack? What is the government going to do about this? These were questions that left me speechless, but God gave me the strength to answer them in a way that made my students feel safe. Toward the end of the conversation, one student asked me if I was scared. He said, "I would be scared if I was Arab Muslim, because everyone would be angry with me for what has happened if those who did it are Arab. I am scared for you."

This comment assured me that my students cared about me, but made me wonder, *Will they continue to do so, after watching the nonstop news broadcasting?* "What do you think I should do?" I asked the student. His response was, "Don't go home alone." Ten- and 11-year-old children knew exactly what I was going to face as an Arab-American Muslim woman who wears the *hijab* (head scarf).

After the students went home, a colleague of mine, Rose, offered to take me home. She walked me to my classroom, helped me pack up my things, and walked me down to the main office. In the office, the principal, Judi, was waiting for me. "If you don't feel safe enough to come to work tomorrow, I understand," she said. In denial, I looked at her and said, "You're overreacting!" I tried calling my house again, but there was no answer. Leaving the building, I realized that I was going to walk out into a new world that was filled with challenges I never dreamed of.

As Rose and I were driving home, a man waiting for the light stared into the car directly at me with deep contempt and rage. He pointed his finger and wagged it up and down while he yelled and carried on. My worst fear, of becoming an outcast and being hated for who I was, was becoming a reality. The look on his face was very frightening and made me wish I could disappear.

For the rest of the ride home, I scrunched myself down in my seat and thought about my family. I was very anxious to find out if Mohammed made it home. I also thought about all those families whose loved ones worked at the WTC and how they must be feeling. I thought about all the firemen and police who were out there on duty, and those who rushed to help. My final thought was about my son Yousif, a national guardsman. Was he going to be called in or not? The thought of his going to the site of the tragedy scared me to death.

We finally reach my house, and Rose waited for me to get inside. As I walked in the front door, I called out my children's names, and they came running into my arms, first Shifa and then Mohammed. I turned to look for Yousif, and my husband broke the news that our son had been activated by his unit. I fell on my knees and cried like a baby. "How could you let him leave?" I asked my husband. "What if something happens to him?" My husband sat next to me answering my questions. Mohammed got me tissues, and Shifa got me water. I finally pulled myself together and went up to my room, where I sat on the couch in a daze.

At around 6:30, the phone rang. It was the school board president of District 15. He had called to request my assistance and input on how to deal with the tragedy. As I was explaining to him that I had obligations at my school, the superintendent grabbed the phone from him to stress how important it was for me to join her cabinet to give them a heads up on how to make sure everyone feels safe. She also explained that she would call the school to cover my class. My husband asked to join me and to be given a spot in the district parking lot to ensure my safety.

Later that evening, filled with despair and hopelessness, my husband picked up the Quran and began to recite my favorite chapter, "The Most High," which describes God's grace toward humanity. Listening to his mellow recitation soothed and calmed my heart. And that's when I realized I needed to engage others and myself in the process of healing the hearts of humanity. I knew then that I would be facing adversity like never before. My only defense was to become empowered and empower others to create wider civic participation that would lead to acceptance and respect. I couldn't let what had happened destroy what was left that was good. I did not want to let go of the hope that we can all live in peace and harmony, even in a time filled with such uncertainty. A quote from the Quran became my inspiration:

O mankind! We have created you from a male and a female, and made you into nations and tribes, so that you may know one another. Verily the most honored of you in the sight of Allah is [he who is] the most righteous of you. And *Allah* has full knowledge and is well acquainted [with all things]. (Al-Hujurat, the Private Apartments, 11:13).

Months later, living out the realization that had come to me when I heard my husband reading, I was working as part of a team that was building cross-cultural awareness in the schools with the largest populations of Arabs, South Asians, and Muslims in Brooklyn's District 15, including P.S. 230, the school whose community would eventually come together to create the mural.

Getting to this point had involved overcoming a great deal of fear for me. On September 11th, I and other Muslim women had lost our safety and security. We became very limited in our daily routines. I, for one, became a self-imposed prisoner in my own home for months. I was afraid to go out in public while wearing the hijab. My husband became my escort; he drove me to work and drove me home. He did everything I needed to get done outside, because we feared for my life. We were afraid of someone attacking me physically or verbally, since it had happened on several occasions to other Muslim women.

Despite the fear and anxiety I felt every time I thought of my son Yousif, I knew I needed to keep myself busy. That was the best way for me to deal with my grief and sorrow. I needed to listen to those who were still angry, scared, and frustrated, as well as to the voices of those who felt excluded and marginalized. I realized that everyone needed the space to express his or her thoughts and feelings and to be heard, regardless of their faith or cultural background. I traveled across the city to speak at churches, synagogues, and wherever else I was invited.

I was on a mission to retrieve the integrity and dignity of Islam and Arab-Americans, as well as South Asians who had been adversely affected. As a mother, a daughter, a sister, and a teacher who takes every moment of life as a teaching and learning experience, I found comfort in educating others about Islam and Arab-Americans. I wanted people to know that we cannot condemn a people or religion for the wrongdoing of individuals who acted on irrational feelings and committed acts that are non-Islamic. My whole life evolved in developing and nurturing communities, resilient communities filled with respect and admiration for others, so I did not crawl into a shell or stumble under the weight of this tragic event that was beyond comprehension. The choice I made was to help build bridges between communities, an endless task that needed to start somewhere.

In the weeks after the attacks, I was a classroom teacher by day, but at night and on weekends, I was a community organizer arranging cross-cultural events and interfaith gatherings, as well as demonstrations opposing the detention of innocent people. "With our rights as U.S. citizens come responsibilities," I would say when I spoke at public gatherings. "We must not let history repeat itself. We need to become the generation that breaks the vicious cycles of racism, sexism, and xenophobia. Our destiny is in our hands, now more than ever, and we need to come together and stand as one for social change."

This volunteer work took all my time and energy, until I became ill from overexertion. My husband and friends made me realize that I had to make a choice between teaching and my community work. I was torn, because I loved being with my students, but I knew deep down in my heart that I wasn't giving them my all. I also loved serving my community, and I felt that if I didn't do it, I would be letting them down. I made my final decision after a conversation I had with Judi, the principal. "If you continue as a teacher, you will impact a group of children," she said. "If you choose the community work, you will be impacting communities. Follow your heart."

Breaking the news to my students was the hardest thing I ever had to do, but after I spoke to them, my heart was filled with joy, because they truly understood that I couldn't keep doing everything I was doing. They knew how involved I was in the community, and they were very proud. Precious, who is as precious as her name, said, "We could never forgive ourselves if something happened to someone because you were with us instead of being out there helping people in schools and in the community." Every now and then, they still call me. It's amazing how children can help you identify what's important in life.

In November 2001, District 15 and I wrote a grant to the Christian Children's Fund to sponsor cultural diversity education that would build cross-cultural understanding in schools and in the broader community. The funding finally came through in January 2002. I worked half of the time in schools and the other half in the community, organizing and facilitating workshops. At that time, immersing myself in this kind of work was very therapeutic; I needed to keep busy while Yousif was still away. I enjoyed meeting teachers and students across the district, and I truly felt like I was making a difference in the lives of others.

In search of healing our souls, we look to the things that give us comfort and happiness. Happiness can be defined in various ways, depending on the individual. In my search for healing, I realized that making others happy brought me the comfort I longed for after the tragic events of September 11th. As an individual who had never experienced such trauma in her life, I was able to cope and withstand depression to do the work I felt needed to be done. My purpose in becoming an educator was finally revealed to me. I was driven by my passion for social change.

Working under this grant gave me the opportunity to cross paths with other people who felt the same way. One of these people was Tom Roderick, the executive director of Educators for Social Responsibility Metro (ESR). His commitment was profound. In the months that we worked together, with Barbara Barnes, we implemented a diversity unit that was inclusive to all, with a specific emphasis on developing a better understanding of Arabs, South Asians, and Muslims.

Shortly after September 11th , ESR received a grant from JPMorganChase for bias training in schools. In January 2002, Tom and I met to talk about how to make all this work. ESR had the bias and conflict resolution training experience, and I had the multicultural background experience. By putting our heads together, we came up with a curriculum that integrated literature from the Arab, South Asian, and Muslim cultures into a diversity curriculum unit that was developed to reflect what ESR calls the "4 Rs"—reading, writing, respect, and resolution.

We located the schools that had the largest populations of Arabs, South Asians, and Muslims in District 15, and ended up with five elementary schools in different areas of Brooklyn, including P.S. 230. Our work in these schools was twofold. The first task was to develop cultural diversity appreciation among students, and the second was to engage parents and encourage them to become part of their school communities. Each school was scheduled to receive six classroom workshop sessions and two to four parent workshop sessions.

P.S. 230 was very receptive to the project. The principal, Howard Wholl, arranged teachers' schedules so they could observe lessons and debrief afterward. He involved the school leadership team, teacher specialists, and the PTA in making the program a success. As the work unfolded, there became a wide interest throughout the school. The teachers I worked with were very receptive, especially after seeing their students take an interest in learning about different cultures. News of this work traveled across the two school campuses. The school leadership and PTA wanted to learn more about the work, the teacher specialists wanted to support the work, and everyone in the school community wanted the work to become a schoolwide effort.

One day, the art teacher at P.S. 230, Kathleen Byrne, asked to meet with me to share an amazing idea that she had been thinking about for months but didn't know how to make it a reality: She wanted to create a mural that reflected the unique diversity of the school. As I listened to her, I realized that the mural would be an incredible culmination of all the work I was doing at the school. During our meeting, we discussed her convictions about the mural and the stumbling blocks she had already experienced as she tried to get this project off the ground.

Kathleen's convictions were driven by the loss of her brother on September 11th. On that day, she was working at P.S. 230. When she heard the news that both towers had been struck by planes, she immediately called her mother to ask about her brother, but her mother had not heard anything and was very upset. Kathleen realized she needed to be with her family. She immediately left the school and drove home to Long Island.

When Kathleen walked through the door of her house, there in front of her hanging on the wall was a print of Norman Rockwell's painting *The Golden Rule*, which shows people of all ages, races, and religions gathered peacefully together. She gazed at it as if it were the very first time she had seen it.

Minutes later, she received the news about her brother. Words couldn't express how she felt about the loss. Days and weeks passed, and there was so much anger and confusion bottled up inside her that needed to be released. During those days, however, it helped her to come to terms with her anger every time she looked into the eyes of her Arab, Muslim, and South Asian students. She came to the conclusion that there are good and bad people in every faith and culture. She knew that all her students and their families were good, loving people who wanted a better life.

After hearing Kathleen's story and ideas about the mural, I felt compelled to do everything in my power to make the project come to life. Thanks to my contacts in the district office, I was able to find out what the process was to get approval for painting on the exterior wall of a building. I also went directly to Carmen Farina, the District 15 superintendent. I shared with her the work I had done in the school, and told her we wanted to bring students, parents, and staff together to create a mural that would be a culmination of the cultural diversity work. Within 4 days, we got the approval from the Board of Education Engineer Office.

As I thought more and more about the mural project, I came up with other ideas to celebrate it. In my travels across the city, I had met a documentary filmmaker at the New York Historical Society who introduced herself and mentioned that if I ever had any ideas

Members of the P.S. 230 community work on the mural

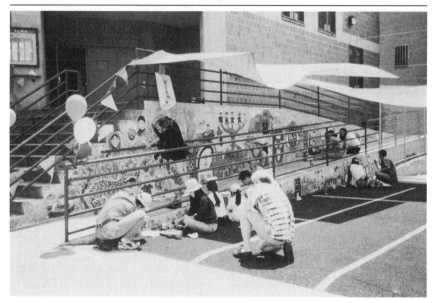

for creating a documentary on 9/11 issues, I should give her a call.
I didn't think we'd ever connect again after that, but I was moved
by her conviction to help others tell their unheard stories. I gave
her a call to tell her about the project, and she was very interested.
I mentioned to her that I had no funding, but that I wasn't going to
let that hold me back from pursuing the idea. I called the school to
share the idea and set up a meeting with her. Everyone was excited
that we were going to have the mural-making documented.

The hard part was finding the money, but I was determined to
make the documentary happen even if I had to pay for it myself. I
needed to capture this moment in history for all who were involved.
I started asking around for foundations that give emergency grants,
but their grants were no more than $500.

The mural-making was only 4 days away, and I kept at it. Then,
in conversation with Tom Roderick, I mentioned that I was on a
mission to raise money for the documentary. He let me vent to him
about my anguish and anxiety. When I finally stopped, he asked me
to tell him more about the project. When I finished, he said to me,

"Debbie, this sounds like a wonderful project that needs to happen, and we can help you with it." I was in a state of shock. That evening, I e-mailed him the cost proposal that the filmmaker, Shawn, had sent me. The following day Tom, Shawn, and I had a conference call, and later that evening, a contract was drawn and signed by all. Two days later, we began to film.

Throughout the process of the mural-making, Shawn was there to capture all the timeless images and the words uttered by every participant, young and old. Everyone spoke from the heart, regardless of how much English they knew or how thick their accent was. They were proud to be a part of something so special and unique that had given them the opportunity to contribute personal things about their culture and heritage.

Ming, who is an immigrant from China, said, "I basically worked on the Chinese dragon, which is symbolically known for goodwill, harmony, energy, and good luck to everyone around the year. The mural represents different people from all of the world. P.S. 230 is all about that, and it's what the U.S. is all about." Ming continued:

> My job has been jeopardized after the tragedy of 9/11. My
> company was struggling for five months, and finally, the com-
> pany had a public auction and they closed the company down.
> I am in the process of locating a new job. That is why I have
> spare time during the week and weekend to basically patch
> up the parts some parents and children couldn't finish. I com-
> pleted them and basically I felt I had to bring the whole picture
> together.

This project gave Ming the opportunity to reflect on life and appreciate what he has to offer. This was his way of dealing with his loss and disappointment about his job. You could see in his face that it was therapeutic and healing for him to be out there painting. He and his family showed up whenever Kathleen was there. He thanked all of us for creating this opportunity for him to contribute his talents.

Aida, a Brooklyn native whose family comes from Puerto Rico, also recounted her experience in her interview for the documentary.

Ms. Byrne welcomed children and parents to color, to sketch things. It was a great time to forget about everything else, to take some time to think about all the things in life I love and that mean things to me and my family, and try to be creative. My daughter worked on "Welcome to Our School." My daughter said, "We have to do a painting." So we decided to think about what was important to us, all the great literature and storybooks we loved to read and learn about. My son drew animals and things that he loved, like lizards. It was fun to help him and encourage him to put his mark on the wall.

Addie, a second grader, was painting a picture of the world on the wall. When asked what it meant to her, she replied, "It's a picture about people around the world, so everybody can make peace." We also asked her, "How did you feel when you were painting the world?" Her response was, "It made me feel like I was making the world feel better." My eyes swelled with tears when I heard her say that. I felt like we had given this little girl the world to make her own. I was filled with joy to know that I had helped give others the joy and comfort that art brings.

Katlin, a fourth grader, was asked, "What does the mural mean to you?" She replied, "It's telling each of us about our nationalities and what each of our customs are. I'm glad that we did this. Now I know more about my friends and their families."

Wahida, a parent from Pakistan who was also Muslim, described the picture she painted and its message. "I paint a view like eyes. In the eyes, I expressed like the world, women are water," she said. "Women are the most important in the world, like if we not exist, you understand the world can't exist. The world would be like zero population. Women are the most valuable person in the world." Wahida also shared with us that she had never painted before in her life, but that she wanted to take part in the mural-making because she wanted everyone to know that women of her culture and religion have a significant role in the world.

Gloria, a parent from Peru, shared her reasons for participating and how much she appreciated the experience. "I enjoyed participating in the mural because I wanted to participate in the school for my son. I think it's a good example for him," she said. "It was very interesting to interact with people from different countries. It was

Three close-up images from the mural, representing the wonderful diversity of the school community

very interesting to learn about other cultures." She also discussed her contribution to the mural. "I chose the woman, because it represent how proud I am, proud to be a woman because we play an important role in this world."

It was amazing to hear the parallels between Wahida and Gloria's stories. Two women from two different parts of the world shared the same ideas. Gloria continued, "I learned about a specific culture. I interacted more with a Chinese lady. They are like us! She's like me! She's very fun! She is the center in her family like me, and they try to raise their kids as successful people, too."

Shanaz, a parent from Bangladesh, was very candid in her interview. "When I first started the project, I'm scared maybe I can do or not," she said.

> But when I started, you saw my picture. I am proud of this picture that I did very well. I did a lot of peoples from different countries, and I tried to explain that after September 11th incident, that we are all here, that we all live here and we are all a part of this community. I tried to make the Muslims, the African-Americans, Chinese, Europeans, and others. I tried to show all these cultures and we live happily in our community.

Her message to her school community and neighborhood was interpreted as she had planned. Aida spoke of Shanaz's contributions by saying:

> I met a Bangladeshi woman who drew a lot of paintings of New York and American life. She painted the Christmas tree. It just showed me that I think that she really loves American things, even though she dresses very traditional and she has a traditional family. I only know her from walking to school, but when I started to see her paint, she painted a city scene, a tree, and I thought, "Wow, she really loves it here," and it made me feel good, too.

In the midst of all her work facilitating and directing the mural project, we finally got Kathleen to give us a few minutes of her time for an interview. She spoke first about her experience on September 11th.

I just remember leaving the school that day and learning that my brother was in the building in the Twin Towers, and I just felt that day I was in such a frantic loss and mess and moral feeling of loss, a great deep sense of loss. I figured if I could feel that way toward everyone that deeply and that intimately on a sad level, I could work to try and flip it over to a happy, more positive experience for me.

Talking about the mural-making, she went on,

It's been a kind of cathartic experience, and I kind of have been able to think through some of my emotions and [try] to grieve for the loss of my brother but also learn more about the world through these people, through all different people. Everyone has had the same experience because everyone was affected that day, and everyone has been coming to work on the project, and everyone wants to know about my brother. They want me to tell them about my feelings of belonging to them. I think this project really needed to be done for that purpose alone, for that connection, to be able to share my complete feelings.

The PTA president, who was instrumental in getting parents to come to some of our workshops, was very proud of being a part of the school and the mural project. "I think this mural can be a role model for other schools. I don't think any one school is as culturally diverse as we are, to be able to share it without any animosity or any problems whatsoever. It just became a joyous experience all the way."

My own family, like many others, has still not recovered completely from the trauma of the September 11th attacks and their aftermath. My son Yousif, working at Ground Zero, experienced something that only grown men in the army usually experience, while he was only 19. Even 3 years later, he still couldn't talk about his experiences. Many months had passed, and his struggle for a normal life was haunted by nightmares and hair loss, which the doctors said was due to mental stress and anxiety. The evil-doing of others has stripped my child's innocence on many levels. My prayer for him as a mother is, "God, please replace the sights and sounds of destruction and uncertainty with visions of peace and harmony."

As my family and I continue to rebuild our lives, it is a comfort to me to know that I have the privilege of doing work that can bring those visions of peace and harmony to others who have suffered. I like to think back on those days of mural-making at P.S. 230 as an example of what can happen when we carve out the time and space for healing: How often do we give our students and their families the opportunity and time to share what is important to them, to engage in activities that help them forget about everything else, and to think about all the things in life they love?

Eleven

The Youngest Witnesses

LOYAN BEAUSOLEIL

I T WAS A BEAUTIFUL Tuesday in September. Edna, my friend and coteacher, and I had been working for a week, making sure the classroom was just right for this first day of school and the 4- and 5-year-old children we teach. We arrived early to the Silver Towers, just south of Washington Square where our downtown Manhattan preschool is located, to make Play-Doh and spend a little time talking and drinking coffee before the children arrived. On the morning of September 11, 2001, before school began, we sat quietly together in our classroom, which was bright, clean, and uncluttered, just like the clear blue sky outside.

School normally begins at 9:00 A.M., but on this first day of school we opened our doors early, at 8:30. Adina and her father came into the classroom as soon as the door was opened, and Michelle and her parents were playing outside in the Silver Towers plaza. Adina excitedly rushed straight toward the warm yellow Play-Doh. After welcoming Adina, I sat with her father, Aaron, and Edna, pleasantly talking about how beautiful the room was with its new coat of blue paint, how excited Adina was to be at school, and what a beautiful day it was.

Suddenly there was a roar and a rumble and the building shook. "What was that?" Edna asked. "It must have been one of those trucks that carry Dumpsters," I said. We have giant Dumpsters in New York City, big enough to park two cars in. They are used on

141

construction sites and for building renovations. When the Dumpsters are being driven around to their building sites—usually in the wee hours of the morning—they make a terrible racket, and the streets shake as they pass, just like a little earthquake.

Only it didn't make sense that one of those Dumpster trucks would be going by at that time of day, but I couldn't think of any other explanation for such a big sound and the shaking of the building. One moment later, a parent burst into the room. "Do you know what just happened?" she asked, her voice trembling. "A plane just hit the World Trade Center." The roar we had heard was the first plane, flying close and low, directly over the 30-story Silver Towers, just seconds before it slammed into the North Tower of the WTC.

We all stood up, Aaron grabbed Adina by the hand, and we rushed out to the plaza where we could clearly see the flaming hole in the building just 14 blocks south and the flying paper and debris, like confetti. Adina was clinging to her father as Michelle and her family came over to us. "What a terrible accident," I said naively. Someone nearby, a stranger, said, "It could've been an act of terrorism." No, I thought, as innocently as the little children I teach—just a terrible accident.

I went back into the classroom to make a phone call to my boyfriend, a photojournalist. It was the last call I was able to make for many hours. When I went back outside, Edna, strong and fearless, was crying. I looked up and, shocked, saw the burning hole in the South Tower. "What happened?" I asked her. "Another plane," she said through her tears. "We just watched another plane hit." Now we talked about terrorism openly in front of the two little girls. My innocent belief in careless pilots melted away as the buildings burned.

Aaron said that he thought he should take Adina home and try to find his wife. He strapped Adina into her stroller and ran off, pushing her downtown toward their apartment and straight toward the burning buildings, just five blocks away from their home. As I watched them go, I thought, Adina is going to look at that big fire all the way home.

Michelle, now the only child at school, was holding tight to her stuffed bunny and talking a lot about the fire and asking a lot of questions—questions that none of us adults knew how to answer. Suddenly she said she wanted to go inside the classroom, that she wanted to start school. It was after 9:00 so we all went inside. I still thought children would be arriving for school. Soon some other families arrived; the parents said that they and their children had watched everything on their way to school, and that they would not be leaving their children at school on this day. Hearing this, Michelle's parents decided she should go home, too. We all went outside together and stood mesmerized by the sight of the giant buildings on fire. Almost an hour had passed since the first plane hit, an hour that felt like an eternity. Time slowed down even more as first the South Tower collapsed and then the North, as if in slow motion, right before our eyes. The Silver Towers plaza was full of people. They screamed and cried and cursed as they watched the buildings fall. All around, people were wailing, but I stayed silent. I couldn't find my voice. Michelle's dad Joe said they were going to get their bikes and ride uptown to Michelle's grandmother's house where they thought they would be safer. Michelle sat silently in her stroller, facing the mushroom clouds of smoke and debris rising into the air, and hugged her stuffed bunny close, sometimes burying her face in the worn body of her beloved toy.

A child of about 8, upset and crying uncontrollably, was quickly ushered past me and into the Silver Towers where she lived. I looked down at Michelle sitting silently beside me, holding her bunny so tightly as if she were strangling it. The image of Adina in her stroller, with her father running downtown toward what was now obviously a very unsafe place to be, popped into my head. I wondered where they were—did they make it home, had they found Adina's mother, were they safe, were they alive? Seeing these other children and thinking about Adina, I suddenly remembered my own 8-year-old daughter. I hadn't thought of her once as the tragedy unfolded, but suddenly she was all I could think of. I didn't know what was going on in the world or even in New York City, and I needed to reach her. I told Edna that I had to find Ezair, my daughter, and that I would come back to work as soon as I got her. I jumped on my scooter and rode east toward her school on the Lower East Side.

Broadway was where I first saw the zombies: the gray people covered in Twin Towers debris and smoke and fear, some crying, some walking, a few trying to talk. Not a single one smiling. I couldn't breathe. My lungs would not accept the air, as if the gray dust was trying to permeate them just like it had the skin of the zombies. When I got to Lafayette Street, it was even worse. There were thousands more gray people making the exodus north, and they would not let me pass. There were too many, too close together, and they weren't stopping for anything. I had to struggle my way through the zombie mass, trying to go east as they moved north. Tears streamed down my face, and I couldn't tell if I was breathing as I fought not to be swept away in the river of fleeing humans.

I finally got to my daughter's school, but she wasn't there. I panicked. The school office was a madhouse. Fortunately, another parent remembered seeing my daughter leave the school with her best friend and his father. A well-meaning friend of mine, he had taken her to his home and then let her watch the ongoing media coverage of the event. When I got there, Ezair didn't hug me or say hello. She didn't dawdle or beg me to let her stay at her friend's house. She quietly and complacently got her jacket and backpack, calmly said good-bye, and walked out of the door ahead of me. The moment we were outside on the street she started to scream and cried that she wanted to go home. She wanted to check on our cats. She asked me if our apartment building was still standing. Our home was on the way back to work, and I took her up to our apartment for a moment so that she could see that our place and cats were okay.

We had always had a view of the World Trade Center from our apartment. As Ezair looked out toward the empty hole in the skyline and the billowing smoke, she commented, "They're gone, they're just gone." She said this many times as if it were a chant, her mantra. She asked me many questions in the 10 minutes we were at our house: "Will our building fall down?" "Are we in a war?" "What happens to children in a war?" For the first time since becoming a mother, I didn't have the slightest idea how to answer her. I lied, as much to myself as to her, as I said everything was fine. I could tell by looking at Ezair that my face was saying something different than my words.

As we walked back to my school, we passed a television that someone had brought outside and set up on the hood of a car. A crowd had gathered, watching the footage on the TV screen with their backs turned to the cloud of smoke farther downtown. This is what people in our Lower East Side neighborhood do—they go outside to socialize, to sit and talk on the stoops, play dominoes, or listen to a boom box playing Spanish music. I wanted to stop and watch, too. It felt safe, like neighborhood and people and community, and I had only seen one brief moment of the coverage at my friend's apartment. My daughter said she wanted to keep moving, that she didn't want to see any more TV, that it was too scary. When I had picked up Ezair from my friend's place, I regretted that she had watched the event on television, but here I was mindlessly exposing her to the same dramatic images she had already seen numerous times.

Back at school the radio was on. I don't remember what it was saying, but it was on continuously. The staff sat around a table in my classroom as Ezair built a tall tower out of blocks. We talked about what was going on, how we felt, when we should reschedule the start of school, and how we would talk to the children. I felt numb. I wanted to start school right away, that minute, and I definitely didn't know what I would say to the little children who would be in my class.

My boyfriend Gabe, the photojournalist I had called after the first plane hit, burst into the classroom in the early afternoon. He was white and gray from the dust of the towers. He was freaked out and pumped up. He had made it to Ground Zero, and the other teachers crowded around and bombarded him with questions about what was going on down there. He paced back and forth on the new meeting area rug and finally sat down in the reading area. All the while, as he answered questions, I could only see the dust that covered his shoes and clothes, his skin and hair. His dark hair turned gray by the dust made him look like an old man. The dust was polluting my classroom, my new rug. By the time the children arrived to school, though, no one would even know that it was dangerously embedded in the rug, only me. I knew that that dust couldn't be safe or healthy for anyone, especially little children. It was now in my classroom, in the rug, on the beanbag chair, in the air. I couldn't ask him to leave, though. He had so much information to share, so many close calls, so many images to describe. It was a trade-off I made: information for the health and safety of my children.

The days between Tuesday, September 11, and Friday, September 14, the day the children returned to school, seemed endless. The skies were silent and empty, devoid of the usual airplane traffic except for military planes, which were too loud, and their sound came after they had passed, so you didn't really know where they were, like loud, mysterious ghosts in the sky; and helicopters, which buzzed dangerously close, spying on us all, shining bright searchlights into apartment windows at night. The streets in my neighborhood were without taxis, cars, trucks, or buses. People could walk anywhere without regard to the traffic signals. Children played in the streets. There were no newspaper deliveries. Big-name places like Duane Reade and McDonald's were closed, but the mom-and-pop stores—the bodegas, neighborhood restaurants, and 24-hour Korean delis—stayed open even as the shelves grew empty. Even the local Middle Eastern food place, the falafel restaurant, stayed open, but they put an American flag up in the window right away as if to say, "We didn't do it." There were police and military blockades all along the major cross streets downtown. Police and soldiers were checking the ID of every person trying to go below 14th Street. If I went uptown, above 14th Street, I needed to carry my passport and my electric bill to get back home, because the police and soldiers wouldn't let people pass the checkpoints unless they could prove they lived or worked Downtown.

I wanted so badly to get back to school, back to work, back to the children, and to start thinking about something else. I had seen how my daughter and her friends could push the horribleness of what had just happened somewhere else as they entered the fantasy world of play. This was something that I and the other adults around me could not do. I thought once school began that time would start moving again, and the second and minute hands that seemed frozen would suddenly move as the children entered the classroom.

Friday finally arrived, the first day that I would really have a class of children. I had spoken with many parents on the phone and knew that a number of the children in my class had left the city with their families. They were in Upstate New York with grandparents or friends, or at country houses. One family just rented a van and left with nowhere to go; they were at some motel. Some families left out of fear and concern for their safety; others had been evacuated from their homes. The families that left town had no intention of being back for the first day of school. The class was going to be small.

Edna and I had talked about what we should do on this first day. Do we talk to the children about the Twin Towers? Do we ask them how they feel? Do we ask them what they saw? Maybe we shouldn't say anything, and just wait and see what happens. That's what we did. That was easiest, the path of least resistance, although the collapsed towers were still burning at full force, so there was no way to ignore the disaster. The putrid stench of burning plastic and chemicals and death filled the air outside. Like an electrical fire with something else mixed in, something organic. We knew we couldn't take the kids outside to play.

As the children trickled in, Edna and I watched as they greeted each other and began to play. Parents are welcome in our classroom, and all of them lingered far longer than usual, as if held prisoner by the air in the room, thick with emotion. The parents displayed gaunt, sleepless, uneasy faces that we all wore for the month following the attacks. They came into the classroom wanting to talk about health and safety, war and terror. They wanted to talk to each other and to Edna and me. But we had decided to focus on the children. We gave out our home phone numbers and told parents that we were available to talk after school, or they could call us in the evening or on the weekend, and the parents said, okay, they would. But it didn't work like that. The Twin Towers worked its way into every word uttered between grown-ups that morning. There was nothing else to talk about. As if jobs and weather ceased to exist. The only things to discuss were crashing airplanes, falling buildings, and the uncertain state of the world. Try as we might, we could not keep those adult conversations out of our classroom that first morning. But the kids seemed oblivious. They were busy playing. Dramatic play was a bustle of activity. Kids had set up a house, and a boy and girl, who had been in the same class the year before, announced that they were getting married. Some children were drawing; others were building with blocks, making nice low buildings, the kind that spread out over the floor—the kind too low for airplanes to crash into.

It was time for morning meeting, and some parents began to leave. Separation anxiety, for the kids, was surprisingly at an all-time low. They were ready to start, ready to be in school, and ready to do something else besides listen to grown-ups on TV and the radio and all around them talk about the Twin Towers. They kissed and waved good-bye to their moms and dads. It wasn't that easy for the parents, though. They lingered with long hugs, clinging to their children, afraid to let them go. Many parents waited in the chairs outside the classroom for the entire school day, unable to leave their little children. I knew just what they were going through. I hadn't felt ready to leave my daughter earlier that morning. The 11 blocks between her school and mine seemed too far apart, and it seemed like I would never get to her in time, if I had to, if it happened again.

School went well that Friday, and the children were excited to be there. There were even brief moments in the day when I didn't think about the World Trade Center, when I thought about block-building or painting or finding the missing piece to a puzzle. At the end of the day Edna and I talked about how wonderful it had been to be with the kids. What a relief to be back at work.

Our class was incomplete, with nearly half the children missing, but we had done it. We had gotten through the day, and that gave us hope. Best of all, the disaster hadn't come up in the classroom. The children didn't talk about it—they were just pre-K and kinder-garten kids, playing and exploring, and they didn't have to think about that terrible day. It was just what Edna and I wanted for our classroom.

Monday came and I was ready. Before we opened the doors, Edna and I talked about what a hard weekend it had been. For me, living Downtown seemed toxic, and Edna could only think about her adult son, who had only a few months left to serve in the Marines. Neither of us could wait to open the door for the arrival of the children, the only people we knew who didn't talk about the disaster all of the time.

We opened the doors early. Many of the children were already waiting outside, and they happily spilled into the classroom. They got busy right away, cheerfully playing with each other. A few parents pulled me aside to tell me how difficult the weekend had been for their children. Sonia's father explained that the fire station right next door to their home, one of the first to respond on September 11, had lost 11 men at the World Trade Center site, men Sonia had known since she was a baby. I listened to the parents and tried to be reassuring. I told them that the children would be fine in school and that they seemed happy to be there. Then we started morning meeting.

We started with a song, using each child's name. There were more kids at school this Monday—families had come back to the city over the weekend—and so the song was longer than it had been on Friday. This was good, more time singing. That's what I thought those children needed—or was I the one that needed that? I had chosen a book, *We Go to Nursery School* by Marjorie Poppleton, to read to the children during morning meeting. I read about children saying good-bye to parents, and eating a snack. Then I read the page, "We build with blocks." Four-year-old Matthew blurted out, "Workers are trying to build the World Trade Center!" Suddenly all of the children were talking at once. They were talking about the World Trade Center, and the jumble of words flying around the room reminded me of the jumble of steel and rubble that could be seen by walking just a few blocks south. Why were they talking about this now? How had one sentence about nursery school triggered it? These kids were so young, why couldn't they just play and sing and listen to the story, like they'd done on Friday? That's what I wanted, playing and singing, a reprieve from the heaviness. I had hoped that the classroom and the little children could provide that solace.

Something clicked in me. It occurred to me that what these little children had to say about the disaster, what they understood and what they saw, was very important. I wanted to be there for them and listen to what they were talking about in order to help each child cope individually. I realized I had to try to write down everything these kids were saying. I asked the children to quiet down, as I leaped up and ran across the room to get a pen and pad of paper. I told them that they would all get a turn to say whatever they wanted. I told them to raise their hands and that they could call on each other until everyone had had a chance to speak. Hands shot up and Matthew, only 4, understood that he should call on someone. He called on Allen, who said, "Yeah, a lot of good workers are building the World Trade Center." Allen called on Matthew's twin brother Lucas, who said, with scorn in his voice, "They will never build the World Trade Center again." Lou said, "They're using a lot of dump trucks." Michelle added, "There was a big fire." Camille filled in some details as she described what she had seen: "There was a big fire when the plane hit the building." Camille went back to Matthew, who added, "The bad guys hit the plane in the building." All the while I wrote furiously, trying to capture every word on the yellow legal pad I held on my lap. Adina, the child I had watched heading toward the flames, who had been evacuated from her home just blocks from Ground Zero, said, "There was a lot of fire, and it was close to my house." Edna and I kept glancing from the children to each other. I wanted to look at everybody's faces as they spoke, but I was afraid to look away from my paper for too long. I just had to write this all down. Lou said, "There are a lot of firemen working to make the building better." Allen added, "A lot of police and a lot of firemen [are] putting out the fire." Allen called on Ann, who had just slowly raised her hand for the first time.

"It's so sad that all those people died," she said.

Silence. Nobody said a word. I looked up from my paper; there was nothing else to write. Silence. Edna was looking at the children. I looked at the children. Their faces showed fear, concern, and confusion. It suddenly occurred to me that they didn't know. Most of the children didn't realize that people had died when the planes crashed and the towers fell. The next day I brought my tape recorder to school. When the children began talking about the disaster again I wanted to be prepared to capture their words and their voices.

Young children use play as a way to understand the world around them. They use creative materials, such as clay, paint, and blocks, to explore and to express their ideas and feelings. From what I could see, these children needed to play more than anything else. Throughout the school year I saw children experiencing play in many forms—outdoor play; play with dollhouses, puppets, and make-believe—to work through what they had experienced on September 11th. Each child played out his or her concerns, curiosities, and fears in different ways and used different materials, as each became more comfortable and confident that school was a safe place to explore these difficult emotions. Some children used play to work through these issues immediately, whereas others only began to explore what they had seen on September 11th later in the school year. The children that worried me the most were the few who didn't seem to be able to play at all.

As a teacher my role was to create an environment where the children felt safe and protected and where play was a priority. The children were given big chunks of time and encouraged to play out whatever they wanted as long as they were not harming others. We created a classroom community where open conversation was valued and where every child knew they could talk about anything. For the children who needed extra help coping, there was always an adult available to them, and there were quiet places designated in the classroom where children could go with an adult if play or conversations became too scary, or if they just wanted to be alone.

I didn't decide to document everything the children did or said that related to terrorism, bad guys, or the Twin Towers. It just happened. I just felt compelled. I understood that it would help me to work with the children, and to talk to the parents about what was going on in the classroom and with their children. For me personally, it became like therapy. I thought that, even though I couldn't change what was going on in the world, I could create a place for the children and myself to feel safe enough to share what we had experienced, what we knew, and what we feared.

I thought about how I had wanted the classroom to be my bubble, removed and protected from the dangerous world right outside. The world we could see and smell burning, just down the street. There were soldiers right across the street, too, keeping people away from Downtown. We could see them from our classroom window. The kids walked past them every day as their parents showed IDs and utility bills to them, proving that they lived nearby. What had I been thinking? That the kids wouldn't talk about this? The destruction of the World Trade Center would come up many, many times that school year. And I was ready with my tape recorder in hand.

Children would talk about the World Trade Center at any moment of the day. During the first part of October, two children, Dakota and Ann, were sitting at a table in the classroom playing with small blocks. Dakota's block tower had grown quite tall, and as she stacked one block on top of the next, she said to Ann, "I think a lot of planes are gonna crash down, are gonna crash into buildings so it could crack down." Ann didn't reply, she just continued playing. Dakota spoke up again, saying, "I just heard on the news that the buildings are cracking down." Ann looked up from her stack of blocks and said reassuringly to Dakota, "It could be that the build-ings are down forever, but it probably will be better."

Throughout the school year, many children talked about and played "Twin Towers." Some played out the disaster with graphic intensity, while others optimistically played out scenes of rescue and rebuilding. Still other children became silent and fearful when children or adults mentioned anything about the destruction of the World Trade Center.

Sonia, the child who lives next to the fire station, underwent a drastic change after 9/11. The year before she had been outgoing and boisterous, but in the year following the attacks she became quiet, reserved, and fearful. Her parents and I remained in close contact concerning the fears she developed both at home and at school. Sonia also began to regress. She even started sucking her thumb, a behavior her parents hadn't seen since she was a baby. One day in November Sonia came into school very upset and afraid to let her father leave. I took Sonia and held her in my lap. She told me, "I'm scared. I had a bad dream last night." When I asked her what she dreamed, she said, "I dreamed I was here at school, and a plane hit this building and nobody got out." At times like this Sonia was always offered a comforting lap, an adult to talk to, and a quiet place or privacy, which she sometimes wanted.

Other children explored their knowledge and confusion about the disaster through artwork, and paint, watercolors, clay, and markers were available to the children at all times throughout the day. On one occasion, Allen was vigorously painting at the easel. He had mixed red and yellow and was moving his entire body as he painted, quietly saying, "Fire, fire, fire." When he slowed down and had covered the entire paper with orange paint, I came up to him and said, "I see you've used a lot of orange." Allen turned to me and said, "A bomb shooted that fire in the building. A guy throwed a bomb." I asked him, "What was the building like?" "It was like, like"—he hesitated—"like our Twin Towers." At times like this I just listened as the children described their paintings, which some-times were so wrought with emotion.

The largest section of the classroom is devoted to the block area. It became apparent what an important part of the classroom the block area would become for some children who had witnessed the destruction of the towers. Both girls and boys built the Twin Towers out of blocks, and at times there would be numerous sets of block Twin Towers of differing heights filling the floor. Some children, like Adina, didn't want to see so many block towers standing. She walked into the block area one day, and seeing three tall, identical, rectangular block towers, she said, as she pointed to one of the buildings, "You know, it would be okay if a plane knocked down this one because there were only two towers of the Twin Towers."

On this day the block area was crowded with sets of Twin Towers.

Photo by Gabe Kirchheimer

It was important that the plane was available to the children who
needed to play with it.

Photo by Gabe Kirchheimer

   Other children built the Twin Towers out of blocks day after day,
like Matthew, who built the towers out of blocks every day for over
4 months. Some days he would readily knock down his block towers, and at other times he refused to take his block structure down,
even at cleanup time, on one occasion stating, "I don't want to clean
Twin Towers! Crash down! Twin Towers crashed down! *My Twin
Towers is standing!*" Matthew, like many of the children, would talk

quietly to himself as he was building. One day, as he built the World Trade Center out of blocks, Matthew said to himself, "This is the giant plane, the plane crashed down into the Twin Towers. The plane have bomb inside it and robbers." He then looked over at Allen's building and yelled, "Watch out because the Twin Towers are so leaning! It's gonna fall down!" He went back to his quiet murmurings to himself, saying, "This airplane is so fast it must crash into the Twin Towers."

Through block play the children were able to explore their questions, recollections, fear, and anger about the tragic events.

Photo by Gabe Kirchheimer

Another time, Leo began flying a toy airplane around the block area. Allen had built a little house of blocks and was playing that little people lived inside. Leo suddenly rushed over and crashed the toy plane directly into the roof of Allen's building. "Stop it, Leo!" said Allen. He then carefully repaired his building and went back to playing. Leo held the plane high above his head, making the sounds of an engine. Suddenly he again flew the plane into the roof of Allen's building. Allen was upset, and as he yelled for Leo to stop, Leo told Allen, "The plane can't stop," and continued flying the plane around the block area. As Allen was again repairing his building, Leo crashed the toy plane into it for a third time. "Stop it!" Allen yelled, on the verge of tears. "The plane can't stop. It's aiming at the building!" Leo yelled back. "I don't want the plane to knock down my building!" Allen pleaded. "But the plane wants to, because it's aiming at the building," insisted Leo.

Many in the class used block play as a way to work through their fears, concerns, and curiosities about September 11. The children constructed such large and tall buildings that year that we had to purchase more blocks to satisfy their need to build.

Even though it was a beautiful fall, we waited many weeks to take the children outdoors to play in our school's little playground. The air quality was still very poor for 3 months following September 11th. The air remained smoky and hazy, and on some days the smell was terrible. We also worried about the sand in our sandbox, wondering if it was safe for the children to play in, if it was somehow polluted with dust and ash from the World Trade Center; the sand was eventually removed and replaced.

We finally took the kids outside in October, despite our concerns about air quality. Using the playground equipment, some children immediately began to act out scenes of people being trapped in a building and being rescued, or dying and being brought to the sandbox. Other children were afraid outdoors, especially when they heard a siren or saw an airplane fly overhead. For these children, we tried to be available to hold their hand, stand by them, talk to them, listen to them, or just let them sit on our laps. There were even days when children became so afraid that we would have an adult take them inside.

*   *   *

During the 2001–02 school year, I set different goals for my classroom than I had ever set before. I wanted to create the most open environment possible where we all felt safe, as a community, to express and discuss what we knew about September 11th. I wanted to provide materials and opportunities to help the children work through their fears through play and exploration. I also wanted to provide ample space and privacy to children who needed more time, and I strove to communicate with parents about the growth their children were making during this difficult year. I wanted to be as nurturing as I possibly could be to the children, the parents, Edna, and myself. That comes easy for Edna, but I'm the let's-get-down-to-the-business-of-school kind of teacher. It just seemed like trying to get these 4- and 5-year-olds to write their names using upper- and lower-case letters was less important than it had been in past years, and the kids did it anyway, even though it wasn't one of my biggest goals for them.

For myself, I also wanted to feel safe and reassured. I was able to find this, to some extent, through recording and writing about the children and the ways in which they talked, worked, and played together; and through the ways they needed me for reassurance and I needed them to help normalize the world around me. We worked together to build a community that supported us all, as best we could, as we tried to heal from what we saw and experienced on September 11th. For the children, the process of talking and playing helped many to find positive visions for the future.

I remember near the end of the school year walking indoors from the playground one morning. Leo, who witnessed the first plane hit the North Tower from a very close distance and remained terribly frightened for most of the school year, said to me, as he noticed a plane fly overhead, "Loyan, do you know what they're going to build at the Twin Towers?" "What?" I asked. He continued, "They're going to build a little garden and a really nice park. It's going to be a little park and there's going to be a little tent shaped like the Twin Towers. There's going to be two little tents shaped like the Twin Towers, and they will be little, and kids will get to go inside of them and play inside." I thought that he knew something I didn't, so I asked, "Did you hear that they're going to build something like that?" He smiled as he looked up at me, and answered, "Well, that's what I want them to build."

Twelve

Voices from the Crossroads

ETHAN LOWENSTEIN

FROM MY CHILDHOOD HOME in Lower Manhattan my mom heard the planes overhead half a minute before they slammed into the Twin Towers. I was in the middle of a research meeting hundreds of miles away in Michigan. I will never forget sprinting up the stairs of the building in a daze, fumbling with the keys to my office so I could get to a phone to call my family. I remember wondering and worrying about everyone I knew in New York that day, including a group of middle school teachers I had been working with as part of my doctoral dissertation.

One of those teachers, Fiona, was too close to the towers to hear the planes before they hit. Fiona wasn't on the phone in her apartment like my mom or watching a TV like most of the country. She was in front of a new group of seventh-grade social studies students in a school with windows facing the towers, which were only a few blocks to the south. Two months after the attack, Fiona recounted:

> Luckily all of the students' parents are alive. One seventh
> grader's mom was terribly burned, and is still in the burn unit.
> But amazingly they're still alive. And they were just coming
> in all day to the school we had been evacuated to. They would
> come in to where we'd walked, and we'd all cry. We're like
> "oh my God." The parents were covered in dust and the kids
> were in a horror, just terrified. A student's parents would show

up covered in gook and smoke, and we'd all cry. They'd go off, and then we'd be waiting for the next one. This continual round of "oh my God." After what they've been through I'm amazed to see my students actually recovering.

Fatima, the only Muslim teacher in her school, in a flash confronted one of her biggest nightmares:

I was in my room doing a lesson and a teacher came over and said, "You know you got two planes in the Trade Center." Honestly my first reaction was, "Oh my God, can it be true?" And then the second was, "Oh, please don't let it be an Arab, please don't let it be a Muslim." Learning from past experience, it's easy to blame Arabs and Muslims in this country as far as terrorism is concerned. With Timothy McVeigh, before you even had all the facts everybody was pointing fingers. It hit close to home.

In Fatima's school community, everyone was pointing at *her*—looking for her to simultaneously play the roles of diplomat, expert, and target.

I am from Pakistan, but they don't realize that I've grown up here and that I consider this to be my home. Two days ago, someone said to me, "So what's going on in your country?" And I got a little angry, and I said, "Well, we're mourning the death of all the people we lost in the World Trade Center." And they just looked at me funny because that's not the answer they were expecting. I am an American citizen. And right now the best way to show citizenship is to support the government and what they're doing.

Ruth is a veteran special education teacher on the Upper East Side of Manhattan with more than 30 years of experience. She describes her reactions on September 11th:

I was in my room getting ready to go and do my job in everybody else's room. And someone just opened the door and said that the World Trade Center had been hit by a plane. And that was hard enough for me to believe—we didn't think that it was terrorism at first. And then I was downstairs and saw [on TV] the building collapse. Then I heard the second one had gone and that the Pentagon had been attacked, and well, at that point I evaluated my whole life and got ready to face my maker.

Ruth didn't know whether her son was near the towers when the planes hit, and remembers trying to keep it together enough to take care of her students.

It took me 3½ hours to get a hold of my son. And I simply wanted just to hear his voice and tell him I loved him because I really did think, "this is it." When my son called me, he said "I love you"—he doesn't do that, and I knew he thought he was dying that day. And he said that when he saw the second plane come, he thought there was going to be a nuclear flash.

I spent 6½ hours of running back and forth because parents were coming in the building. We were locating the kids, matching them with the parents. Making sure we were handing children over to someone that actually was in their family.

Like Fiona, Fatima, and Ruth, 9/11 reoriented my professional life, though certainly less traumatically. No longer a "doctoral student," in many ways I had become an ideal witness to teachers' experiences in New York City during the year of 9/11. Having recently been a New York City high school teacher in a "last chance" school in East Harlem, I knew the ropes. My dissertation happened to be on how teachers teach, learn, and think about democratic citizenship. All of the teachers I had studied were in the New York City area. I was "part of," but had enough distance from, the event to compare teachers' experiences and place them within broader social contexts.

What is instructive about teachers' accounts of teaching during the 9/11 period is not that the craft of teaching was radically changed by the attacks, but that existing and critical dimensions of the work of teaching were painfully and obviously brought to the fore. Every crisis is also a learning opportunity. If we listen carefully, if we truly honor the courageous teachers who taught and nurtured our children during the school year following 9/11, maybe we can discover who our teachers are, and who they need to become in order to successfully prepare our young for the significant challenges of the 21st century.

Teachers and Students in Social Context

One core aspect of teacher professionalism is suspending one's own needs, controlling one's own emotions in order to meet the needs of one's students. Like good parents, teachers learn to put on their game face when confronted with chaotic environments. Ruth speaks about the teachers in her particular Upper East Side school the day of the attacks:

> I don't think it ever leaves you that you're a teacher. I think on that day I was so impressed with the teachers who had people down there, who went in their closets—and you saw what my closet looked like [laughter]—they're flying into their closets and closing the doors to cry. Then they'd come out, wash their faces, and go back to work. It was amazing.

As important adult authority figures in the students' lives, in the days, weeks, and months after 9/11, teachers bore the emotional brunt of the significant impact of the attacks on their students. Students experienced the trauma individually. Under "normal" circumstances it is difficult to assess the needs of each individual student, and it was particularly true for teachers like Fiona during the year of the 9/11 attacks. Several months after the attack, Fiona stated:

> Today a student handed me a note saying that he wanted counseling. I couldn't believe it because he seems so fun, he's been leading tours of the school, he's been into this and into that. When he told me he wanted the 9/11 group counseling, he said, "I don't even know what's wrong; I'm just sick, and I'm not sick."

But there was also a collective impact on students that cut to the core of who they were as adolescent Americans. An important aspect of teaching is identifying cultural currents and riding these currents to construct opportunities for students to construct knowledge from who they are. Many teachers I've spoken with in the last decade have pointed to an increasing distrust of adult authority on the part of children. Can we be trusted as stewards of this country's institutions, its democracy, and the physical environment? Can we keep our children safe, secure, and hopeful? This distrust was accentuated by the terrorist attacks. Fiona reflects:

> I can remember our first couple days of school. Teachers would come into my class and say, "Wow, they are so awesome for you—they do exactly what you tell them." That was out the window. It was gone. And I could sort of see it because I talked with a therapist and she was saying that the kids are angry at adults in general because they feel let down. And they may not be able to voice that or say it, but at some level they always looked at adults as protecting them and shielding them. Even though we got them out of the building, and they were safe, still they're angry at so much of what happened and we're the ones that are there every day still facing that anger, basically. And it's not that they're mean or they yell at you or anything, it's just you can see that they're testing and they're pushing more than I think they would normally push—more than I've ever had kids push.

Though the event created anger and fear, it also created hope, and the possibility of a society with renewed civic and communal commitments. Ruth recalls that some students were angry, but others

> want to have hope that we could take this mess and build toward something better because they have seen and they have experienced that we are better. We New Yorkers now value our policemen, we don't shoot at our firemen when they come to save us. We are blown away that they ran in when we ran out. I don't know anyone who isn't stunned by that.

What and how teachers teach is not solely dictated by who students are and what they need, but who teachers are themselves. Teachers do not give up who they are when they attempt to meet the needs of their students. Through the lens of 9/11, it becomes

very clear that teachers' culture, personality, and beliefs all filter
what and how teachers teach and also how students will respond to
them. All teachers who went into the closet to compose themselves
that day did not have the same identities. In a conversation with
Fatima, during an intense week of professional development with
Facing History and Ourselves several months before the attacks,
Fatima foreshadowed:

> A lot of my own history as far as being a Muslim keeps com-
> ing into my mind and how so many of the world terrorists are
> Muslims, and I'm just afraid of heaven forbid these people
> ever do gain some footing as far as international power is con-
> cerned. What the heck is going to happen in this world? And as
> a Muslim I feel responsibility and obligation.

Fatima does not leave her fears or sense of duty at the classroom
door but brings them to her teaching. She also brings her own experience with racism during a similar social context:

> When I was in middle school, I faced some racism. Talk about
> sticking out like a sore thumb. We were in social studies class
> and we were talking about the Gulf War and the teacher was
> just saying something about Hussein and how cruel he was be-
> cause he used yellow gas [on] his own people. At that moment
> I felt like, "Okay should I defend all Muslims there or should
> I just keep my mouth shut?" So the guy [sitting behind me]
> taps me on the shoulder and he goes, "So was that one of your
> relatives doing that?" And I was an angry child. I was about
> to throw my chair back. . . . I didn't care. I didn't say anything,
> I just laughed and said, "You don't know much." I'm sure the
> teacher heard it too or something but didn't do anything. And
> that angered me.

When we reflect on what to teach and how to teach it, we first
look to our own personal history:

> I brought those experiences into my classroom obviously.
> Now even if I hear a student say "shut up," I address it. Be-
> cause one thing leads to another and then it escalates. I say to

my students, it's okay to have your own views and opinions as long as you're not putting somebody down to make yourself look better. The kids get that.

Ruth, a teacher with a strong Jewish and antiracist identity, also cites an incident from her childhood as fundamentally shaping her approach to teaching:

> And I was raised in a home that was very open-minded. When the first Black family came into Crown Heights where I grew up, it was my elderly grandmother who went to greet them with baked goods. When she stood up there—and she was very respected in the Jewish community 'cause she was probably the only old lady that was in the temple morning, noon, and night—and so when she stood on the steps, she knew what she was doing, what she was getting into, because she felt the tension of the neighborhood. And [people from the Jewish community] were outside [the Black family's] house, and they weren't there to say "hello." And she turned to them and it was a Friday night, and she called them by name, and she said "Sarah, you should be home getting ready for the Sabbath. What are you doing here?" Well, so you know yelling nigger was not on the list of what you're supposed to do on Sabbath [laughter]. So . . . she called out other names, and I just remembered as a kid 'cause I never had thought of my grandma as tough or strong 'cause she's a tiny little thing. And always *davening*, you know, always praying to God. I didn't know she really spoke that much to the rest of us [laughter]. But there she was. And also I remember my mother never baked. So just the idea that they had gone to the bakery during the week [and] that was only something you did on Sunday and the whole thing—it was so intense. And we were the first White family to be friendly to the kids in their family.

The Demands of Diversity

Many schools across the city were faced with the sometimes hidden but ever-present realities of community intolerance and racism. Ruth continues:

In my school, at the beginning, the Muslim girls did not wear their scarves, they were so frightened. And there were bad instances outside the school. There was some harassment of the kids. . . . And my students and I talked about the difference between a Muslim and a terrorist, a Black person and a criminal and how many people don't see that.

As a White antiracist, Ruth is the teacher that Fatima and many Arab- and Muslim-American students throughout the country never had. Like other socially committed teachers in urban areas, Ruth sees it as her job to regularly take notice of, and advocate for, students who are underserved by schools as they are currently designed. She states:

Well, my Arabic student told me that I was the only Jewish teacher who had a discussion with her about the fact that she was Arab and I was Jewish and about what's going on in the world. I was the only one to ask her, "Do we need to talk or make you feel better?" She was in my after-school program and she couldn't start immediately because of Ramadan. Her mother wrote me a note saying that she would send her once she could pick her up once the holiday was over and they weren't eating at that hour. So she announced to me in class one day that she'll be coming in after school because Ramadan was over and I said, "Isn't that interesting," I said, "Hanukkah is over." And she stopped, and she looked, and she said, "Do you think the world will ever let us celebrate together?" And the next day I got a season's greetings card signed by her mother and her father and her brother and her sister. Amazing. But first she took off her scarf, and I asked her to bring it back and asked her if I could help her put it on and that I would make sure that she was safe.

Ruth took a stand as an isolated individual, but how well are our schools designed to support an increasingly multicultural democracy in the complex global context of the 21st century? The attacks of 9/11 were a real test. What a help it was for a new teacher with whom Ruth was working to be able to draw on her rich personal and professional experience in the days that followed the attacks. Ruth reflects,

Two days later you were back in the class and you were expected to answer questions. A little girl in the sixth grade said
to me, "why don't they like us?" I was working with a teacher
in one class. It was just her fourth day of teaching in her life.
She was so happy to see me! [laughter] "Can you do this with
me?" she asked. She was sweating bullets. As strange as it may
sound, this was not new to me because I've done riots, I've
done gangs.

Meanwhile, Fatima's students were asking a different set of
questions. Fatima had to navigate the tension of being a Muslim
worried about her own safety and a teacher dedicated to helping
her students grow.

My students' first reaction was to say, "We have to take action."
So I said, "Well what do you want to do? Do you want to go
kill all the people in Afghanistan? Is that going to solve the
problem?" They said, "No, but we need to take some military
action." I said, "Against whom?" And they said "The Middle
East." Then I pulled down the map and said, "Well, here's the
Middle East." And it finally dawned on them that you cannot
generalize. That's something you learn at Facing History.[1] One
of the first things that we learned at the Facing History seminar
was [how people divide the world into] *we versus them*. And I
brought that point up. Because one of the kids who was really
scared of me said, "Oh, why don't we just bomb any country
out there?" And I was like, "Whoa, you know it's like there
are people there." [Some students were like,] "Yeah yeah, they
killed 5,000 of ours let's kill 10,000 of theirs." And I said, "Okay,
so what if they retaliate and they kill 20,000—what are you going to do? Wipe out the whole Middle East?" And they're like,
"Yeah, we could do that. We got the bombs." Oh, my God!

All students, especially adolescents, respond positively to teachers' authenticity. But authenticity for teachers of color (as well as
White teachers with resistant racial and cultural identities) can be

---

1. Facing History and Ourselves is a professional development program that is specifically designed to help teachers think about issues of human behavior and democratic citizenship.

high-stakes, risky business. Appropriately confronting the complex issues of democracy in a community whose values do not always reflect the democratic purposes of education is incredibly difficult, given the isolating professional environments that most teachers maneuver within. Fatima continued:

> And then I moved them slowly very gradually. It was so scary for me because I knew that if some of my kids had been a little bit older they would've been out there trying to find all the Muslims and Arabs in their community and do something. It was that scary, their anger. And not because they didn't know why they were angry. It's because of what they see on TV and what their parents were doing. No one took the time to explain things.
>
> So I had to be very careful as to how I put the questions out, because they're kids. They will misinterpret, they'll hear what they want to hear, you know, and that's it.
>
> I definitely understood what happened in the 1930s in Germany. Just a very small inkling of it, but I definitely understood.

It was important to teachers like Fatima, Ruth, and Fiona, all teachers with strong commitments to the democratic purposes of education, to confront, head on, the dilemmas and issues of being an American in the 21st century. But having strong social commitments by itself doesn't necessarily make one a great teacher.

Confronting America

Our racial and cultural identity, the identities of our students, the historical and cultural contexts in which we teach—all affect how we teach about democracy and confront issues of cultural difference and pluralism in classrooms that in our country are becoming more and more culturally diverse. If we expect teachers to support our democratic institutions, how do we in turn support them?

None of the teachers I spoke with cited state standards, high-stakes tests, or school or colleague support in helping them with the meat and potatoes of teaching—organizing instruction around essential questions and concepts, translating these questions and concepts within particular student and teacher contexts, and finding rich materials to use in this translation. All of the teachers, to one degree or another, received professional development support from Facing History and Ourselves. Fatima talked about the value of the program to her:

> And I think that especially for me because I've never been comfortable in my own skin for such a long time—I'm more comfortable with who I am now than I was even last year or the year before. . . . Facing History made me look at myself and my history and my family's history and how that is affecting me now and how that's making me a little more comfortable to talk about things. You know especially with what happened on September 11th, especially with being a Muslim.

In fact, one of Fatima's primary tools for countering anti-Arab and anti-Muslim propaganda was to project for her students a strong, deep, and honest sense of who she herself was. A Facing History program associate had visited Fatima's school and given her the moral support and encouragement she needed. "Just talk it out with the kids," he said. "Use your personal experience. Don't be afraid." Fatima told me that it was an unwritten rule in her school "not to discuss too much in depth." Instead you were supposed to send students to the crisis management team. Fatima thought the rule was idiotic, because teachers know their students best. "Why would the kids trust someone they don't know?" she said.

Though it was against her labor contract, Ruth, a special education teacher, was often asked to substitute-teach on days when many teachers were absent. Drawing on a Facing History lesson, she used the time productively to help her students ask critical questions about the media messages with which they were being bombarded. Facing History had made Ruth ask herself whether the U.S. government had started to use some of the same propaganda techniques as the Nazis.

Ruth's predisposition toward democratic education, her understanding of the historical context, specific lesson materials, and the needs of her students produced a poignant and timely learning opportunity for her students:

In class I asked [my students if a house flies] the American
Flag daily, is that propaganda? And then I said, "Okay, try and
remember September 10th—do you remember seeing a lot of
flags?" And the children replied, "I don't remember seeing
any flags." "What does the flag stand for?" "United we stand,"
[one kid said]. And so another kid said, "Boy . . . that's [a] slogan, it's propaganda." "But do you agree with it?" "Yes." "So
is propaganda a good thing and a bad thing?" So they came
to the conclusion that it could be either, which again means a
moral responsibility to a person in democracy because then
they have to think whether it's good or bad because they're being pummeled all the time with messages. 'Cause I said, "What
is this thing, the right to vote? Do you get propagandized before you go in there, do you think it influences the way people
vote? What's your responsibility as a citizen in a democracy?"
And one kid was talking about how the media is giving so
many messages right now, they don't feel they can trust anything. . . . So when you vote you might vote for someone who
says the media has to be controlled, so it came out throughout
this lesson.

Fiona reflects on her pedagogical thinking and the themes that
emerged from her eighth-grade American-history class as they
struggled to make meaning of the events around them. Fiona picked
up on similar themes, concepts, and questions as Ruth—themes,
concepts, and questions that Facing History had helped her to identify and organize in the immediate months after the attacks.

It's interesting because I was doing Facing History on September 11th. I was doing a lot of the community building, and of
course when the attacks happened, we came here and right
away [we looked at issues of identity] and creating the "other."
We did the identity charts,[2] and then I took from the newspaper
an article by a Muslim woman who's now an American citizen,
It was really perfect for this because she gave her identity—
[she said] this is my identity, but now because of September

---

2. In this type of identity chart, the student draws her or his picture in the center of the
paper, draws lines from the picture, and at the end of each line lists an element of her or his
identity.

11th, this is what's being tacked on to me and this is what society is labeling me. And then I had the kids speculate about how her identity changes if society looks at her and sees a terrorist and sees an evil person and sees this anti-American. What happens to her love of New York and her citizenship in the United States?

Unlike Fatima and Ruth, Fiona and her students had actually had to relocate to another school building. The direct trauma of the attacks and the relocation took its toll on Fiona and her students. They had become different people, with changed needs, in a different America. Fiona reflects:

There are so many times that I see a glimmer of my old self and go oh, oh yeah, I used to be like that. And then it falls apart. You just can't get your whole thing together. Even though it's two months after 9/11, it's just not together. And how can it ever really be back together when we're not home, we're not in our building. They're not in their real homes.

The opportunities to learn, which she and her students created, began to change as the term progressed:

I originally planned to use the theme of racism and creating the "other" to lead me through the whole year, and that was going to be my theme for the year. And then after September 11th and after talking about all these issues and the racial profiling and everything, the kids said to me, "Do you know, we just can't really handle hearing more depressing stuff about America. We keep hearing that we've done so many wrong things. We really want to hear some good things that we've done." And so I said, "Okay." So I chucked out my theme and I thought, well, I'm too mentally a wreck to really put out a whole new theme for the year. . . . How am I going to do this? And then I started putting together this constitution [curriculum], and I needed something that would be their essential question or what are they trying to get from the whole thing, and I came down to power and the use of power.

Fiona herself was forced to confront what it means to be an American, and she brought that to her teaching:

I don't think I ever really sat down and thought this is what makes Americans, Americans. And it's hard when you sit down and try and figure it out because there's no one thing because we're all so different and we still maintain all our own cultures when people move here. So what's connecting us together? What are those threads? That's, I think, maybe one of the big differences that I'm using now.

Fiona helped her students develop a more inclusive and hopeful sense of community membership:

Facing History definitely helped with talking about issues of community. . . ." I had students first draw their own picture of what they viewed community to be—and then they put their pictures together in a group. We then reflected on it, talked about it, and came up with some very interesting ideas. [Weeks later, after we had received gifts and letters from all over the country and world, my students asked me if they could do the community pictures again.] They said, "Now we sort of see each other as being part of a country, as being part of a large whole." Before, when they would do their pictures of community they would draw their family or they would draw their friends and none of them really expanded out of it. After doing the second version of our visual depiction of community, my students then began to see, "Wow, we're not just our little school, or our little family."

Remembering School

Teachers all have the moments and students they remember. Students also fix certain parts of the year in their minds, in the narratives of their life stories. What students and teachers remember helps us to understand what they consider to be the most meaningful and important dimensions of teaching and learning. Fatima explains:

My relationship with this graduating class will be different from any of the others I will ever have, ever.

Now I'm actually wrapping up. At the beginning of the year I have students write a letter to me introducing themselves. I just had them write a letter to me talking about their most memorable moment with me. And a lot of kids mentioned the group discussion after September 11th because I made them sit in a circle so they could face each other while they were speaking—you've seen the room, it's small, so it's so hard for them to do that. So they loved that and they remembered it.

This year we had more discussions as a whole group. During the discussions about 9/11 there was no note taking or anything. The whole point was to get their anger out.

My kids are at the age where they're just figuring out who they are or beginning to. So it's really interesting to see how much they've matured from September to June. You know where their priorities are.

I was the only Muslim in the entire school on staff. So students were turning to me for answers. That meant I had to brush up on everything I knew. Students came to class with questions to me like, "Does Islam teach hate?" I said, "No, it doesn't." The literal translation of the word *Islam* is "peace" or "to submit." You know if you're submitting you are not vengeful. There is no room for hate. My brother told me about an article that said that the majority of the hijackers were from a radical sect that, if you look back historically, had attempted to kill the prophet Mohammed, too.

This year I felt that I was in a position of power. Here I am. I'm able to explain to my children what their parents cannot because I am a Muslim. At the same time it put a lot of pressure on me. I'm a target and that's such a scary feeling.

Unlike Fatima and Fiona, who are at the beginning of their careers, Ruth is near the end of hers. A child of the civil rights movement, having faced many social crises throughout her professional life, Ruth remembers the year within that context.

It's been a crazy year. But I often wonder if I didn't have 32
years of teaching, I mean how could I do the job?

   I came in here over the age of 50 toward the end of my career, and I had no idea how I'd be received. . . . What coming
to a new experience at this stage of my career has taught me
is: who you are is what you teach. And whatever you say is
weighted by the children by who you are. Whether you have
authenticity, whether you don't discriminate, whether when
you have something racial in your head, you identify it and
that you know you have to work on it and that you say it. You
have to be a work in progress. You have to, in your gut, believe
in the process of education.

Standing at the Crossroads

The experience of teachers during 9/11, and how this experience
reflects critical dimensions of the work of teaching, reminds us that
"curriculum" is not a fixed object, but a dynamic process, a continually shifting relationship between teacher and student identities,
knowledge, and interests; learning materials; and the social and
cultural contexts within which teaching and learning takes place.
As any one element of the relationship changes, the curriculum
necessarily changes. We are faced with a choice as Americans, educators, and policy makers—do we use teachers' experiences during
the school year of 9/11 to recognize the incredible complexities of
this process and support teachers' attempts to meet the demands of
diversity that confront the America of the 21st century?

   Our society itself has made many questionable choices since
9/11. In a short period of time we have witnessed an intensification
of the so-called War on Terror, two wars on foreign soil that have
not yet ended, the horrors of human rights abuses in Abu Ghraib,
as well as a focused and thinly veiled domestic war on our country's poor and disenfranchised. To support these efforts we have
also witnessed the development of a sophisticated and efficient cor-
porate and political propaganda machine. I have a sinking feeling,
and I know that I am not alone. Though we are born into strong
social institutions, in the end we choose who we are and collectively what our society will look like. Maybe every generation has

the feeling of standing at a crossroads. As I complete this chapter, I certainly do.

In my current work as a teacher educator at Eastern Michigan University, I feel an urgency that is difficult to suppress. The last day of teaching my secondary methods class, I listened closely to the echoes, the voices, the lessons of the courageous teachers I worked with during the year of 9/11. As a Jew whose wife is from a family of Holocaust survivors, I simultaneously heard a different set of voices. I do not typically lecture, but I gave my students one that day. I told them that citizens and teachers living in a democracy have been faced with important choices concerning how to raise their young and these choices have had undeniable consequences for that democracy's cultural and political institutions. I told them my family's stories and handed them a timeless letter written by a Holocaust survivor to every future generation of teachers:

Dear Teacher:

I am a survivor of a concentration camp. My eyes saw what no man should witness:

Gas chambers built by learned engineers.

Children poisoned by educated physicians.

Infants killed by trained nurses.

Women and babies shot and burned by high school and college graduates.

So I am suspicious of education.

My request is: Help your students become human. Your efforts must never produce learned monsters, skilled psychopaths, educated Eichmanns.

Reading, writing, arithmetic are important only if they serve to make our children more human.

Though not completely analogous to our current context, as individuals and as a society, we certainly have some important decisions to make regarding our schools.

Thirteen

Question Marks
All Over
the City

LIA FRIEDMAN

T HERE'S A POSTER in my dad's office that says, "1 + 1 = 3?" He's a mathematician, but I guess that's irrelevant. The poster has to do with two waves merging and becoming a set of three, which has no philosophical connotations whatsoever. Yet I find myself thinking about that poster a lot, in relation to what it means for something to be finite, set in stone, one right answer and one wrong.

The only answer I have ever been able to come up with is that there is no black and white. September 11th and the aftermath were flooded with questions, bigger ones than we could answer. There was us, and there were the evildoers, clear right and wrong ways of life. There were the patriots and the terrorists, and nothing in between.

On September 11, 2001, my city was attacked. I was a sixth grader at The Center School on the Upper West Side, and 100 percent assured of my maturity and worldliness. I was walking through the gateways to our tiny, one-floor school when I first heard the rumors in the hall. "Yo, somebody crashed a plane into the Twin Towers!" Was that just a rumor? And even if it wasn't, did I care? Later, I sat in homeroom, in 328 where the lights were never on, with my brand-new journal and a pink pen.

. . . 9/11/01

To my advisor:

Our principal just came in to tell us about the kamikaze attacks on the World Trade Center. I just can't help wondering if
there is a reason behind it. Maybe if the planes were sighted,
someone saw where they were from. I wonder what will happen next. There was a bombing in Washington too. . . .

My dad came to pick me up even earlier than if it had been a half
day. I fought with him half the time. "I don't need to go home! This
is the second day of school, I want to hang out with my friends!"
When we were home, he turned on the television and watched it
for a long time. "Can I watch cartoons now?"

Looking back on that afternoon, I can't believe how young I
seem. People say that America lost its illusion of protection when
the World Trade Center was bombed, but I felt even more untouch-
able. My friends were afraid to fly, afraid to take elevators, the subway, afraid of the streets . . .

I wanted to take a plane across the country, as if to say, "Look
at me! I'm not afraid!" And I wasn't. I'm still not. That is the most
surreal part of the entire ordeal; looking at myself and wondering
why I'm not afraid, why I'm not grieving, why I became less of a
patriot in the following months. Everyone had a different way of
dealing with the closeness of the attacks, and mine was to be strong
and angry.

There was one afternoon in Hebrew school, when we were discussing the war in Israel. My teacher was telling us about a bus of
children who were killed in a bombing. As he listed the atrocities
committed by the Palestinians, I wanted him to tell us that the Israelis were doing it, too, that this was not a one-sided conflict. This
was a teacher—and a person—whom I respected greatly. He never
mentioned it.

At that point, I began to consider that adults were never going
to tell me both sides of the story. At what point, I thought, does
personal bias interfere with learning? The single most overused
word in a social-studies–related classroom is *culture*. We are constantly reminded that everyone carries his or her own culture and
heritage with them. But this is always used in the positive context

of diversity; we are never told of how biases and prejudices are carried along with it. It took me a long time into my academic career to realize that educators are people as well, with their own blemished histories. Is there any way to truly know two sides of a story? And even if we hear two different perspectives, is there any account that is entirely objective? But most of all, can we even accept a different view, brought up and educated in a certain way, and is there anyone who can teach us to do so?

I've begun to think now that teachers were too careful about letting their opinions out and telling us what they were going through. Maybe there is a point where bias is a good thing to hear, if we can recognize it for what it is, accept it, and see all the feelings that are floating around, so we can pinpoint what exactly it is that we are feeling.

All I remember about that time were phone numbers to call for help on the #2 train; messages all around me that what everyone was going through was normal. But I didn't know what I was going through. The one comment from a teacher that touched me more than any politically correct statement ever could was when my social studies teacher commented, off the record, that after she heard the news, she went into the girls bathroom, got down on her knees, and started praying.

That was the year that I dropped out of Hebrew school. I had to explain to myself and others many times that I simply didn't feel any spiritual connection, and that I found it hard to say words that I didn't mean. I remember a distinct thought that passed through my head in the months between September 11th and the time at which I stopped going to the temple. I had an assignment in social studies, world religions, on thoughts about God. I felt the need to be politically correct, and mention the fact that faith is what keeps people alive; keeps their flame burning in times of adversity. Underneath that, I felt a desire to rip that from them, to tell everyone who could hear me that we as a race of human beings shouldn't have the privilege of that faith, because of how horribly we have abused it. I thought about the members of my congregation, if they could be capable of killing another human being for the sake of the ideology so important to their lives. I wanted to say that I didn't believe in God and I considered myself lucky, because I wasn't trapped in a false sphere of comfort.

. . . Three Years Later

It was hard to relate to people who had suffered a loss, simply because I hadn't. Who was I to tell them what they should or shouldn't feel, all because I had this anger inside of me, anger at religion, at the thing that I blamed for this tragedy? In the first few months of school, during a chorus rehearsal, my teacher stopped the class. She's very melodramatic, so it wasn't at all unusual. However, she began telling us about a graduate who had come to visit her earlier that week. He was working for the armed forces, on missions so secretive he couldn't even tell her about. I began to groan inwardly; this was going to be one of her "Proud to Be an American" interludes. But I listened, because her sharp eyes would notice me the minute I began to drift off. Suddenly, she was asking the chorus to remember a previous first soprano section leader, who used to sit two rows in front and three seats to the side of where I sat then. This was a girl who had been killed on September 11, 2001. The visiting graduate had brought back a plaque in her memory. I have never felt so close to the the terror as in that moment. I can imagine the girl singing, taking attendance, handing out numbered sheet music. It took me so completely by surprise, for I'd never encountered anything like that before.

Being so sheltered myself in middle school, it was hard to imagine my new and intimidating high school in the midst of the horror. There are echoes of that day all over Stuyvesant, and I have to remind myself that for some people, it's not such a distant thing. In the first month of school, there was a day of commemoration that students were invited to attend. I can only imagine looking out the windows and seeing black smoke, walking across the Tribeca Bridge every morning and looking out over the highway and remembering the chaos of Downtown.

This graduating class is the last to have experienced that day at the school. Today in the hall I listened to a senior talking to my friends. He was talking excitedly about his own freshman year. He was talking about what it felt like when the plane hit, a rumbling that he could feel in the building. I wasn't quite sure that he was talking about September 11th, but he confirmed it when another friend asked. He seemed so casual, and I wondered if in school and also in our lives, we make it casual because of our politics, and also so we can't feel the pain.

"September 11th" is a household term. 9/11, Ground Zero—these are phrases that we connect with a certain day, place, and feeling. I wonder if, in learning, they have become as anonymous as other dates we learn about, even though the wound is still so raw? We sit in classrooms learning about the Koran, the U.S. government, and how airplanes work, but we never seem to discuss how all these things are interconnected. There are forums and support groups all over the country to discuss the impact that September 11th had on our lives, but the rigorous curriculum has no room for feelings or real insights. Is that senior removing himself from an experience too close for comfort, or is he a product of the New York educational system, where knowing is more important than understanding?

One Friday afternoon, I was walking with my friends from school. We were walking to a friend's house; there were about 20 of us. We walked past a huge fenced-off area with the sounds of sirens clinging to it. Only after someone mentioned that this was Ground Zero did I make that connection. It had seemed so distant before this, the infamous Ground Zero, spoken with capital letters. There it was. If I tried, maybe I could see it from the Tribeca Bridge as I walked out to lunch every day. This was the Ground Zero that people had died in, where others had dug through the rubble for months, where all the construction plans I'd seen in the newspaper were going to take place, the mass grave of all the faces who stared out at me from the signs in Times Square for so long.

As I think about that place, which for all I knew could have been a random courtyard, it becomes easier to identify with all the angry and vulnerable people, easier to be a New Yorker and also a victim. There are question marks hanging throughout the city, on the gates of empty courtyards, on the walls of the Times Square subway station, and in all the classrooms. We don't know the answers to the questions; we are afraid to answer them. We either tread too carefully or place blame where it does not belong. There exists a lingering "why?" from which we have diverted ourselves. And that fifth W is the one that schools cannot—or haven't tried—to teach.

Fourteen

Rediscovering Compassion in the Classroom

AMY MARTIN

The clearness of the blue sky does not look true today. We stand there, rigid, under this blue sky in the schoolyard waiting. Anna's knuckles tighten around the straps of her backpack. My mind is filled with the left and right punches of my thoughts, and yet, somehow, I find solace in wondering what is inside Anna's backpack. I wonder what she is clutching onto: empty lunchbox, yesterday's unchecked homework, books for tonight's reading. They are all there, these second-grade relics from a morning that seems like worlds ago. There is no homework tonight. We look at the yard entrance, and I think about what I had said today. I think about what I should say now. Do I say that your mother will be here? We stand and we look. The sounds of helicopters and sirens push at the edges of our heavy silence. What do I say? Anna watches anxious students melt into their parents' arms.

Into the schoolyard gate comes Anna's mother. With heavy footsteps, she rushes up to us, and the urgent words stumble out of her mouth, "What did you say to them? You didn't tell them, did you?" What did I say? What do I say now? Anna's mother waited for my words, and I said: "Yes. I told them two planes had crashed into the Twin Towers, and the people there and all over the city are working together like a community, like we work together here to help each other. Yes, I told them. I told them this is why some parents are picking their children up early from school." Anna's mother exhaled and responded, "I didn't know parents were picking up their children early. I'm going to seek a professional's advice before I talk to my children about this. I don't know what to say."

THE SPACE IN BETWEEN the question and the answer is where we can redefine categories of meaning, and in the process, create new ones. The process is what interests me most. September 11th is an event that pulled me out of an underappreciated sense of everydayness. As I walked in the streets of Manhattan in an attempt to get to Queens that day, I walked with an awareness that every person I passed was focused on the same despair of knowing that our everyday reality had been violently redefined. I wondered if an equal act of incredible peacefulness could hold our attention. I wondered about the forums for building compassion in my classroom that could possibly lead to some sense of peacefulness. *Compassion* is a word that has picked up unfortunate political associations with our current government. Nonetheless, the compassion that I am interested in is the kind that takes root from the word *feeling* and thereby invites the imagination to *feel* along *with* another. To feel a range of emotions: joy, anxiety, happiness, pain.

As I gathered together with my students on September 13th, I realized that what I had to say was not nearly as important as what I do for my students to listen to one other. Here I will share some of the forums in my second-grade classroom that assisted us to understand each other and ultimately, to create new meaning in our daily lives. I will explore the roles that community meeting, writing workshop, meditation, and conflict resolution had in building our sense of compassion during the uncertain climate after September 11, 2001.

P.S. 116 is a vibrant school located in the heart of Manhattan, down the street from the Empire State Building. It is a school comprised of a young, hard-working staff. We have over 800 students in grades K–5. The students and parents come from all parts of the world and from various socioeconomic groups. Yet the students remain separate according to their placement in the school's tracking system. The result is two Talented and Gifted (TAG) classes per grade and approximately three general education classes per grade.

The general education classes have students from a variety of ethnicities who come from a range of socioeconomic backgrounds and who have multiple learning needs. The TAG classes are characterized by White students who come from middle- to upper-middle-class backgrounds and have an active parent base. Arguably, this parent population has created a powerful history that continues to hold the school's tracking system in place. These parents have played a significant role in changing our school over the years and have helped to make it a well-funded, highly desired institution.

The tracking system continues to be a sore point among our staff; some believe in maintaining the system to uphold the learning styles of different students, and some are curious about what would happen if the system were challenged. The question remains: would the upper-middle-class parents in TAG leave to send their children to private school, or would the hard-earned reputation of our school continue to draw parents and children who want an exceptional education with a truly diverse classroom, not just a diverse school with separate classrooms? I continue to struggle with this question as a former teacher of TAG students. Currently, I am enjoying the challenge of teaching a variety of students as the school librarian.

On September 13th, the day we returned to school, we had a faculty meeting to share our questions and worries about what to say to our students who were arriving at 10:00 A.M. "What if students ask why it happened? What if students start to cry and say that they are scared? What if parents tell us not to talk about it?" Our school principal and our guidance counselor suggested that we begin our day with a community meeting in each classroom. It was to be a meeting for students and family members to voice what was on their minds. I was fortunate to be spending a 2nd year with my students and their parents because of our school's looping system (teachers and students can choose to advance together to the next grade). Although my students were familiar with community meeting from first grade, it still felt like an incredible responsibility to lead a meeting on an issue that held the entire world's attention.

So, on the morning of September 13th, we gathered in our classroom and sat in a large circle. It became clear that my students had been exposed to a range of information. The meeting began a conversation of questions that had no immediate, clear answers. In the presence of parents and administrators, the children shared comments and questions that were the unwanted silent companions of all the adults:

> "I saw people jumping from buildings and then the towers fell."
>
> "Who could have done this to us? Will it happen again?"
>
> "I couldn't sleep last night. I kept thinking about how tall my building is and if it could be hit, too."
>
> "I saw on the television that two planes crashed into the Twin Towers and it was not an accident. Another plane crashed close to the White House and one crashed in Pennsylvania. How many people died?"

I did not attempt to answer their questions. Instead, I invited them to respond to each other and to use the space of our community meeting to articulate what was going on inside their hearts and minds.

The space to be heard and acknowledged opened them up to take the chances necessary to live the solutions to their questions and concerns. In *The Little Prince*, Antoine de Saint Exupéry explains, "It is only with the heart that one can see rightly; what is essential is invisible to the eye."[1] The Little Prince learned that to know the fox is to create ties with him. This distinguishes the fox from the hundred thousand other foxes. Knowing the fox is a process that required patience of the Little Prince to act at certain times and thereby create rites. Particularly after September 11th, community meeting, like the meetings between the Little Prince and the fox, became the predictable time for the children to sort through life's unpredictabilities, and in the process create the tools needed to trust themselves and each other. Having the space to ask those questions somehow allowed us to continue to rebuild the comfort of our everyday learning habits. Our community meetings became, more than ever, a safe, consistent space for students to name their fears and to realize that they were not alone. During this time of

---

1. Orlando: Harcourt, Inc., 1943, p. 86.

great uncertainty in the world, our weekly gatherings became a reliable place to slow down and to check in with ourselves.

One example of how community meeting nurtured the students' sense of empathy involves the story of two particular students, Malcolm and Thomas. They both joined our community after school had begun (Malcolm in first grade, Thomas in second grade). Malcolm is African American and Thomas is Japanese American. Malcolm arrived in December of 2000, and in an effort to be heard, he often grabbed or pushed children when he had a problem. For a few weeks, examples of different situations were brought up during community meeting that involved Malcolm. He denied them; an all-too-frequent refrain of his was, "No, I didn't." Within the next few months, Malcolm began to realize that no matter how much he denied having any responsibility, the problems were still there. He realized, also, that he did not have to wait for others to bring up concerns; he could set the agenda, too. When he began to name the problem, a shift occurred. At a community meeting Malcolm shared, "I don't like it when I ask to play and I am told 'no, go play with someone else.'" I asked the class if anyone else has ever felt left out. Several hands shot up into the air. Knowing that he could be listened to as someone with concerns that others also experienced opened Malcolm up to hearing suggestions. This time when a fellow student offered, "I would play with you, Malcolm, if you didn't push me to get into a game," he nodded and replied, "Next time, I'll ask."

Malcolm's sense of responsibility came to fuller fruition when Thomas joined our classroom. Thomas transferred into our class in January of second grade because his school was temporarily relocated due to its proximity to the World Trade Center. In addition, Thomas and his family had to relocate their home. When Thomas began to demonstrate disruptive behaviors that were similar to the ones Malcolm had shown during his transition into first grade, Malcolm offered advice. Thomas's name continued to resurface in community meeting for reasons involving pushing and shoving. Malcolm eventually announced, "Thomas, I used to get into trouble and say I didn't do anything, too. Then I started to tell people what was making me mad instead of pushing and shoving. Maybe you could try this, too." Malcolm's bravery in sharing his self-awareness with Thomas helped him to not feel alone, and slowly he began to make more friends. The open forum of community meeting allows children to negotiate difficult situations that need time to be recognized and changed.

When the children began to write in their notebooks for the first time, many entries contained the questions that were weighing down on all of our minds. Like too many precious stones in their pockets that couldn't be tossed aside, they asked, "Why did this happen?", "Will it happen again?", "How many people died?", and "Who did it?" But it was one of my more reticent and sensitive students, Michela, who asked, "What about the Afghan children? Do they need food? What can we do?" When she shared her notebook entry with the class, she received a variety of responses. Some children also shared their concern for the safety of the people in Afghanistan, but Lewis asked, "Why? Why should we send them food? What good would that do when we're the ones who got attacked first?" Rather than attempting to give them answers, I praised them for asking their questions and for listening to one another. I pointed out that we could have different ideas and still be in a community together. Michela later developed her entries into a published piece about her concerns about Afghanistan. She shared it with parents and students at our publishing party. Many parents commented on how surprised they were to read a second grader's concerns about a topic that they had difficulty discussing. Particularly during the tenuous climate following Semptember 11th, the students' notebooks became vital passageways for them to travel in between the world they were living and the world they were creating.

If community meeting and notebooks are a place for children to name and to identify their world, then meditation is another opportunity for children to reimagine what is possible. Following the loud and crowded daily experience of lunch and recess, the children need a moment to slow down and be in a quiet, still place. For this reason, I began doing a brief meditation with them in first grade.

Meditation is an opportunity for children to direct their attention to their internal reality. It allows them to sift through the daily details of external stimuli and to realize what is left, what matters. Meditation is a brief moment in time that becomes a creative tool on which they can rely to experience and then change intense feelings such as fear, pain, and anger.

To start our class meditation, I led the students to sit quietly for a minute. During this minute they were invited either to close their eyes or keep their gaze fixed on one place. Once they became comfortable with this ritual, I used visualizations from an exceptional resource on children's meditation, *Spinning Inward*.[2] The visualizations help the children to be led to a comfortable internal space where they can make choices, ask questions, and create answers.

The students continually requested a visualization that involves choosing to walk down either a path in the forest or along the ocean. Eventually, they are guided to envision a person walking toward them. The person could be someone they know or someone they would like to know, but it should definitely be someone they trust and believe in. As the person is approaching, the children take time to formulate a question that they would like to ask. Upon meeting the person, they ask the question, and they can either get an answer or choose simply to talk. After the conversation is over, they say good-bye, and the children open their eyes. After each meditation, there is a brief sharing session, and the responses were always varied: "I feel more relaxed. I was able to ask about my father, who is away right now." "I talked with my grandmother, who is sick. I told her that I hope she gets better." "I found out how to make an invention to slow down time when you are having fun!" As the children's experience with visualizations deepened, they shared the duties of leading and offered the community their own ideas for journeys of self-discovery.

France Morin, a former curator at the Museum of Contemporary Art in New York City, explains, "Attaining a state of focused concentration could nurture the heightened powers of perception and creativity essential to full self-realization."[3] During the time after September 11th, the children created visualizations that invited

---

2. Maureen Murdock, Boston: Shambhala, 1987.

3. *Quiet in the Land, Everyday Life, and Projecto Axé*. Salvador, Brazil: Museu de Arte Moderna da Bahia, 2000, p. 39.

opportunities for creative departures. For example, Catherine especially enjoyed leading the class to imagine entering a room with three paintings: one painting is blue, the second painting is green, and the third painting is red. The children were asked to choose a painting to enter and to explore. During the share, the children offered how it felt to go inside different colors; some chose to linger in one and some chose to go into all of them. Their choices usually reflected a feeling they wanted to experience: calmness, excitement, intrigue.

Visualizations seemed to help students outside of school, too. One parent shared that when her daughter hurt her finger while cooking, she said, "I'm going to take a quiet moment." Another mother explained that when she expressed feeling stress and tension, especially following September 11th (her husband worked in the World Trade Center and safely escaped the buildings), her son advised, "Mom, you should meditate for a silent minute to feel better. We do it every day after recess, and then we feel different."

By middle of the school year, P.S. 116 was invited to participate in conflict resolution training led by Educators for Social Responsibility (ESR). One teacher from each grade participated in training for a program known as the 4Rs (Reading, Writing, Respect, and Resolution). This program is designed to work with the increasingly demanding needs of teaching literacy while simultaneously strengthening the students' ability to solve problems. During the training, teachers from across District 2 brainstormed ideas, discussed texts in the 4Rs curriculum, and explored the conflict-resolution lessons. The lessons exposed me to a new set of tools that I knew would engage my students and open them further to understand each other's perspectives.

Following the training, we were guided by an ESR staff developer, Emma Gonzalez, who helped us to implement the lessons in our classrooms. Emma's enthusiasm and flexibility made it possible for me to invite another second-grade class into our room for the conflict-resolution lessons. This gave us the opportunity to bring together a multitude of experiences and perspectives for the students to negotiate. Jane Hsu (their teacher) and I led read-alouds together of the books from the units. The discussions expanded the children's thinking outside of their usual classroom talks. Jane and I saw the potential for coteaching across the division of TAG and General Education and explored as many opportunities as we could find. Eventually, we were coteaching writing units as well as read-alouds, and taking excursions outside of school together. The results were that not only did the children hear ideas from those they usually only saw at recess, but they became more acquainted with each other and saw the potential for building new friendships.

One example of how conflict resolution clearly bridged the gap between students who may not be familiar with each other, is when Jane and I read aloud from a picture book entitled *Angel Child, Dragon Child*.[4] The story is of a Vietnamese girl who moves to America. It explores the troubles she has with a school bully. When the two main characters are asked to write about their problem, a shift occurs. At this turning point in the story, I asked the students to turn and talk to a neighbor to discuss what caused the bully to change. Thomas's partner shared, "My partner said that when the girl told her side of the story, the bully started to understand how she felt because of what he did. He started to see her as a kid like him." Thomas, who was introduced earlier, had to negotiate redefining his life after September 11th: a new home, a new school, a new set of friends. For him to make an observation about the story and to have it heard in a large group setting, seemed to demonstrate that he was realizing he wasn't alone, that he, too, could be understood.

I have described some of the ways that I attempted to rebuild the comfort of everyday learning in my classroom following the events of September 11th. Community meeting, writing workshop, meditation, and conflict resolution served as guides in a time of great uncertainty. However, this uncertainty served as the most useful guide of all. It has reminded me that learning is never finished, that it is an ongoing process. This liberated me from feeling the burden of having the answers, of saying the right words. Instead, I worked with my students to live through the uncertainties and in the process, try, again and again, to understand one another.

---

4. Michele Maria Surat, New York: Scholastic, 1989.

Learning

Learning is like the moon growing 'till it's full.
Learning is like an unraveling snake turning every strange
    corner to the end.
Learning is like a star growing 'til day.
Learning is like magic lasting 'til the last day of our lives.

—Michela Garabedian
Second Grade
June 2002

Fifteen

The Doorway to Change

LORRIE MANN

I THINK OF MY CLASSROOM doorway as the threshold of crisis. Over the years, I've stood below the lintel of my doorway to receive disastrous news enough times that I think I might be learning to use these experiences as I would a gift.

Many years ago as I was teaching, an announcement came over the P.A. system to lock all classroom doors and stay in the classroom. Alarmed, I went to the door and peered out of the doorway window. Catching sight of a lone teacher with her hands up to her face, I did not heed the warning and I opened the door. She was sobbing. She told me that our principal, Mr. Daly, had been shot. He had gone out to check on the safety of a child who had left school after having a fight. Later when more news reached the school, we found out that while on his way to the child's home in the housing projects, Mr. Daly accidentally stepped into the crossfire of a gang-related gunfight. He had been killed by a bullet in his chest. We had lost our beloved principal in the matter of a moment. Our hallways were still, and the shock of disbelief reigned for many days to come.

Most recently, the bad news came on September 11, 2001.

As I answered the knock on my door, a colleague whispered to me, "How can two planes crash into the World Trade Center?" "What a bad joke," was my immediate response, but as I couldn't think of a punch line, I slowly realized that she wasn't kidding. The rush of nerves from my stomach to my toes felt familiar, and I had a seasoned sense of confidence that I would be able to keep my footing and a cool head about me.

I teach Pre-Kindergarten at P.S. 15 in the community of Red Hook, Brooklyn. My kids didn't need to know a thing. We talk and we play and we learn how to live with one another every day, but Pre-Kindergarten children learn through their daily activities and are not required to "know" any body of facts as yet. In that respect I was off the hook. Yes, the kids could probably sense that there was tension in the room when I paused too long before answering their simple innocent questions. "Are we going to choice time now, Ms. Mann?" "Ah, no, ah yes, ah maybe," is what I came up with. When their parents began to come to pick them up before the end of the day, they didn't wonder why. They had barely learned the routines of life at school. They were going to be able to cope with a change of routine.

In fact, the kids who attend P.S. 15 are not used to routines at all, and they also know more than one would expect about coping. For a variety of reasons, mostly having to do with parents with poverty-level incomes, many of their home lives are unstructured. Most of the students live in the Red Hook housing projects. Built in the 30s by the Works Progress Administration (W.P.A.) 12 city blocks worth of tightly compressed buildings, some towering to 14 stories, provide housing for a majority of the 11,000 residents of Red Hook. Famous for being one of the city's largest and earliest housing projects, they are infamous for being crime-ridden. To alleviate the cramped quarters due to extended families sharing apartments, lots of the kids run free in the hallways without any supervision. The hallways are where the young children start their street-life education, meeting older kids who are ready to join gangs.

P.S. 15 is right across the street from the western boundary of the projects. Sometimes I park my car on the projects' southern boundary of Wolcott Street. I walk alongside these looming buildings, and as I cross the street toward P.S. 15, a two-story 60s-era modern structure, with no more high buildings on the horizon, I have a sense of relief and of hope. I know that if I keep on walking a few more blocks west, I will have a full view of the New York harbor, and I can make eye contact with Lady Liberty. (P.S. 15 is the closest

New York City school to the statue.) I sometimes wonder if during the kids' journey to school, they feel the same westward-ho sense of freedom and possibility.

Now, though, on this day, as the children gradually cleared out of the room, I looked back remembering the cataclysmic event that happened on December 17, 1992, when we lost Mr. Daly. It also happened suddenly and violently, but we did get through that horrible shock, and we proceeded to grieve and to heal.

Thus it happened after 9/11, too. Not many days after the initial shock, our school began preparing for memorials and expressions of condolences. We reached out to our local fire companies and police precinct, inviting them to a memorial service. Our chorus sang, poems were read, and two cardboard-box constructions resembling towers displayed a variety of images symbolizing themes of hope, faith, brotherhood, diversity, and community strength. The students made postcards and sent them to children in the schools in Pennsylvania and Washington, D.C.

Creating a memorial is a part of the healing process. It's almost a promise to yourself that you know you'll get better but you'll never forget. A memorial ceremony took place at P.S. 15 after we lost our principal. Our school was renamed in his honor. We are now called The Patrick F. Daly School, not only because he died tragically, but also because he had an indescribable amount of care and concern for the children of Red Hook.

In part, this is why my first emotional response when I heard the news of his death was of overwhelming anger. Of course I was infuriated by what happened, but I was also angry with Mr. Daly. Both our staff and children needed him. The children who attended P.S. 15 could not lock out the violence that surrounded them at home when they entered school, but Mr. Daly had been successful in changing the tone of our halls. What had been danger zones were now corridors full of beautiful displays that he encouraged the children to create. Classes now walked in a relaxed orderly way in a peaceful environment.

This fragile balance was also achieved because Mr. Daly enlisted our school as one of the first to pilot and adopt the Resolving Conflicts Creatively Program (RCCP). When it was developed, the highlight of this program was to teach children mediation skills in order to avoid conflicts that result in violence. Clearly it is particularly appealing to administrators and teachers in schools where maintaining order is a difficult task, but I think Mr. Daly recognized that the soul of the program was what our kids really needed.

In its nascence around 1984, RCCP was dubbed the Peace Program. (I think that must be why Mr. Daly embraced it so readily.) Perhaps too quixotic a word for the times, the name was dropped, but the concept of peace, as a way of living, remains the underpinning of the program. He believed that by learning how to communicate better, understand and articulate their feelings, think critically, and work together to build a fair and just community, the children of Red Hook would be better equipped to face the vicissitudes of their world around them.

The loss of Mr. Daly was actually a major one for the entire Red Hook community. Besides being a model for the children, he was a figure who projected a sense of calmness and security beyond the doors of the school. Every day he stationed himself at the corner outside the school at dismissal time. Tall and stately, with his arms outstretched to walk a preschooler or two across the street, he appeared as a beacon of almost religious status. It seemed like everyone in Red Hook knew Mr. Daly, even though he had a soft-spoken, deferential, gentle manner and was often described as quiet. With his death the stability he brought to the school was threatened, and the community lost a figure that at least represented stability to them.

In the days and weeks that followed I tried to understand my feelings of anger. Assuming that the rest of the faculty was as indignant as I was, I thoroughly expected that we would band together to take some action against this violence, but nothing developed.

In my head, I began reiterating the word *guns*. They were ubiquitous in this neighborhood. Although the kids wore school tee shirts imprinted with the school slogan "Peace Begins with Me" and their teachers tried earnestly to instill this feeling in the kids, they went home and lived in close quarters with guns and gun violence.

At first I felt helpless. To even think of attempting to stem the flow of guns into the hands of utterly irresponsible violent people seemed impossible. Then I did a little research and found an organization called Handgun Control in Washington, D.C. I called them, explaining my story, and they invited me to meet with them.

I hopped on a train and already felt invigorated and relieved now that I had the possibility to take some action. Interested and responsive, the people at Handgun Control referred me to Congressman Charles Schumer's office; he was then a New York representative and a strong advocate for gun control. After a few weeks they contacted me and asked if our school could send two student representatives to speak about our tragedy at the hearings for the Brady Bill. Two of our sixth graders did just that. Since it has been passed, there is strong evidence that the Brady Bill has been very effective in undermining gun-running operations that used to transport guns bought in the South up to the northern states for resale.

At the time, I didn't realize that I was channeling my anger toward positive action, and as time went by, my residual anger subsided. I resumed teaching RCCP every year, some years with more emphasis than others, depending on the needs of the children.

Typically our lessons are presented in a workshop format. The students participate in a number of interactive exercises, focusing on one of the themes of the program. Each lesson starts with a gathering to break the ice, making the comfort level high and allowing for more risk-taking during the lesson. As a prop, we often use a soft, squishy stuffed globe called a Hugg-a-Planet. Standing in a circle, we toss it to each child. When he or she catches it, everyone shouts that person's name. It is a very affirming game. Often we break down into smaller groups for more intimate discussions. The groups are formed by using random selection procedures. For example, the class might count off in a sequence of one to four repetitions. Then all the ones, twos, threes, and fours would form their own groups. It's amazing how many children can make new friends by following this simple strategy. While children are in groups, they might all be asked to respond to a question such as, "How have you been treated unfairly today, and how did it feel?" Each student in the small group would have an allotted time to share this experience with the other members of the group. Sometimes rules are imposed like "No interrupting." A small group member might be asked to retell someone else's response to the question to the larger group. A follow-up question might be, "What did you do about this unfairness?" Using this approach, children are placed in a position where they might get acquainted with people who might otherwise have remained unfamiliar. They are able to learn good listening skills, to contemplate the concept of fairness, to examine their feelings, to empathize with other, and to reflect on their assertiveness skills. There is also time during the lesson for the children to evaluate what they've learned. I've always found these lessons to be a dynamic way to practice living a moral and ethical life.

In addition to the workshops, for many years after Mr. Daly's death, I gathered the class regularly so they could share kind acts that they performed. We would list them on chart paper and call them "daily" deeds. Often I would tell the children personal stories of how Mr. Daly never let a day go by without doing many nice things for the people around him. Frequently he did them anonymously. One early morning he left brand-new dolls on the table in our housekeeping area; this was during a time when the school itself could not afford such things.

Gradually Mr. Daly's presence wasn't as strong in the school as the kids who knew him aged out and went on to other schools, as did many of the staff. Although I always operated on the premise that the themes of the program are important, my enthusiasm varied from year to year. As the school's atmosphere became even more temperate thanks to the strong and kind principals who succeeded him, I lolled into a moderate state of complacency.

But in the days after I received the news at my door of the 9/11 tragedy, I found myself having to deal with that intense outrage again. Whatever I could think of doing certainly wouldn't be enough. I had swelling emotions regarding how vitally important it was for the whole world to be able to recognize the differences among us and embrace everyone without bias and prejudice. What we were doing in the classroom no longer seemed enough, and I didn't see air-dropping RCCP pamphlets over the Middle East as the answer, either. Nonetheless, I carried on our lessons of peace with a renewed fervor.

With regularity, I kept on thinking of one particular lesson. I started deeply examining why I felt it was particularly relevant. It is a lesson that tells the story of Little Red Riding Hood from the wolf's point of view. It turns out that he had some valid complaints about Little Red Riding Hood since she was littering his home, the forest. In turn, I started reflecting on how things got to the point at which 9/11 happened. What does our country look like through other people's eyes? Do we need to change? Are we able to change? These were big questions for a classroom teacher to deal with. Even so, I always found the word *change* to be very challenging. I started thinking back to an education course I had taken years ago. It seems that we tend to be comfortable with our old ways of thinking. But when our old solutions to problems don't work, we are intuitively attracted to newer levels of understanding. We are both attracted to and resistant to change. In order to grow, we reconcile these conflicts, accept new solutions, and participate in the balancing act between the old and the new called *equilibration*.

As I stood in my doorway while pondering these notions, I had a practical task to achieve. I had to think of a phrase that represented an RCCP theme that reflected the work in our classroom and then put it on a banner to be placed around the outside of our classroom door. Fortunately both of the principals that succeeded Mr. Daly have been ardent supporters of RCCP, and each year the teachers are requested to do this.

For many successive years I displayed the phrase "We are a helping and caring community." This just didn't seem right anymore—I suppose I was ready for a change. In fact, while standing in the doorway, I realized that the continuity of our daily routines and practices was greatly disrupted and changed when I received tragic news more than once right in the spot where I was.

I didn't put anything up for a while. I thought a little bit about the significance of a doorway, particularly mine. It is a threshold, an entrance, a beginning. The dictionary calls a threshold "the lowest level of intensity at which a stimulus can be perceived as a turning point"—or maybe a tipping point. Maybe that was it. My doorway signified a place where change was possible. Now the task seemed clearer. Not only do I want to teach kids to see others' points of view, but also to look at themselves, both individually and collectively. Are changes needed? If so, make them happen! I could have posted "We take action" or "Do it," but by some other inspiration I simply wrote above my door, "Bother." I liked it; it had an edge to it. Basically it is a response to the question, "Why bother?" It is to answer a certain complacency that many of us had both before and even after 9/11, but personally it rings of a sense of urgency and profound responsibility. *Now* will always be the time to do something in order to make significant changes; later will not do.

The kids in my school are often on the receiving end of changes. Family members come and go. Families move and come back. Some of their lives are like rocking boats that seem to need plenty of ballast just to keep afloat. I used to think it healthiest to close my eyes at 3:00 since we as teachers can't create that stability for them outside the classroom. Now, though, after 9/11, everyone must be able to deal with change. Our sense of stability as a nation was so dramatically altered after this event. The issues of safety and protection rose in our minds; fear and vulnerability were dominant feelings. The concept of our country as a haven of security disintegrated with the tumbling of the towers. It was a strange feeling, but it was as if we were all passengers in that rocking boat.

The Red Hook project towers once bore a miniature resemblance to the Twin Towers that shadowed above them. As symbols, the twin towers could have evoked feelings of greatness, perhaps superiority. From our vantage point in Brooklyn, they almost had a parental presence. A parent, a leader, a principal, a tower can disappear in an instant.

Even though my reaction to the news of 9/11 was tempered with an understated confidence that we would be able to cope, it was worth it to try to understand the value of the things that we had done before. When our tangible symbols disappear, it helps to hold onto something as a replacement—a kind of temporary surrogate. Mary Manti took over as principal after Mr. Daly's death. With a deep understanding of our needs, she proceeded to organize a memorial, set up displays, and commission a mural replete with motivational quotations.

With a retrospective glance as I've posted my banner "bother" above my door, I've come to realize how we as a school have matured since the initial quotation was posted over a mural in our lobby. It was a quote from *The Prophet* by Kahlil Gibran. It said, "Would that I could be the peacemaker of your soul, that I might turn the discord and the rivalry of your elements into oneness and melody. But how shall I, unless you yourselves be also the peacemakers."

The mural illustrates adults, children, and babies gathering flowers and passing them to each other. They share the work and the fruits of their efforts. Over the years the mural has gone through some transfigurations. Now the Gibran quote has been replaced by a list of all of the community outreach programs with which the school is currently involved. It now bears the title Strength Through Collaboration.

Sometimes it helps to read the walls to see how far we've come. As a school, we chose to develop a philosophy of interconnectedness. In this respect we can even serve as a micro model for a more global philosophy. We didn't choose to buttress our fortification, but in our grieving and vulnerable state we sought to reach out and we now have a multitude of programs supporting us.

Not long after 9/11 we invited a number of schools across the nation to fly kites for peace. One bright balmy spring afternoon, dozens of our children sent up their creations to the breeze. Expressions of peace on earth rolled across the sky. It turned out to be an exhilarating experience.

With all of these good wishes for peace floating in my mind, I always return to my doorway. Ultimately it is behind that door where the work toward peace takes place. "Bother" forces me to bear the responsibility of teaching children that they have the power to redirect their negative feelings and use them as a motivating force to make changes in their lives.

For example, we worked on a couple of practical issues. The children created signs that we've posted in our windows asking the ever increasingly noisy truck traffic to consider our need to concentrate. The class also learned that some of our neighbors have formed an organization called GAGS (Groups Against Garbage Sites) in order to stop the city from locating a noxious garbage transfer station in Red Hook.

Most of all, though, "bother" insistently beckons me to remember to always be alive to feelings and needs. This sounds so basic and essential, but it is easy to revert to quotidian habits and miss the synaptic connections that can be made simply in sharing a glance with another person. I try very hard to help my children read their internal feelings out loud. They need to be more conscious of themselves in order to communicate their feelings and needs in the first place. Near the doorway I have displayed an emotions poster that charts photographs of children with different facial expressions and the word for that feeling. How simple but astonishingly effective it has been in helping the children verbalize what is in their hearts.

We are currently making our own photographic display. The camera has caught us amazed, proud, sympathetic and enthusiastic, as well as surprised, edgy, and wary.

At the end of each day the children take a moment to reflect on one feeling they have had during the course of the day. One little boy who has had a particularly hard time getting along with the others said that he felt proud that he helped clean the dramatic play area.

Discerning our genuine feelings and articulating them, as well as voicing our needs and our requests in a way that evokes compassion and a willingness to connect, is like learning a new language—and it is perhaps even harder for adults than it is for children. It is hard for a teacher to shed the armor of authority and single-minded purpose, especially when words like *standards* and *accountability* are part of our daily lexicon. Yet if teachers do want to serve as models representing connectedness and interdependence, it is important that we communicate in the same manner with which we teach our children to communicate.

In the post–9/11 period it has become clear that dichotomous cultures are confronting each other more with a sense of resoluteness than of resolution. It seems to me that the simpler route is to hold your ground unswervingly when forces are acting upon you. It seems like the harder and more complex task, but possibly the more rewarding one, is to merge with those forces so that there is mutual satisfaction. This way intuitively seems more mature, more evolved, and more lasting.

Over 20 years, I've received many sad and often shocking stories in my doorway, and they do serve to galvanize positive action for behavioral change. But these kinds of changes take place over time. Evolution is subtle, slow, and sometimes unnoticeable. One morning this spring, as I stood in the doorway greeting the children upon arrival, one mother had not one but two children in tow. She had recently accepted a foster child into her family, and she, too, would now be a member of our class. After the children settled into their seats, the mother stood back and explained that there had been some difficulties that she was dealing with during this adjustment period. She spoke about how she was encouraging the children to use their words to settle their disputes and to try to see each other's point of view. She was speaking the language of RCCP. This particular parent grew up in a large, well-known Red Hook family that had over the years established a reputation for being contentious and combative. Taking a look again, I realized that over time in an unperceived way, changes were actually taking place in the community. Positive attitudes were taking root.

This exchange was such a motivating reward for me. It has supported the need I feel to *bother* to awaken in my students feelings of empathy, compassion, respect, and a desire for resolution. I have to *bother* to help my students develop ways to go about effecting change in their lives based on their needs. Hopefully by making changes, future crises will be avoided. Hopefully more people will be convinced that *to bother* is a good thing—to put forth that extra energy—to push. When people knock on my door with inquiries about the sign, I usually answer that I'm glad that they "bothered."

Sixteen

Unknowingness

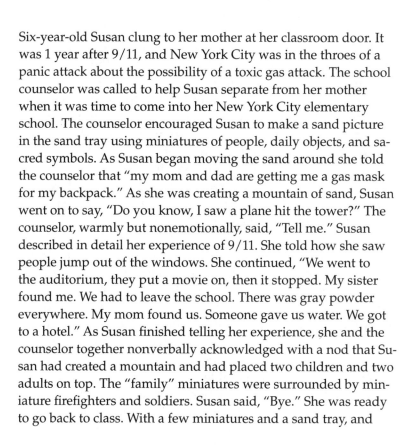

ROSALIND WINTER

Six-year-old Susan clung to her mother at her classroom door. It was 1 year after 9/11, and New York City was in the throes of a panic attack about the possibility of a toxic gas attack. The school counselor was called to help Susan separate from her mother when it was time to come into her New York City elementary school. The counselor encouraged Susan to make a sand picture in the sand tray using miniatures of people, daily objects, and sacred symbols. As Susan began moving the sand around she told the counselor that "my mom and dad are getting me a gas mask for my backpack." As she was creating a mountain of sand, Susan went on to say, "Do you know, I saw a plane hit the tower?" The counselor, warmly but nonemotionally, said, "Tell me." Susan described in detail her experience of 9/11. She told how she saw people jump out of the windows. She continued, "We went to the auditorium, they put a movie on, then it stopped. My sister found me. We had to leave the school. There was gray powder everywhere. My mom found us. Someone gave us water. We got to a hotel." As Susan finished telling her experience, she and the counselor together nonverbally acknowledged with a nod that Susan had created a mountain and had placed two children and two adults on top. The "family" miniatures were surrounded by miniature firefighters and soldiers. Susan said, "Bye." She was ready to go back to class. With a few miniatures and a sand tray, and a caring and trained staff member, Susan's emotions of anxiety and fear were expressed, contained, witnessed by a trusted other, and symbolically transformed. She created an internal reality that settled her emotions and allowed her to return to her classroom.

MY CAREER AS A Jungian psychoanalyst, working primarily in my office and teaching analysis and sandplay therapy to therapists, suddenly changed on 9/11. It brought me back to the schools, exactly where I had started some 30 years before as a middle school teacher. On that Tuesday morning, I was plunged into a state of what I call "unknowingness." Unusual circumstances—a doctor's appointment in the midst of my workday—had put me in my car at 10:00 A.M. where I learned about the World Trade Center attacks over the radio. Located just 12 miles due west of the Empire State Building on the "first mountain" outside of New York City, our New Jersey town of Montclair looked to the World Trade Towers for a point of orientation. Attacked, the distance between us and them collapsed. When I looked east, I saw them on fire. A doctor's appointment made no sense at all.

Without thought, without planning, totally driven by instinct, I found myself parking illegally in front of my town's local high school where I had been involved as a parent, a volunteer, a teacher trainer, and consulting psychotherapist for many years. I heard my own voice say, "Go in." The principal, in the midst of the chaos, noted my presence, asking, "Can you do something? I have all the kids whose parents work in the World Trade Center area in the library." Nodding yes, I proceeded more or less unconsciously up the stairs to the library.

The library has double glass doors. From the outside, I saw 60 to 70 kids centered on a TV. Sixty to 70 kids who did not know if their parents were alive. The enormity of the situation drew me back into consciousness. I took a deep breath and entered the space of unknowingness, where a sense of control is suspended, where our markers of predictability and security have been removed. In profound moments of unknowingness like on 9/11, the tension of not knowing is almost unbearable.

In the library, the atmosphere was intense, as though no one was breathing. Breathing would have meant we were in our bodies and experiencing our feelings. It was impossible to take in the reality of the moment. Yet in this state of contained panic, school administrators were doing their jobs, they were on the phones, desperately trying to locate the students' family members. The kids were mostly focused on the TV, trying to figure out what was happening. For the next hours, I emotionally and physically held kids, some of whom I had never met before, some of whom I had known since they were 4, in a state of not knowing.

A young woman sat at a round library table all alone, studying SAT words. She had just arrived from Taiwan. It was her 2nd day in the school. When I approached her, she told me that her father worked on the 103rd floor of the first tower that was struck. She was sure he was dead. In a singsong voice, she told me he would not want her to be sad. We talked about the possibility of not really knowing whether he was dead or alive. Could we wait and see? I suggested. It was easier for her to imagine that he was dead than to tolerate not knowing.

I noticed a group of girls, all cousins, wailing in a corner. They were unable to speak. "Can you pray?" I offered. Yes. They began praying, saying over and over again that they knew, they just knew their aunt was alive. . . . But?

A lanky 17-year-old boy, who looked vaguely familiar—he must have played lacrosse with my son—was sitting alone, and agitated, throwing pencils at the table. He looked in the opposite direction as I approached him. Intuitively, I knew he was not going to speak with me. I asked, "Does anyone know who his friends are? Could you find them?" "Yes." Before a friend was found, his younger sister came into the library crying hysterically. He pulled himself together for her. When the librarian reached their mother on the phone a few moments later, they walked out hugging.

Then, most terrifying to me, I noticed my son's best friend across the room rigidly standing in front of the TV. My son appeared. After a quick hug, I asked, "What's with Alyssa?" "Her Dad's on a plane," he said, "and there are still five planes unaccounted for." My heart sank. I held Alyssa as she cried. I struggled to remind her that we did not know, we just did not know yet about her Dad. In addition, her good friend Linda had just heard moments before from her mother that her aunt was pulled out of the rubble dead. How do I hold a different possibility for Alyssa? She was losing it. I had Alyssa call her mother every 15 minutes. It gave her a focus.

We all held Linda, cried with her, and Alyssa kept phoning Mom. Her father was not on a missile plane. He had landed safely in Chicago.

A voice summoned the girl from Taiwan to the office over the loudspeaker. *Oh my god, what does this mean?* I walked her downstairs. Her mother was standing at the main office sobbing; in her broken English it was difficult to understand what she was saying. Was the girl's Dad alive or not? He had been getting a cup of coffee on the 30th floor. He was safe. Unknowingness resolved for the moment.

Being able to hold this unbearable tension, the tension of the opposites—of life or death, safe or not safe—and thus staying in unknowingness was a profound struggle for all of us. Timeless literature and spiritual beliefs offer support and direction in crisis. As I worked with myself to stay calm and be totally present in the situation, a quotation from the *I Ching*, number 5, "Hsii" (Waiting or Nourishment), came to mind. "It is only when we have the courage to face things exactly as they are, without any sort of self-deception or illusion, that a light will develop out of events, by which the path to success may be recognized."[1]

In my practice as a therapist, holding the tension of opposites is a daily work, one in which one waits, with a faith that the transcendent, the "light" that will illumine, will appear. My practice and training as an analyst had developed my mind and heart to wait, to be in unknowingness, to have the courage to face things exactly as they are, and to trust "that a light will develop out of events." Yet never have I felt so put to the test, so pushed to the very edge of my own limits, than on Tuesday, September 11th, when the opposites were life and death.

Since September 11th, we have come to consciously live in a place of unknowingness. Of course, in reality even before 9/11, we never knew what would or could happen to us at any given time. (An important note here is that much of the world and some minority groups within the United States had lived with this reality for some time.) But on that date we became aware as a collective society that we could not guarantee our children's or our own safety. This produces anxiety.

---

1. Reinhard Wilhelm, *The I Ching or Book of Changes.* New York: Bolligen Foundation and Princeton University Press, 1968, p. 25.

*   *   *

While I was concerned about individual students in the library, I was also aware of the level of tension and chaos we were all experiencing. When I returned home after the 1st day, overwhelmed and unable to sit still, I went to my e-mail. I found messages and help from my colleagues from all over the country, the members of the Sandplay Therapists of America (STA). Sandplay therapists work with clients, using a standard box of sand and miniatures, to activate the psyche's own natural healing process. The sandbox itself is a standardized 21-by-30-inch wooden box filled about halfway with soft sand. The bottom is painted blue, to represent water. The miniatures are culturally, ethnically, and spiritually diverse figures and symbols, usually 5 inches or less in height, and represent both daily and spiritual life.

People using sandplay are encouraged to allow themselves to deeply settle into their own sense of reality and allow themselves to use the miniatures to express their internal worlds. This activity begins the process of working through deep issues. Additionally, in my role as a therapist, I have seen that during moments of intense emotion or trauma, a person's psyche will express his or her most urgent and immediate feelings and experiences. When using the miniatures and the sand, both in working through deep issues or expressing concretely and/or symbolically current trauma, the sandplayer feels soothed and contained. And by working kinesthetically with both emotions and images, the right side of the brain is accessed and worked with. Current neurological research shows that to heal trauma it is necessary to process the trauma information that the right brain carries. Sandplay facilitates healing on this level.

Over and over again, there were e-mails asking what I needed, people asking if they could be of help. I thought to myself there must be a way to take some of the elements of sandplay therapy and use them in this crisis. I knew that sand and the miniatures could be used to express emotions and experiences that were impossible to put into words. Sand and miniatures could be part of the process of accessing, expressing, and containing disturbing emotions. Because sandplay does not require any particular skill, people are comfortable giving it a try. It is hard to make a mistake using sand

and miniatures. Could the Sandplay Therapists of America actually provide enough miniatures, representing the different aspects of life in a multicultural way, and several sandboxes to allow its benefits to be shared in my community? To my astonishment, the STA members responded with a resounding effort.

Within 2 weeks, over 2,000 miniatures inhabited my dining room. All of the miniatures were given in a spirit of healing; many came with notes containing moving stories. Each package felt as if it had been wrapped with love. When I realized something was missing, I would send an e-mail and someone would send me what was needed. Before long, I had five complete sets of miniatures. I placed the first sand trays and miniatures in the Montclair High School and Montclair's town drop-in counseling center.

People coming in for counseling at the town's drop-in center created an ongoing collective expression of the terror and horror of September 11th. Police, firefighters, and various municipal employees also used the sand tray. I used the sandplay tray and miniatures with volunteer therapists, encouraging each person to choose a miniature and experience its symbolic value of their experience of 9/11. I offered them a brief training for the adaptation of sandplay therapy that I was creating in the moment. Although we were using the basic materials of sandplay therapy, we were not focused on deep-seated issues or long-term treatment. Rather, the goal was to give people an opportunity to immediately respond in a healing manner to a current trauma. I wanted to use the power of symbols to hold, contain and transform an unbearable situation.

Another sand tray and miniatures were placed at Montclair High School. As we were setting up the sand tray and miniatures in a walk-in closet in the hallway between the vice principal's and nurse's offices, the vice principal asked a boy who was walking by whether he would like to place something in the sand. The boy chose a figure of Jesus and an angel and set them both in the center of the tray. This expression touched us. What had this young man done? He had created an image, using the symbol of Jesus that resonated deeply within us all.

As a part of the school district's response to 9/11, a few days later an in-service processing training for all of the child-study teams, psychologists, and student assistant-counselors was scheduled. It was my job to help process the events of September 11th.

We all acknowledged how difficult it was to help people when we ourselves were so anxious. We needed to be able to contain our own responses so that we could be of use to our students. To help us help ourselves, each person selected an image that reflected his or her personal experience of the terrorist attack. Each participant placed her or his miniatures in a sand tray. It was an incredibly moving experience. We saw towers turned over, Superman toppled over, babies buried, skeletons half buried, and ambulances and police vehicles all around. And somehow, as horrible as the image was, we all felt deeply touched and more relaxed. We could go forward with our day a little more clearly. Our emotions had been expressed, contained, and seen by ourselves, as well as being witnessed by others.

Fortunately, at that time, I also had the opportunity to speak about the theoretical value of symbols and explain how trauma research has found that images are one of the key methods of integrating traumatic experiences. During a traumatic experience the left brain, which is responsible for language and rational thought, shuts down. The right brain manages the trauma by splitting it into fragments. The bits of the trauma are *refound* in images, intense emotions, and body sensations. One of the best ways to help a person process the trauma is to help her or him access and express the images and emotions of her or his experience. When these are not expressed either verbally or nonverbally, they manifest as symptoms in the body. Part of our nature as human beings is that we are able to *think symbolically*. Our unconscious can tap into a vast reservoir of images and symbols that express what we in our more conscious selves cannot express verbally. When images hold deep meaning, they become symbols. A symbol evokes more than it can possibly mean literally and concretely. It points to a meaning, yet leaves a certain openness, a mystery, an unknown that gives us room to project our personal associations into. Jesus and other collective religious symbols were frequently called upon to bring solace during those moments following 9/11.

For those counselors who were interested, I offered to assist in setting up sand tray and miniature collections in their schools. People were fascinated by the offer. They were curious about an organization that would provide these materials for them and their students for free. I trusted that once people experienced the power of working with symbols/miniatures in a contained space, they would want to use it to help their students. During the processing session, a social worker asked on the spot for a setup and directions for using the materials.

As I am told, a nurse from one of the elementary schools in Manhattan was visiting a nurse in the freshman building, saw the sand tray set up, and became curious. She told her school social worker about it as well as a group of nurses at their next meeting. The school social worker went over to the high school and visited the sand tray. She then called me and asked if she could have a setup. Another social worker saw it at her school and called me as well. In time, a grassroots movement developed, leading to the placement of sand trays and miniatures in all of the schools in town. Within a month the head of Pupil Services called and said that the staff would like some training in the sand tray and miniatures. At that time I realized I needed a name for this adaptation of sandplay and called it Symbol Formation.

I was invited by the head of CASEL's (the Collaborative for Academic, Social, and Emotional Learning) satellite program at Ground Zero to share the Symbol Formation experience of the Montclair school system. The staff of District 2, the Ground Zero school district, immediately saw the potential benefits for their students. Initially, they were particularly concerned that those with a more nonverbal culture were not having their needs met with the more standard debriefing techniques. Within a year, sand trays and miniatures were set up in 17 schools. District 2's staff became so impressed with sandplay's value in dealing with 9/11 experiences, for both its nonverbal and verbal children that they requested training to deepen their understanding of symbol formation and the potential of sandplay therapy. They saw it as a way to help district children also deal with all of the ordinary traumas and anxieties that they experience in daily lives.

It feels like, in a split second, my professional life changed. I had started in the classroom as a middle school teacher and eventually served on the faculty of a college's education department. Now I was walking the halls of schools again. I had come full circle. I had the opportunity to bring my psychological knowledge and experience back to the classroom, where at that earlier time I had worried about what kept children from learning. I was thrilled to be deeply engaged with real-life issues as they face our children in the moment. Living with unknowingness has always been a fact, a fundamental reality of life. For me, creating an adaptation of a psychological process that could work in a school was profoundly satisfying. I intuitively knew then, based on my understanding of the symbolic process and the capacity of the psyche to hold feelings in images, that it was possible to express and to contain intense emotions and go on with the necessary tasks at hand.

We, even as caring and compassionate adults, cannot remove the anxiety in our society. However, we can offer opportunities for ourselves and our children to access, express, and contain those most difficult emotions so we can go on with daily life. When we use miniatures to express raw emotions, we move into a symbolically expressive process. This process actually helps us distance ourselves from the emotions, and create safer internal worlds. This type of symbol formation leads to a stronger and more resilient person, who can better tolerate life's unpredictabilities.

Yet I have not given up my life as a psychoanalyst. It is too important to me as well. Rather, I am holding the tension of two different professional lives. I do not know how this will resolve itself. I probably cannot go on doing both forever; it is too physically demanding. So I live in a state of unknowingness, waiting for the glimmer, the new direction to emerge.

Seventeen

A Teacher's Journal

STACEY FELL-EISENKRAFT

September 11, 2001

THE 4TH DAY OF SCHOOL in New York City's Chinatown. I greeted my sleepy, lumbering eighth graders and pointed to the directions on the board: "Please line yourselves up in the order of your birthdays. This task must be accomplished without talking." After a few groans and some grumbling about "more community building exercises," the students began to push back their chairs and stand up.

BOOM! The noise from an explosion filled the classroom. We collectively froze as the windowpanes rattled and the floor beneath us gave a quick shudder. The students immediately looked toward me, and I scrambled to think of something reassuring to say. Phillip took advantage of my pause to joke, "Wow! The gods must be angry today." His humor relaxed the other students, and they resumed their emphatic gesturing and pointing. Phillip's simple joke haunts me now. Later that day, I jotted it down along with the following question: *How could we have known that at that very same moment we innocently laughed at Phillip's joke, thousands of people, just one half of a mile to the west of us, were experiencing such unfathomable terror?*

I did not notice Lauren, a first-year humanities teacher whose classroom is directly across from mine, until she grabbed my shoulders to get my attention. Her face had drained of its color, and her lips were trembling as she said in a strained voice, "One of the Twin Towers just exploded!" Before I could react, Lauren spun around and ran back into her classroom. Over the shuffle of my students, I was immediately aware of the chaos that had erupted in Lauren's room. Her students were pressed to the windows, climbing on chairs, climbing on desks, pointing and shouting, screaming. Other students remained in their seats where they buried their heads in their arms. The girl who was sitting closest to the door was hunched over her desk, her shoulders heaving as she sobbed.

Shocked by the state of the students in Lauren's classroom, I glanced briefly at the three student teachers, Robert, Elizabeth, and Lynne, who happened to be visiting my classroom on this day. "Just a minute," I motioned to them before crossing the hallway to Lauren's room. Lauren was standing by the doorway, her arm around the shoulders of a girl who was shaking her head violently as Lauren pleaded with her to stay in the classroom. I made my way to the large wall of windows that looked directly out on the World Trade Center.

Lauren's students grabbed at my arms, pulling and pushing me toward the windows, screaming for me to look, to see what they were seeing. I stumbled back at the sight of the enormous gaping hole glowing with red-orange flames. Thick, black smoke poured out from the unnatural opening in the side of the building. I squeezed my eyes shut, feeling physically ill as I thought of the people who must have been inside the building.

The students were shouting a strange mix of questions at Lauren and me: "Is this real? Is this a movie? Why are you crying? Do you think it's a bomb? Are people dying?" As I tried to respond to the students, I spotted Robert, Elizabeth, and Lynne standing uncertainly in the doorway, some of my students hovering behind them. Lauren and I quickly conferred. There was no way we could continue our lessons and decided instead to turn on the radio and listen together with our two classes.

The student teachers tried to convince the students to take a seat while Lauren and I fiddled with the radio, searching for a news station. Just as they were starting to succeed at ungluing the students from the windows, a new round of screaming erupted among the students. "I saw a plane! I saw a plane! Look! The other Twin Tower is on fire!" Tim was holding the sides of his head, shaking in disbelief at what he had just seen. Other students nodded numbly, agreeing that a plane had just careened into the second tower. More students broke into tears and begged to go to the office to use the phones.

Lauren found a news station and turned up the volume. The students drifted away from the windows to crowd around the radio. Many of the students, who speak English as a second language, struggled to follow the rapid speech of the newscasters. We regularly turned the volume down to highlight bits of information and to answer their questions. We all kept our gazes trained on the scene of disaster just outside the classroom windows, trying to make sense of the broadcast.

"Look at the things falling, Stacey," Mae said quietly, pointing to the burning towers.

The other students joined in quickly: "People—people are jumping!" There were pained cries, and most of the students turned quickly from the windows, too afraid to face such a horrific scene.

"Why don't they wait?" Chris asked out loud. "Aren't people gonna save them?"

"We're watching people die," one of Lauren's students whispered, squeezing her eyes shut.

"The towers must be falling," Amy reasoned. "Stacey, do you think they'll fall down? Will they fall down on us?" With Amy's urgent questions, fresh panic swept through the classroom.

Another group of kids observed the flood of pedestrians moving through the streets below our school. People were crossing the Manhattan Bridge by foot, glancing back again and again as they exited the city. "Why are they leaving? Are we going to get bombed?" Jose asked. Students demanded to know why we were still in our building. How could it be safe to stay in Chinatown when it appeared that everyone else in the city was leaving? Diana accused the school of "keeping us hostage."

I have never been at such a loss to answer my students' questions. I could only think to myself:

This situation is horribly, horribly wrong. It is wrong that my students are watching this tragedy unfold before them. It is wrong that more than 45 minutes has passed since the first explosion, and there have not been any kind of announcements

or directives for the teachers. It is wrong that we can only
watch the mass exodus and wonder if we should join them. It
is wrong that smoke and debris are seeping into our building,
and we have no means to comfort the students.

I asked the three student teachers to go downstairs to the main
office to speak with the administration. Lynne quickly returned to
the classroom to tell me that it was extremely chaotic in the office,
that the lobby and office were packed with hysterical parents, and
all of the phones in the office were ringing. The principal had asked
that Lynne, Elizabeth, and Robert stay there to help. Later that day,
Elizabeth wrote the following about her experience that morning:

> Parents were already flooding into the school to find their chil-
> dren and take them home. Pamela Chin, the assistant principal,
> approached me. If I felt unsafe or if I was worried about friends
> or family, she told me, I should certainly leave. "But if you can
> stay," she said, "We can use you."
> I stayed. I answered phones and talked to parents. "Every-
> one's okay here," I would say. "We are all safe." Some parents
> cried or worried about what would happen if they couldn't
> get to the school by 3 P.M. I felt the second tower fall, but I kept
> on answering phones. It was frustrating not to hear the radio
> or even to run outside and look, but I was grateful to be doing
> something useful, even if it was just telling mothers and fathers
> in a calm and steady voice that their children were safe.[1]

At a complete loss for how to continue the day, Lauren and I pulled
down the window shades and encouraged the students to open their
journals or sketchbooks. Writing, as well as painting and sketching,
became our media for addressing the overwhelming fear, anger,
and sadness that had settled over the classroom.

September 17, 2001

It has been 5 days since we have seen each other. I was shocked
to come face-to-face with the Red Cross shelter when I entered

---

1. M. Shaw. (2002, March). "What Does It Mean to Be a Teacher When the Walls Are Falling Down?" *English Journal*, pp. 15–17.

the building this morning. I had wrongly assumed that if school was reopening, it was because the Red Cross shelter was either not needed or was relocating. The lobby of our school has become a communications center, as an octopus of wires and cables snake around the showcases. The gymnasium is a field of cots, and the lights are perpetually dimmed for the sleeping rescue workers. A steady stream of volunteers and doctors swings through the front doors of the school.

The other public schools, which resumed classes on Thursday or Friday, had delayed openings to allow the faculty to meet before the students arrived. The schools in Chinatown and Lower Manhattan—the ones that stayed closed the longest and whose students and teachers feasibly suffered the most trauma on September 11th—did not have a delayed opening. How does that make any sense?

Our administrators personally called everybody on staff last night—nearly 100 people—to request that we come to work earlier than usual to meet for 30 minutes before the first bell. Most of the faculty showed up for the meeting, but it was far too rushed; there was no way for it to be about bringing the community together. As the first bell approached, the staff became increasingly anxious about facing the students again.

A colleague stood up to suggest, "Of course we all need to talk to our children about what happened, but we should stick with the factual information and not let our responses become emotional. The students are probably as worried as we are. If they ask us whether or not we feel safe, our job is to reassure them that you do." *Not let my response become emotional??* Ironic tears sprang to my eyes as I turned her suggestion around in my head.

I was still processing the faculty meeting when the first bell rang. The students seemed hostile when they walked through the classroom doors. They demanded to know why the Red Cross "took over" the school and complained that it makes them feel like Chinatown has been bombed. The talk quickly switched over to what the United States should do to get "them" back. Many of the students talked about "World War III." Phillip entered the classroom holding the biggest American flag I have ever seen, and asked me where he should hang it. Eileen shouted, "Yeah, we have to show them that these colors don't bleed!"

I am completely taken aback by Phillip's flag and Eileen's comment. In this time after the attack, it has been difficult for me to adjust to the wave of patriotism that has washed over the nation. Everywhere I turn, I come face-to-face with yet another American flag. I wonder about the psychology at work behind the flag-waving and the way this sweep of nationalism seems to discourage people from taking a critical perspective to the events. I had naively thought that I would not find this same patriotic display in Chinatown, because our students do not tend to identify as American. Normally, when I ask students about their nationality, most students agree that they are Chinese, regardless of their actual citizenship.

Yet in light of September 11th's events, my students are suddenly more American than ever. This phenomenon perplexes me. My students, who are both people of color and recent immigrants, all live below the national poverty line. Their life stories speak to the complex ways in which issues of race, gender, and class intersect. They hold fast to their Chinese identities because they are proud of their heritage but also because there doesn't always seem to be room for them in the taken-for-granted definition of the word *American*. Overnight, this appears to have changed. The "Attack on America" (CBS News) seems to have presented my students with the opportunity to become instantly American, in a way that citizenship papers and green cards do not. The recipe for being a proud American is relatively simple these days, and my students are pleased with themselves for figuring it out.

At the same time, for some of my students, this crisis has forced them to acknowledge the different parts of their identity. As Lily wrote in her journal, "Here in New York, it's my hometown, even though I was born in China." Last Tuesday, when Lily read from her journal in class, several students agreed that the tragedy made them realize they do "feel American" even if they always think of themselves as Chinese. I wonder how the attack on New York will continue to affect the ways the students define themselves and the ways they negotiate the different worlds in which they live.

September 20, 2001

The students walked into first period talking about "them" again: how we should "get them back" or "bomb them" or "get revenge on them." James made me cringe when he repeated a particularly obnoxious *New York Post* headline.

"Welcome back. We really need to talk," I told the students, motioning them over to the discussion area. It is not comfortable or practical to squeeze a class of 30 eighth graders onto a rug, but it is the only way we can see each other's faces and hear soft voices, absolutely necessary for having a class discussion. The students settled on to the rug, and I invited them to talk about what was on their minds. The students' questions centered on the threat of war and how to hold the terrorists responsible. I noticed that most of the students were using *Afghanistan* and *Muslims* and *Osama bin Laden* and *the terrorists* interchangeably. It seemed obvious to me that we needed to start by clarifying the meaning of the terms and labels that have seeped into all of our vocabularies over the past week.

I started the discussion tentatively, asking the students if we could hold all of the Afghani/Muslim people responsible for one person or one group's beliefs and actions. Amid the grumbles, my student teacher, Robert, jumped into the discussion and reminded the students that White, Christian men were responsible for the last major terrorist attack to take place in the United States (Oklahoma City). "Did we blame all of the Americans who happen to share these men's ethnicity and religion?" Robert asked the students.

"Muslims are different from Christians," David blurted out, not answering Robert's question but representing a good portion of the students' thinking. There were murmurs as some students added to David's statement and others asked what "Muslim" meant. I listened intently and scribbled furious notes, anticipating how much we have to learn together right now.

"And Americans were angry when that happened," James replied, "but the Muslim people right now are cheering." I know the images to which James was referring, because I have seen them over and over on the news, as well. In fact, when the television stations first aired the footage, I could not help but think that such images would be an effective tool for gaining most Americans' approval in case President Bush takes military action.

The task before me seems overwhelming. I need to teach my students to take a critical lens to the news coverage: Why were those images of cheering Pakistanis aired? What images weren't aired? I need to show them the alternatives to military action, ideas that are not making the front page of *The New York Post* or the news desk of the television channels. I need to push them to examine the prejudiced beliefs that are circulating and the kinds of bias that they, themselves, hold.

September 21, 2001

I pointed to the Albert Einstein quote I had copied on the board: "Peace cannot be kept by force. It can only be achieved by understanding." I told the students I was bringing Einstein's words to their attention because they might offer us new ways of thinking about the current events. I asked the students if they had thought about the United States using something other than military action in response to the September 11th events. The students broke into small groups to share their thoughts and then reported back. Eileen spoke for her group: "It's not fair that the terrorists can make Americans suffer. We should make the countries they live in feel the same thing." Some of the other groups reported similar responses. The classroom air already felt thick with vengeance when Chris stated smugly, "Well, it's an eye for an eye."

On the brighter side, I did note one important change today; the students spoke of *the terrorists* or of *Osama bin Laden*, rather than of *Muslims* or of *Afghanis*. When Amy slipped and started to say, "If Afghanistan hadn't bombed us . . ." the other students quickly corrected her. Robert and I must have explained this in a way that made some sense to them yesterday. However, there is still a lot of talk about how the people who live in Afghanistan with Osama bin Laden deserve to suffer the way we are. It is hard for me to listen to this talk—they sound so bloodthirsty! I have to keep reminding myself that, for one thing, they are echoing the sensationalist media by which they are surrounded. I also have to remind myself that they are hurting right now. My students are seething with anger and that makes them want to lash out—I understand this feeling, because personally, I am having to find ways to work through these same feelings of grief and anger. Yet somehow I am doing this without calling for violence. What process have I had to go through and do I continue to go through to arrive at this place? How can I push on my students' thinking? This is where I need to start our next class.

September 22, 2001

"Look, Einstein's still here." Matthew pointed to the board as the students drifted into class this morning.

We returned to our discussion on the rug, and I found myself speaking as earnestly as I ever have to my students: "I want you to listen carefully to something I've been thinking about since we met yesterday." I scanned their faces, seeing the way they reflected my own seriousness. "Yesterday, I could hear how angry many of you are. Something really terrible has happened just down the block from us, and now we are all suffering. I want you to know that I feel just as angry as you do." As I spoke, some of the "teacher tension," which I so often hold, seemed to fall away; I was appealing to the students, showing them that I—another human being, not just the teacher or the adult in the room—do share their feelings. I waited, leaving some space, and a few of the students tried to describe the depth of their anger. "This is the most scary thing that ever happened to me and my family—I'm pissed," Diana summed up.

When the student talk returned to a call for vengeance, I raised the following issue: "If we know how badly this hurts, do we want other people and their families to experience the same kind of pain we are going through? Will bombing Afghanistan lead to peace?" Again, the students formed small groups and debated the question.

The class came back together, and James quickly informed the class, "If the bombers care about their country, they shouldn't have done this to us."

David reported for his group: "Well, my group thinks there are people who are innocent who live in the same country as Osama bin Laden." Robert and I immediately made eye contact; we were both aware that the tone of David's comment had definitely departed from what had been said in class up until this point.

Misty quickly responded, "Yeah, since innocent people live there, I don't think the country should get bombs."

"Maybe if you don't bomb, they won't stop," insisted Jose.

"Maybe bombs won't stop it," Cindy spoke up for the first time during a class discussion. She nodded toward the Einstein quote and geared up to continue her comments. Robert and I leaned forward in anticipation.

At that moment, a fire drill interrupted our discussion and ate up the remainder of the class period. There has been at least one drill, sometimes two, every week since the World Trade Center attack! (We normally have one drill every 6 weeks.) But, for the first time this week, I feel a bit of hope, a bit of faith in the possibilities of our classroom talk. I see some of my students shifting, trying out different perspectives.

October 7, 2001

We are spending a lot of time pouring over the newspapers together. My students often complain that they are caught "in between," as they have forgotten so many Chinese characters that reading is laborious in their native language. At the same time, their lack of fluency in English causes them to struggle with reading in English, as well. Yet my students' families usually expect them to keep the whole family informed of current events and school happenings, because they are the generation who is being educated in the United States. In turn, my students rely on me to explain a range of matters that they and their families find confusing. Often students linger after class to show me rental agreements, jury duty notices, or household bills that their parents have handed to them.

The first few days after the attack were especially difficult on our students and their families, because they were completely disconnected from all of their usual means of gathering information. None of the Chinese newspapers, which many of my students' parents read, were making it down to Chinatown, and without teachers to explain the English news, many of the students and their families felt especially isolated.

Overnight, our school was transformed into a Red Cross shelter, a place where the rescue workers could go between their shifts for showers, meals, and rest. The shelter was also designated as a place where the Chinatown community could go for assistance. All across the school building, the Red Cross had posted "Disaster Relief" signs. My students have recounted similar stories of their parents entering the school in search of phones or information about assistance, only to find that the relief workers had not been supplied with translators. Colleen wrote in her journal: "It was confuse for my mom. It's good for us that the teachers were telling people where to go and what to do." Some of the bilingual administrators and teachers, who understand what an important link the school provides between the community and the city, showed up at the school during the 5 days it was closed to address the needs of the school's families.

Over and over again, as we have flipped through the newspapers, which seem to be taking over our classroom, my students and I have noticed that most of the families profiled in the news do not represent the experiences of those who live in Chinatown. Questions of equity and justice bubble to the surface when Tony reads about a family who has relocated to their New Hampshire vacation home out of fear that the smoke and fumes will make their children sick. Tony notices how near to his own apartment the address of the family's abandoned residence is. "Who decides where it's safe to live?" Misty asks me after class.

Weeks after the attack, many of my students continue to live without electricity, hot water, and phones. I have heard several students complain that their tap water is running "more brown" than usual. They wonder if Chinatown will ever be serviced and express acute awareness of the imbalance that existed long before this attack. "Nobody ever cares about Chinatown. We'll be the last place they fix—if anybody remembers," Diana lamented when her peers demanded to know when Verizon planned to fix the school's phone lines.

The lack of phone service is definitely taking its toll on the community. Many restaurants—the same restaurants that employ most of my students' working relatives—rely on takeout orders and banquet reservations. Without phones, business in Chinatown's restaurants has declined dramatically, and many employees are losing their jobs.

I have heard Verizon's spokesman say on Channel 2's news that he is aware of the economic impact the lack of phone service has on Chinatown, and he encourages all Chinatown businesses to keep reporting phone outages. However, as my students point out, many of the neighborhood's business owners do not speak English and do not know whom to call for help. The students have also complained that the mobile Verizon trucks around Chinatown are only free for the first 3 minutes. The calls that the students are helping their families make to welfare, unemployment, and other assistance offices take much longer than 3 minutes. My students are showing signs of stress and exhaustion as their families face even tougher financial issues than usual. All this to contend with, and their parents are relying on them more than ever to help navigate this mess.

October 9, 2001

Robert and I are really trying to push the students to take a critical lens to the media surrounding them. Today we brought in five news articles, all from different newspapers and magazines. In groups, the students examined the five articles. We asked them to analyze the articles, headlines and pictures. The focus questions for their analysis was: "If you only read this article, how would you think that people in Afghanistan and nearby countries are reacting to the action that the United States is taking? How does it change or challenge your understanding when you read the articles against one another?"

It was a really difficult task! Matthew eventually asked if the articles were written from different perspectives. His question gave way to some talk about what perspectives are included when students learn about history from a particular textbook and who gets to make such decisions. James was immediately bothered by the question, because he seems determined to hold on to the notion that popular news sources and textbook history are truth. He announced that my class gives him a headache, because I "always have to make everything too complicated." When we returned to our reading of the articles, James read halfway through the article about Afghanis, who are fleeing from their homes, in anticipation of American bombs, before he pushed it away, mumbling that he "didn't want to know." When I pressed James to explain what was disturbing him, he told us, "I don't like to read this kind of stuff. The situation just stays simple if I don't think too much about it. It's better like that."

Diana was really quick (as usual) to respond to him, shooting back: "That's not better, that's just ignorant, 'cause you just don't want to know all the sides." James merely shrugged his shoulders in response, making a show of how determined he is to not "think too much about it."

I do not think that James was reacting so much to the news that the article was reporting as he was to his sudden (uncomfortable) awareness that his political views may be overly simple. Of course, he may also just be trying to push away any reminders of the way his family has been so affected by the events of September 11th.

As a classroom teacher who believes in the potential of curricula and pedagogy to impede or to bring about social change, one of my goals is to push my students to be as self-reflective as possible. I want them to visit and revisit their emotional responses and ways of thinking. Ultimately, I want to see them distance themselves from taken-for-granted assumptions and recognize their own participation in oppressive discourses. Many students, like James, become resistant along the way ("I don't like to read this kind of stuff" and "it's better like that"), because it can be so painful to personally engage in this kind of critical thought. I am aware that now, more than ever, I must create space within the curriculum for students to work through this messy process.

October 16, 2001

I am finally starting to understand the physical toll that working in Lower Manhattan is taking on me. These are the symptoms that I notice: my throat is sore, my head throbs, and my eyes sting. By the end of the day, my eyes are swollen and too sensitive for anything but the dimmest lights in my apartment. Last night, I woke up at 2 o'clock in the morning because my pillow was soaked. My eyes were burning and had been tearing while I slept.

Today, I was meeting with Jessica in her classroom when she jumped up to use eye drops. She swiftly applied the drops and then resumed our conversation, but I felt I needed to point out to her that I am having trouble with my eyes, too. I am suddenly aware of how little opportunity teachers have to talk with one another. My school does not have an equivalent to the office water cooler, a gathering place where the work community exchanges information.

I am left wondering how many of the staff members at my school are suffering from health problems that may be related to the smoke wafting over us. I have also found myself dismissing my concerns, telling myself that these physical ailments are probably just the result of all of the stress we have endured over the past month. Various air tests supposedly show nondangerous levels of asbestos and carbon monoxide, so perhaps I am working myself into a frenzy over something imagined? Then I catch myself in that line of thought, because in a way, it does not actually matter to me if the symptoms are related to poor air quality or related to stress over the seemingly poor air quality. Either way, we are suffering.

Yesterday, David wrote to me in his journal: "Things had started hard this year. School closed about 3 weeks ago. Phones not working and people is getting out of work. Too hard to keep surviving. We can easily give up after this horrible attack on the World Trade Center . . ."

I believe teachers and students should not have to endure the anxiety of being in such close proximity of Ground Zero. No amount of air testing will show the emotional burden that people like David are carrying.

October 17, 2001

The Daily News published an article entitled "Stuyvesant Students Sickened" in today's news. According to the article, the parents called a meeting with teachers and administrators because their children are suffering from "severe headaches, rashes, and burning eyes and lungs." Stuyvesant parents have enlisted environmental consultants and are threatening to pull their children from the school.

Who will advocate for my students? The parents of my students work 14–16 hour days in Chinatown's sweatshops and restaurants. They do not have the energy or money or English—they do not have the power—to demand answers from the school.

Amy happened to bring the article from *The Daily News* to class to use for our discussion of current events. In the written reaction she prepared, Amy wrote, "I feel bad for those kids. . . . Because of the events that happened in 9/11/01, the students can't learn and go to school regularly. That is very bad for their education. I know it hurts a lot to have headaches because I got headaches almost every day."

How many of our students feel sick? When their parents return home so late in the evening from their work in factories and restaurants, can they assess their children's health as some of the Stuyvesant parents have been doing?

Again, I wonder, who will advocate for my students in China-town?

Postscript: August 2005

I can remember the heaviness with which I wrote that last journal entry. I had arrived on the first day of school with a carefully mapped curriculum, and 4 days into the school year, I had found myself seriously derailed. On September 11th, Lauren and I made the decision to put our lessons aside and to listen to the radio with our students. When I finally resumed my planned curriculum, I often felt as though my teaching was nothing but a weak attempt to distract the students from the chaos in their community and their homes.

By December 2001, the bitter smoke that had been threading its way from Ground Zero through Chinatown and the surrounding downtown neighborhoods began to dissipate. However, the cleaner air did little to lighten the burdens of the students. During lunch periods and after-school activities, I heard story after story of families who were in crisis due to the high unemployment rate that continued to plague the community. To make matters even more complicated, some of the families were reluctant to pursue assistance due to fears about their immigration status.

Acutely aware of the disconnect between my planned curriculum and the students' lives, it was a relief to begin one of my favorite units: an intergenerational writing workshop. For 8 weeks, we visited a senior center on East Broadway to exchange stories about growing up in what has traditionally been an "immigrant neighborhood." If nothing else, I reasoned, the new unit would lend extra sets of ears to the students who needed to talk about coping in their post-September 11th world. The warm and attentive seniors with whom we partnered did just that for the eighth graders, but they also provided the unique and invaluable perspective of having lived through other historical crises. Some of the seniors were Holocaust survivors, and all of them had experienced war times. They mesmerized the students with their stories and discussed how their lives were forever changed by their experiences.

Some of the students grew quite close to "their" seniors, bringing small gifts of artwork and writing letters in between our scheduled visits. Others maintained the appearance of cool indifference to the project—or even complained about having to "hang out with old people"—but were nonetheless reluctant to leave the community center at the end of each visit. Most remarkable was the awareness many of the students began to develop that the hard times that they and their families were experiencing were not simply personal ordeals but part of a larger collective story/history about living through September 11th and its aftermath. They began to imagine that one day they might even be the seniors who shared their narratives with visiting eighth graders.

These new understandings marked a turning point in my teaching practice. They empowered me to seek out more opportunities for my middle school students in Chinatown to use oral history in creative contexts. I began collaborating with a colleague and two educators from the Columbia University Oral History Research Office to establish an oral history curriculum at the middle school.

From 2002–2005, we introduced the students to the concept of oral history and its place in historical inquiry. The students learned to conduct interviews and use audio recording equipment. They worked together to build a collection of oral histories from the Chinatown community on the topic of September 11th and the different ways that people who live and work in the neighborhood experienced the events. The students' project was particularly relevant because it answered a call from the Museum of Chinese in the Americas for documentation of the impact of events on Chinatown. The museum, which directs a September 11th Collections Project, elected to include the students' interviews in their archives and invited the students to create two exhibits about the stories the youth and adults told about their experiences of September 11th and its aftermath.

Today, looking back at my journal from 2001 and reflecting back on the development of the oral history curriculum, I see a complicated journey: being a teacher in Lower Manhattan on the day of September 11th, choosing to scrap my planned curriculum because it suddenly seemed irrelevant in the days and months after September 11th, searching for ways to address the events within the setting of the classroom, realizing that oral history and storytelling could be a way to make sense of the students' experiences, and finally creating an oral history curriculum for the middle school students in Chinatown. I do not mean to imply that I arrived at the ultimate solution to teaching and learning about September 11th. Instead, oral history was just one of many possible curricular and pedagogical responses that took place in the years following September 11th, each one informed by my previous experiences and each one raising new issues, dilemmas, and bringing old beliefs into question.

Eighteen

The Morning After, and the Mourning After That

MICHELLE FINE

September 12, 2001

YOU CAN TELL who's dead or missing by their smiles. Their photos, shockingly alive with joy, comfort, and pleasure, dot the subways, ferries, trains, and Port Authority Terminal. They died before they could know what *we* now know. The not-dead travel on subways and trains filled with hollow eyes; no smiles; shoulders down. Thousands dead and still counting, and that's without the undocumented workers whose families can't tell, the homeless men and women whose families don't know. Each evening, millions of nightmares startle and awaken, alone and dark, throughout the metropolitan area.

The air in the city chokes with smoke, flesh, fear, memories, clouds, and creeping nationalism. My niece, a bus driver on Wall Street, describes the plume of smoke "chasing me down the street" as she abandoned her bus. Now a flood of flags, talk of God, military and patriotism chase us all. Searching for an icon of meaning— the flag worries, it feels like draperies for war. Even the dove and peace symbol, my students tell me, feel like generational imperialism. We blanket this terror with our memories of Vietnam, just to make it familiar to those of us who remember the 60s—taming our own terrors.

My friend Maram Hallak, originally from Lebanon, now teaches psychology at Borough of Manhattan Community College, in a building damaged, in part, by the World Trade Center attacks. As we cried today over the mounting deaths, she carefully explained to me,

> To you this is an assault that shakes your world, like a woman raped by a stranger—out of the blue. But for me, and others from war-torn countries, this attack echoes with so many in our past. For us, the experience is more like an incest survivor. Each pain is deep . . . but they are different.

Appreciative of Maram's honesty, and shamed by the U.S.-centric "horror" that I and others were expressing, I was similarly comforted and discomforted by loving e-mails from friends in Northern Ireland, Gaza, Australia, Israel, and New Zealand. I realized that I don't e-mail them every time a bomb goes off in their countries. How much do I/we collude in the imperial calculus of whose body/whose tragedy/whose land counts more?

Switch channels: a student's husband is gone; neighbor boys are orphaned; children waited at school for parents who never showed up; cars sit idle, still, in commuter parking lots.

We've learned the vulnerability of isolation. Bush and colleagues walked out of the environmental meetings in Kyoto, the racism meetings in South Africa. Isolated and privileged, a dangerous combination. The Fantasy of Invulnerability as we build a global empire—one more product made in the U.S.A.—in ruins.[1]

And the Days Immediately Following September 12, 2001

Agoraphobia—formerly unfamiliar to me—is now a warm buddy.

As in the streets, the air in the academy is getting thin. To raise questions about the horrors of terrorism and U.S. imperialism in the same breath becomes a betrayal of patriotism, a disregard for those who sacrificed life. Many work to separate grief and critique,

---

1. The opening of this chapter was adapted from an article originally published in *Qualitative Inquiry*, 2002.

as though we can't mourn as we consider critically what the United States might have done to contribute to the mass hatred that surrounds.

What counts as dissent has swollen beyond recognition. Flashes of Japanese internment, McCarthy, and Vietnam haunt. A timely e-mail from the Black Radical Congress—brilliant and powerful—was passed around with scores of others. This one provoked a protest. Complaints to the provost, followed by more e-mails about academic freedom. A speak-out at CCNY, followed by nasty newspaper coverage, followed by pressure for us all to rally around America. We are forgetting that dissent is woven into the fabric of the United States.

The air is getting thinner. Intellectual surveillance constricts narratives and talk. Stretchy capillaries of surveillance penetrate public talk. Muslim cab drivers try so hard to convince that they are loyal, good citizens. An Indian shopkeeper has handwritten a sign explaining to potential customers, "Please, we are Indian not Arab." A national hyperbole of patriotism drums out dissent, discourages collective self-reflection. Edward Said clarifies when he writes, "Peace cannot exist without equality: This is an intellectual value desperately in need of reiteration and reinforcement."[2]

September 14, 2001

The PATH train stopped. In a tunnel. No apparent reason. I couldn't breathe. Anxiety replaced my more typical early morning obsessive review of what I must do for the day. "Is there no air on this train?" I am afraid to ask the man who stands so close behind me that I can feel his breathing on my neck. Beads of sweat populate my forehead. "Will I faint?" I check out my neighbors, my "self" splitting rapidly into two and then three: "Come on, everyone else is breathing." "In fact, they are *reading*." "Are you *really* reading?" I say nothing.

"Is this an okay way to die? Will it happen fast? What will happen to Sam and Caleb (my sons), David (my partner)? Mom?" A sign for Christopher Street—we're through the tunnel.

---

2. "The Public Role of Writers and Intellectuals," *The Nation*, September 17, 2001, p. 28.

Those of us who live or work in New York seem to be having trouble writing, talking, or holding in our minds at the same time thoughts of lives lost, families, and communities devastated, and the political and economic relations of terrorism, U.S. politics then and now, racial profiling, and anxious worries about what's coming next. It's not easy for people to talk together, or even to speak within ourselves. As we dig through the rubble, searching for words, bodies, and clues, I am struck by the common reaction in so many different bodies walking the streets: the hollowed, empty eyes, refusing contact, the dark shadows beneath, the sweaty hands and heads, the feverish reading, the dreams. Death, ghosts, orphans, analyses of U.S. imperialism, Middle East politics, and the fears of what's yet to come line our insides. And yet most hesitate to ask *why*. Since September 11th, mainstream media have covered—albeit partially and not impartially—who, what, how, where, and when. The coverage rarely interrogates why. Why the United States, why now, why those buildings, why the mass hatred? Why terrorism, why mass destruction, why this form of international assault?

You can't be in New York, New Jersey, the United States without hearing thickly wrapped nationalist discourse. Echoes of the xenophobia that swallowed Oklahoma City at the time of their tragedy. It is as though the nude and shivering terror embodied in the American people steals warmth and comfort from the flag and religion. But these ideological robes falsely unify and flatten the jagged, conflicting perspectives percolating within the American (un)conscious. The long reach of nationalistic ideology bleeds into conscious and unconscious thought and talk—preemptive justification for war. The seepage into schools, racism, law is unimaginable.

October 8, 2001

As we prepare to bomb Afghanistan, few dare to speak. On September 15, 2001, Barbara Lee, a brave representative from the Ninth District of California, is the lone Congressional voice against the War Powers Act, which would provide President Bush with the unchecked ability to mobilize the military. In an interview less than 1 month later, she speaks of the fear of being alone, and the power of speaking for so many who would not speak:

It never dawned on me that I would cast the only vote against this resolution. Many members asked me to change my position. They were friends and they said, "You do not want to be out there alone." I said, "Oh, no don't worry. There will be others." When there weren't I said, "Oh my God. . . ." I think that, when I cast that vote, I was speaking for other people in Congress and outside Congress who want a more deliberative approach.[3]

Men and women—and children—living on the bottom of the class, race, and ethnic stratifications called America know more about domination and exploitation, because they experience, see, care for, anticipate, and have to study those with privilege. As Toni Morrison has written, they know too intimately how (and on whom) the "system" operates.[4] Now they dare not speak aloud— not in public institutions and not in schools. Yet students carry such knowledge, wisdom, fear, and desire in their inquisitive eyes; disengaged stares; rude outbursts; and hands waiting to be called on. Do we dare listen?

October 15, 2001

Working-class university students, particularly students of color, are beginning to mention brothers and sisters who have "gone away"—to Pakistan? The Gulf? Afghanistan? "They call but can't say where or how they are." Undergraduates in ROTC, high school students in Junior ROTC are "on deck." Undocumented immigrants are being promised citizenship if they serve. Students in poor high schools are being recruited with promises of travel, education, and "saving" America. Usually poor or working class, White, African American, immigrant, Latino, Asian young people who "enlist" are typically trying to pay for an education, secure an extra income, support too many people with too little.

---

3. "Barbara Lee's Stand," *The Nation*, October 8, 2001.
4. *Playing in the Dark: Whiteness and the Literary Imagination.* Cambridge, MA: Harvard University Press.

August 12, 2005

A 15-year-old student named Basil, who attends a racially and ethnically integrated, middle-class public high school, says, "When I walk down the street, I know they're thinking I may be a terrorist."

Over the last year, I joined colleague Selcuk Sirin of New York University, in conversations with Muslim-American youth in the New York metropolitan region, in a small effort to bear witness to the collateral damage at home, in the bodies and souls of U.S. Muslim-American youth, a small but deeply affected part of the great mass of people for whom Barbara Lee was compelled to find a voice.[5] These young people, aged 12 to 18, were unsuspecting teenage citizens of the United States of America—until 9/12/01.

Between then and now, our nation has invaded Afghanistan and Iraq, exchanging Osama Bin Laden for Sadam Hussein. We have constructed, detained, and abused at Guantanamo; passed the Patriot Act; and orchestrated mass detentions of Muslim Americans, including some young people under 18. We have elected George Bush to a 2nd term, witnessed the atrocities of Abu-Ghraib. Estimates range from 25,000 to 1,000,000 Iraqis who have been killed, as we near the 2,000 mark for number of American soldiers killed.

"How do you know they're thinking you might be a terrorist?"

"I know," Basil replies, his voice dropping. "I just feel constantly violated. . . . even if they say nothing."

As the Muslim-American youth talk to us, they tell us—one of us Turkish and raised Muslim, the other a Jew from the Northeast United States—that on September 12, 2001, they were evicted from the moral community of psychological citizenship in the United States.[6] From that point forward, maybe before, these young people and their families have experienced a relentless undertow of challenges to their psychological well-being, social relations, and public life; placed at once under intense surveillance and rendered fundamentally invisible as human, critical, engaged citizens.

---

5. For full article, see Selcuk Sirin & Michelle Fine, "Hyphenated Selves: Muslim-American Youth Negotiating Identities on the Fault Lines of Global Conflict." Unpublished manuscript.

6. Susan Opotow, "Conflict and Morals" (2004). In T.A. Thorkildsen & H.J. Walberg (Eds.), *Nurturing Morality*. New York: Kluwer Academic/Plenum.

Mariam, age 18, told us:

> I remember that day [9/11/01] my father drove home a num-
> ber of children from school, a religious school. As he dropped
> them at the elementary school, where they would meet their
> parents, the police were there, taking names, phone numbers,
> and licenses. That was frightening enough, but as we drove
> off we found ourselves in a big traffic jam, and some woman
> screamed out of her car, "Why don't you just go home?" I knew
> then that everything was going to be different.

These young people describe daily walks to school, being on the
streets, at the mall, in the library, on the bus, escorted by the specter
of *terrorist* (for boys) and *oppressed/uneducated* (for girls). Living in
the new "world," they were now outsiders within their own communities and schools. We heard stories of airport delays, dates broken because "my parents wouldn't understand," tongues bitten in
history class for fear of being sent to the principal for a dissenting
opinion. Abid, a sophomore at a public high school, told us, "My
history teacher got mad when I challenged him about the war. . . .
I think his son is fighting there." Ahab, at age 11 the youngest and
smallest in our discussion group, joined our conversation with a
whisper: "I don't like it either when people think me, or my father,
is going to throw a bomb."

When we asked whom they turn to, in the face of these difficult
adolescent interactions, they explained: "I don't really tell my parents. They have enough to contend with." Salma elaborated with a
story about her father and his job. Originally from Macedonia, Salma's father works in the food industry at a major hotel. Importing a
long and deep history of hiding his Muslim identity, at the hotel he
remains silent about his ethnic and religious commitments. Asked
by the hotel chef to "taste" a new chicken dish dipped in wine, he
politely refused and later told his family that he told the chef he
was "allergic to chicken." Salma laughed, "Dad, this is America.
You can say you are Muslim, and you don't drink wine." And then
turning to the focus group, she continued, "My parents hide everything, but we're free here." Protecting parents from knowledge of
persistent discrimination and "parenting parents" about U.S. ways

In Omar's identity map he shows himself shedding tears for racism.

of life appear to be two of the related labors of adolescent hyphen-ated selves.

We asked these teens to draw identity maps, to reveal how their "American" selves and their "Muslim" selves overlap/interact/ negotiate life in the United States post 9/11. As the identity maps reveal, Muslim-American youth craft *hyphenated cultural selves* in a sea of contested global relations and representations. *How* young people negotiate at the hyphen varies widely, and often by gender, class, and type of schooling (public, religious, home schooling). But they all have to negotiate.

Consider the map created by Omar who, at age 14, humanizes what we heard from so many of the young men we interviewed: the fractures of being Muslim and being American have seared him in half, filling him with "tears for racism," a frown, a severed soul. Living with the haunting ghosts of "terrorist" looming around him, he, like so many young men, feels swallowed by a representation he can't actively resist, lest he embody the hegemonic trope—young Muslim man filled with rage. To resist, he tries to contain the anger, to protect himself and his family.

Selina, age 15, draws a distinct yet equally powerful visual narrative of fluid selves—American and Muslim—at the hyphen, voicing what so many of the young women told us. Actively refusing to separate the currents of Islam and America that move through the river of her body, she (like Marian, next page) nevertheless recognizes the distinct pools of water from which they gather a fluid sense of identity, rightfully claiming both currents

Selina draws a narrative of fluid selves.

at the same time, decorated with smiles and (in color) a beautiful blending of shades. Not at all naïve to the flood of stereotypes held about Muslim women as uneducated, oppressed, or dupes of religion, these students look for ways to educate those who stereotype and "don't know any better."

Many of the young people mentioned times in school when everyone "turns to me, like about the war. Like I am supposed to educate them." We asked if they mind being singled out as an authority. Most said no, they didn't mind, although they were a bit discomforted by the attention. Amira offered an elaborate retort:

Marian illustrates her blended identity.

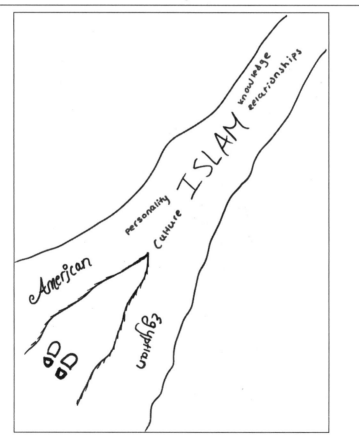

I guess it's better that I educate them than they stay ignorant.
I want to tell them there is more to know than just today, them
alone, the mall, boys, music. I want to tell them to learn about
what's going on in the world. But they don't watch the news
or read the paper. I listen to CNN, Fox News, Al-Jazeera, and
French news every night. So maybe it's best that I do answer
their questions. There is a big world out there, and I personally
believe I am just one small dot in this world. There is something much bigger than any of us. I wish the American students understood that.

Both boys and girls are equally frustrated by the absurdity of
questions tossed their way (are you a terrorist? why do you dress
like that?), but the girls are nevertheless eager for others to "just
ask me a question—don't assume I'm gonna throw bombs . . . or
I'm an uneducated woman!" They want the opportunity to share
themselves, to teach, and to change minds.

We thought that Muslim girls who are veiled and therefore more
visible would have a more difficult path than [relatively invisible]
Muslim boys, but we were wrong. Amira helped us understand
what seemed initially like an anomaly: "I finally figured out what
to tell people about the *hijab*. I wear it like a bicyclist wears a bike
helmet. It protects me from danger, and it gives me the freedom to
wander where I dare not without it. Then they leave me alone!!"

Filled with confidence and wonder, the young women voiced
concern that "people are afraid to talk to me because I wear a *hijab*."
They nevertheless seek contact with a larger world. When asked,
"If you were on MTV, what would you tell other teenagers about
being Muslim-American?" they were eager to tell their peers:

"Yes, we shower!"

"No, we don't swim in a *hijab*!"

"It's not that my parents won't let me go to the dance, I don't
want to go!"

"We use cell phones, and can tuck them in. Look—I'm hands-
free!"

Jabor contrasts his understanding of his two worlds.

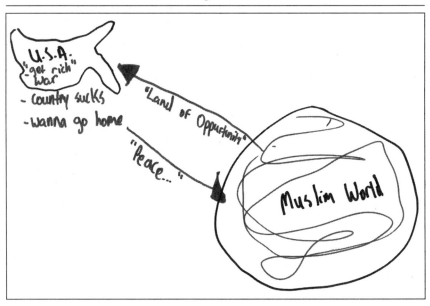

In contrast, in our discussions with the young men, hyphenated selves were splintered with the weight of the world; split open with the searing knife of global conflict. As Omar (earlier) and Jabor (above) articulate in their identity maps, so many of the young men view the United States as an oppressive force on their souls ("get rich," war, country sucks). Some wax eloquent with a mystifying romance ("wanna go home") to return to their "homelands of peace." This is despite the fact that an overwhelming majority of the participants were born in the United States and have very limited, if any, real-life experiences outside of this country.

Adamant about the splits between the United States and "Muslim countries," Adnan wrote on his map, under "U.S.A.": "Land of opportunity, rich, war, get drafted and die." On the other side of his map, the heading reads "Muslims in Other Countries" and under that is written: "People are accused but are not hurt or no action is taken against them. Muslims love each other and take care of each other. Land of peace." Torn between the land where they live and are persecuted and a strong imaginary picture about peace abroad, taunted often at school and on the street, these young men try to prove the stereotype wrong and so struggle to contain the anger, the rage, and not fight back.

While so many of the young men—as teens—come to see themselves as homeless or displaced, most of the young women—like those shown above—present themselves as transnational citizens or citizens of the world. And still, all yearn for a conversation, in school and out, with educators and peers about the global conflicts they carry in their souls.

Like the Arab and Muslim students with whom we spoke, many students today may find themselves part of the "collateral damage," exiled from mainstream culture. As teachers, we are charged with the responsibility of helping all students find a voice, and guiding them toward a deeper understanding of the multilayered circumstances that define a complicated, and often difficult, world.

If we do not teach about conditions of oppression and terror (State- and corporate-sponsored, interpersonal, domestic, and suicide bombs), even in times of relative prosperity and peace, we relinquish the space of public education to the globalization of terror, greed, fear, obedience, and silencing. By so doing, we surrender democracy, hollow the souls of educators and youth, and threaten our collective futures.

Today's students will become tomorrow's voters, policy makers, and world leaders. With such important responsibilities to look forward to, they deserve an education that interrogates what they know, and what they need to know.

About the Contributors

Debbie Almontaser is currently Coordinator of External Programs for Brooklyn Public Schools. As a multicultural specialist and diversity consultant, Ms. Almontaser facilitates teacher and public workshops on Arab culture, Islam, conflict resolution, cultural diversity, and Augusto Boal's Theater of the Oppressed around the city. Ms. Almontaser also serves as a consultant for Nickelodeon's Muslim American Series Project, Independent Production Fund on the Islam Project, Islam Access Project, the Muslim Communities Project, Columbia University, and Educators for Social Responsibility, among others. She sits on the board of The Dialogue Project, Women in Islam Inc., Youth Bridge of New York, and the Brooklyn Borough President's New Diversity Task Force. She is also a co-founder of Brooklyn Bridges, the September 11th Curriculum Project, and the We Are All Brooklyn Coalition. Ms. Almontaser co-designed and developed a curriculum for the Muslim Communities Project at Columbia University and for Educators for Social Responsibility/Metro. As a Revson Scholar at Columbia University, Ms. Almontaser took courses from the International Center for Cooperation & Conflict Resolution at Teachers College and received a certificate in conflict resolution.

Loyan Beausoleil received her M.S.Ed. from Bank Street College of Education. She is the director of University Plaza Nursery School (UPNS), located in downtown Manhattan, where she is also a teacher of 4- and 5-year-olds. Since September 11, 2001, Ms. Beausoleil has been working to document the lives of young children who witnessed the destruction of the World Trade Center. She has presented the Youngest Witnesses project at numerous conferences and colleges (www.youngestwitnesses.com), and has produced a DVD of children discussing their hopes and fears as they view proposed models of the new World Trade Center.

Ms. Beausoleil loves teaching and spending time with children. She believes strongly in the value of play and its ability to facilitate learning and healing, and she encourages children's exploration and growth through playful interactions with their peers. She lives in downtown Manhattan with her daughter Ezair, and loves biking, hiking, and the outdoors.

Marygrace Berberian is a board-certified and registered art therapist and licensed social worker. She has established and developed art therapy programs for at-risk children and families in community-based organizations throughout New York City. Currently, Ms. Berberian is the Director of Art Therapy for the New York City Public Schools, instituting the practice of art therapy into Downtown schools. Her work on 9/11 has appeared in *Psychoanalytic Social Work, Pacesetter*, and *Art Therapy: Journal of the American Art Therapy Association*, as well as the book *Understanding Mass Violence: A Social Work Perspective*. Ms. Berberian has presented at cross-disciplinary conferences nationally and internationally, and has appeared in a number of documentaries. Ms. Berberian is committed to supporting the resiliency of New Yorkers, personally knowing a great deal about the struggle to persevere.

Isaac Brooks came to teaching as a second career after 8 years mastering the dark art of advertising. After graduating from Teachers College, he taught in public schools in Greenwich, CT, Tenafly, NJ, and Hunter Elementary School for the Gifted in New York City, before he joined the staff at Manhattan School for Children as a fourth-grade teacher. After the 2001–02 academic year, Isaac left MSC to teach middle school at the Horace Mann School, where he's been teaching English and history ever since. One of his favorite courses, called "City Visions," examines the history of the United States through the lens of New York City's growth. He is also passionate about teaching writing, which he believes is all about revision—because great writing is crafted, not born. A life-long Sinophile, Isaac has been studying Mandarin Chinese and stayed in Hohhot, Inner Mongolia, People's Republic of China, for a month during the summer of 2005. He and his wife, Della, have two children—one in college and the other in high school. In their spare time they like to sail on the Hudson River on their boat, "Feng Shui."

Abigail Deutsch was a senior at Stuyvesant High School on September 11, 2001 and graduated in June, 2002. She is now completing her final year as an English major at Yale University. Abigail spends her time reading, writing, singing, laughing, and convincing others to be English majors. She has worked for the *Yale Daily News Magazine*, the *Yale Literary Magazine*, the *Yale Review*, and *The New Yorker*, and has won awards for academic, poetic, and nonfiction writing at Yale. After graduation she hopes to write and teach.

Claudia DiSalvo received her B.A. from State University of New York–Brockport, and soon after began her teaching career at Long Island's middle and high schools. She completed her Master's Degree in Educational Administration at New York University. Interested in working with and developing programs for diverse communities, she became a NYC Board of Education health and physical education teacher. She joined the Bureau for Children with Retarded Mental Development and served on many educational committees concerned with improving Special Education programs. After this, Claudia briefly left the education world to go into business, but found that she missed the school community and joined the teaching staff at the School of the Future. In 1993 she became the acting principal of the Professional Performing Arts High School. Claudia then worked for District 2 as a Special Assistant to the Pupil Personnel Director, until retiring in 2002. She continues to consult and work with the NYC Department of Education, Region 9.

Ada Rosario Dolch served as principal of the High School for Leadership & Public Service for 9 years. At present she serves as a member of the Supervisory Support Team for the Council of Supervisors and Administrators. The events of September 11, 2001, have afforded Ada the opportunity to present to school administrators at various forums throughout the United States on the topic of Preparedness, Response, and Recovery. Most recently, Ada traveled to Herat, Afghanistan, for the ceremonial opening of a school she helped build, and for the dedication of the school's garden to her sister Wendy, who gave her life for our freedom on 9/11. Ada is wife to Norman, and mother to Lauren, 24, and Amy, 19.

Stacey Fell-Eisenkraft collaborated with 8th-grade students in Chinatown to design and carry out a community-based September 11th oral history project. She is also a doctoral candidate in the Department of Curriculum and Teaching at Teachers College, Columbia University, and has gone on to research the different ways her students used the oral history curriculum to voice their critical insights about their lives and their community. In 2005, Dr. Fell-Eisenkraft completed and successfully defended her dissertation on the subject of September 11th and youth in Chinatown. Two weeks later she gave birth to twins. In addition to her new career as a parent, she continues to conduct research, write, and work as a staff developer at several middle schools in New York City.

Michelle Fine is the Distinguished Professor of Social Psychology, Women's Studies, and Urban Education at the Graduate Center of the City University of New York. She has been funded by Rockefeller, Spencer, Ford, Pew, Leslie Glass, and Open Society to design Participatory Action Research projects with youth and "elders" in schools, prisons, global human rights organizations, and local communities. Recent publications include *Working Method: Social Research and Social Injustice* (with Lois Weis), *Off White: Essays on Race, Privilege and Contestation* (with Lois Weis, Linda Pruitt, and April Burns), and *Echoes of Brown: Youth Documenting and Performing the Legacy of Brown v. Board of Education* (Teachers College Press, 2004).

Lia Friedman is currently a student at Stuyvesant High School (Class of 2008). She is an amateur potter, guitarist, and shower singer. She feels extremely lucky and proud to be part of the Farm and Wilderness community.

Tom Goodridge taught the Special Education class depicted in his chapter at a Harlem elementary school for 11 years. He obtained his Master's Degree from The Bank Street College of Education, where the importance of play and developmental learning are emphasized. Currently he volunteers as Director of the Garden Project at the same school, which seeks to connect city children with nature through a school garden. Tom is pursuing a Ph.D. at Union Institute and University in the interdisciplinary field of Ecological Learning. His research investigates the role that direct contact with the natural world plays in the development of urban children.

Maxine Greene is the William F. Russell Professor of Philosophy and Education (Emerita) at Teachers College, Columbia University, and Philosopher in Residence at the Lincoln Center Institute for the Arts in Education. Presently she teaches classes in aesthetics and education for Teachers College and for the Maxine Greene Foundation for the Arts and Social Imagination. She is past president of the American Educational Research Association, the American Educational Studies Association, and the Philosophy of Education Society. She has written about 100 articles and forewords, as well as six books, including most recently *The Dialectic of Freedom*, *Releasing the Imagination*, and *Variations on a Blue Guitar*.

Dalia Hochman holds a B.A. in History from Yale University and is currently a Ph.D. candidate in Educational Policy at Columbia University. After teaching in the New York City public schools for several years, Dalia is currently teaching at Vassar College in Poughkeepsie, New York. Dalia would like to dedicate this piece to her parents, sisters, and grandmother, who helped her through September 11th and beyond.

Linda Lantieri has over 35 years of experience in education as a teacher, an administrator, a university professor, and an internationally known expert in social and emotional learning, crisis intervention, inter-group relations, and conflict resolution. Currently she serves as the Director of Project Renewal, a project of the Tides Center. She is also co-founder of the internationally recognized Resolving Conflict Creatively Program (RCCP). Linda is co-author of *Waging Peace in Our Schools*, editor of *Schools with Spirit: Nurturing the Inner Lives of Children and Teachers*, and a contributor to *Educating Citizens for Global Awareness* (Teachers College Press, 2005).

Patricia Lent was born and raised in Virginia. In 1982, she moved to New York City to pursue a career in dance. She performed with the Merce Cunningham Dance Company from 1984 to 1993, and with White Oak Dance Project from 1994 to 1996. In 1998 she joined the faculty of P.S. 234, where she has been teaching 2nd and 3rd grade ever since. She can often be found in Central Park leading young birders on walks through the Ramble.

Ethan Lowenstein is Assistant Professor of Curriculum and Instruction at Eastern Michigan University. Earlier in his career he taught social studies at an alternative high school in East Harlem, and received the New York City Board of Education Teacher of the Year Award for Alternative High Schools. Now, 5 years after 9/11, Lowenstein remains obsessed with the same question he had then: How do we facilitate teacher development in education for social and political responsibility? Lowenstein is currently exploring this question while working on a large scale evaluation of the nationally acclaimed organization, "Facing History and Ourselves." He will soon co-author an article with a number of his students about the Arab American Experience, based on a collaboration with the Arab American National Museum and a group of 4th and 5th graders in Detroit. Ethan lives in Michigan with his wife, Margo, and his two daughters, Ruby and Jasmine.

Lorrie Mann has been an early childhood teacher at P.S. 15 in Red Hook, Brooklyn, for 21 years. Prior to and during her teaching career, she has been a practicing artist, wife, and mother of two daughters. She has also been running the Prospect Park loop for 11 years and counting.

Amy Martin has been a teacher at P.S. 116 for 8 years. Currently she is the school librarian. She has contributed writing to Educators for Social Responsibility's *Teachable Moments*. Amy loves reading and writing, but also makes time for other forms of merriment, including dancing, cooking, knitting, and yoga. She would like to thank Tom Roderick, of Educators for Social Responsibility, for his encouragement and support of her writing.

Rosalind Winter is a Jungian analyst and a member of Sandplay Therapists of America and the International Society for Sandplay Therapy. She serves on the Faculty of The C.G. Jung Institute of New York. Ms. Winter continues to train and supervise the psychological staff of the NYC's Ground Zero Schools in Symbol Formation (an adaptation of Sandplay Therapy for institutions). Her 9/11 work has been applied to other large-scale traumas and has lead her to consult and speak nationally and internationally on large-scale collective trauma in the wake of Katrina and the tsunami in Sri Lanka. On this topic, Ms. Winter has authored "September 11th: The Day and the Experience," in the *Journal of Sandplay Therapy*, and "Reflections on September 11th," in the *Journal of Jungian Practice and Thought.*